Putting
FACES
on the Data

Dedicated to
Jim
who is always right beside me.
—Lyn

Dedicated to
Harry, anonymous donor
—Michael

LYN SHARRATT
MICHAEL FULLAN

Foreword by Sir Michael Barber

Putting
FACES
on the Data

WHAT GREAT LEADERS DO!

A JOINT PUBLICATION

CORWIN
A SAGE Company

ONTARIO
PRINCIPALS'
COUNCIL
Exemplary Leadership in Public Education

learningforward

CORWIN
A SAGE Company

FOR INFORMATION:

Corwin
A SAGE Company
2455 Teller Road
Thousand Oaks, California 91320
(800) 233-9936
Fax: (800) 417-2466
www.corwin.com

SAGE Ltd.
1 Oliver's Yard
55 City Road
London EC1Y 1SP
United Kingdom

SAGE India Pvt. Ltd.
B 1/I 1 Mohan Cooperative Industrial Area
Mathura Road, New Delhi 110 044
India

SAGE Asia-Pacific Pte. Ltd.
33 Pekin Street #02-01
Far East Square
Singapore 048763

Printed in the United States of America.

Library of Congress Cataloging-in-Publication Data

Sharratt, Lyn.
Putting FACES on the data : what great leaders do! / Lyn Sharratt, Michael Fullan ; Foreword by Sir Michael Barber.

pages cm
"A Joint Publication With Ontario Principals' Council and Learning Forward."
Includes bibliographical references and index.

ISBN 978-1-4522-0258-7 (pbk.)

1. Educational tests and measurements—Case studies.
2. Effective teaching—Case studies. I. Fullan, Michael. II. Title.

LB3051.S44 2012
371.26—dc23   2011053438

This book is printed on acid-free paper.

Acquisitions Editor: Arnis Burvikovs
Associate Editor: Desirée A. Bartlett
Editorial Assistant: Kimberly Greenberg
Production Editor: Cassandra Margaret Seibel
Copy Editor: Amy Marks
Typesetter: C&M Digitals (P) Ltd.
Proofreader: Jennifer Gritt
Indexer: Sheila Bodell
Cover Designer: Michael Dubowe
Permissions Editor: Karen Ehrmann

SUSTAINABLE FORESTRY INITIATIVE
Certified Chain of Custody
Promoting Sustainable Forestry
www.sfiprogram.org
SFI-01268
SFI label applies to text stock

14 15 16 10 9 8 7 6 5 4

CONTENTS

LIST OF FIGURES AND TABLES

FOREWORD

In this new book, Lyn Sharratt and Michael Fullan have performed a vital service for progressive education reformers around the world. They have shown not only that good data and good teaching go together but that success is possible only if in fact they do go together.

For many years, a powerful strand of the culture among educators has been skeptical about data, sometimes even rejecting it altogether. Great teaching, in this view, is about inspired individuals walking into a classroom and, through force of personality and knowledge of subject, engaging the students who happen to be in there. And of course we can all remember in our own lives teachers who did exactly this, so it's a story we're inclined to believe.

Moreover, it is argued, the data are at best limited and often out of date, and because so much of what makes great education great is hard to measure, the data force a reductionist perspective on schools and turn teachers into technicians.

Sharratt and Fullan demonstrate convincingly the flaws in this perspective. There will always be uniquely inspired teachers who rise above the mere mortals around them, but what the authors show here is that, if we want whole systems to succeed with every child—which is indeed the challenge of the 21st century—then we need collective capacity; and collective capacity involves teachers in each school and between schools engaging in serious conversation of what good teaching looks like and how it is achieved. For that conversation to be successful, evidence is required; and if the evidence is to go beyond the anecdotal, then good data are essential. Above all, Sharratt and Fullan demonstrate the vital two-way street between assessment and instructional improvement.

Of course, any data in any field have their limitations and learning from the data requires insight, analysis, and imagination. Data alone rarely make clear what needs to be done; rather they provide the basis for informed professionalism, the kind of professionalism that insists that, however good a teacher or school or system was yesterday, it should strive to be better tomorrow.

What makes the argument in Sharratt and Fullan's book so powerful is their emphasis on putting FACES on the data, reminding us that the numbers represent real children and young people striving to make the most of themselves as they prepare for an uncertain future. This perspective applies not just at the level of the classroom and the school, but also at the level of the district and the state or province. In my own experience of bringing the data to bear on domestic policy priorities at No.10 Downing Street, I tried always to remember that, however aggregated the data, they represent real lives—every 1 percent increase in the reliability of trains represented a million extra journeys that started and finished on time; every 1 percent increase in children reaching the standard in English or mathematics at age 11 represented 7,000 more children ready to succeed in secondary education; reductions in drug abuse represented so many family tragedies avoided; and so on.

Sharratt and Fullan bring this perspective to bear excellently not least because, in addition to writing about education, both have direct experience in education reform at different levels in the Ontario system, Sharratt in a senior position in the York Region District School Board and Fullan as adviser on education to Ontario premier Dalton McGuinty. The reform they have been part of is exemplary in its consistency and success in building principals' and teachers' capacity. Above all, it has delivered results at every level. As this book shows so clearly, using the data at every level, from classroom to province or state, is a vital ingredient of successful whole system reform.

I recommend this book for every educator, wherever they are in the world, who wants to master using data to drive up performance and who believes that every child, every FACE, needs to count and be counted.

—Sir Michael Barber
Chief Education Advisor, Pearson

PREFACE

Statistics are a wonderful servant and an appalling master.

—Hopper & Hopper, 2009

Technology and accountability have generated a data dump on teachers. There is no longer a shortage of information; it's just the opposite—a glut. We tackled many of the problems that arise from too much information in our previous publication, *Realization* (Sharratt & Fullan, 2009). Using the 14 parameters of district-wide success that we developed in our work in the York Region District School Board, we showed how schools and the district as a whole were able to realize improvements on a wide scale. But we did not really delve into the role of data in a deep, human way.

In FACES, we go deeper in our quest to balance and integrate two aspects of school improvement that look like they can't be brought together: on the one hand is the question of how you personalize data for all students so that each is treated as a real person and helped to learn according his or her own individual needs; on the other hand is the question of how you do this for 100,000 students at a time without losing the human touch. FACES does just this, honoring and helping the individual, and improving the system.

We examined three research questions in our work in four countries, Canada, the United States, the United Kingdom and Australia. We asked over 500 educators three direct questions: why put FACES on data, how do we do so, and what leadership qualities would be necessary to lead a system that did this well? Then we asked participants to tell their stories about their work with the FACES that they know. In our work with practitioners, we have come to appreciate that "practice drives practice" or, more precisely, that best practice drives even better practice. Systems need to be stimulated and steered sometimes, but by and large effective practice needs to be unleashed, spread, and further developed.

This book is an account of what good practice is and how to get more of it using data and the FACES of students as the drivers. In Chapter 1, we set the context and show how we and others use data. Chapter 2 examines what we found from our key research questions. Then we focus on assessment (Chapter 3) and instruction (Chapter 4), inseparable conjoined twins. In Chapter 5, we examine the leadership required to make such a balanced and integrated system work. Finally, in Chapter 6, we consider ownership—who is accountable for putting FACES on the data.

So, join us in this journey to find the "wonderful servant" for which the Hopper brothers yearned.

ACKNOWLEDGMENTS

We know that it takes many people to produce a book that will be a meaningful contribution to the educational research literature. All the folks involved in the production of this book are too numerous to mention; however, there are some who deserve special mention for their yeoman-like efforts.

One such person is **Jim Coutts**, an educator himself and a successful businessman, who not only edited the manuscript but also contributed to the content and the data analyses in a big way! Thank you, Jim, for your positive ways of supporting the writing, for being there through the good and bad times of writing a book, and especially for helping to make it happen!

We want to thank **Claudia Cuttress**, a very creative designer who always willingly added a personal and professional touch to the manuscript and helped to record our research data, as well.

Thank you to **Michelle Sharratt**, preservice coordinator for the Ontario Institute for Studies in Education at the University of Toronto, who shared her outstanding teaching expertise and helped to add the current realities in teaching and learning to our work, making it even more precise and meaningful.

Thank you **Jill Maar**, principal of Armadale Public School, a vibrant, thoughtful instructional leader and good friend, who always opens her school to "learning walks and talks" with us, so that we can experience the best practices that she and her staff have to offer—always focused on all students' achievement.

And thank you to **James Bond**, principal of a Manor Park Middle School, who went out of his way to share with us his intentional leadership to ensure that *all* students in his school are achieving.

We thank **Denyse Gregory**, independent researcher, who diligently put unwieldy raw data into a categorized format that we could then think and write about cogently.

Christine Ward, instructional consultant from Scotland, thank you for your invaluable help not only in asking our research questions during your cooperative learning and leadership sessions, but also in highlighting the great practitioner stories from teachers across Scotland to add to our database.

Thank you, **Peter Hill**, CEO of ACARA, for his wisdom and patient determination that we should understand how NAPLAN in Australia works and who is continuously improving data delivery in a timely, meaningful way.

Thank you to the **507 educators** who filled out our research placemat for this extensive data collection. We appreciate that you came from all over the world to lend your voices to this manuscript. We asked you to participate from across the United States, Scotland, Canada, and Australia. Your practitioner voices made a huge difference to our work—thank you, sincerely, on behalf of *all* children.

And, finally, thank you to the **authors of the case studies and stories**, whose eagerness and commitment to tell their improvement stories illuminated the concepts that we were trying to convey in the manuscript. On many occasions, these authors highlighted for us, through example, the importance of being specific where students' achievement is concerned. Nothing was too challenging for these authors in writing about their important and creative work.

We salute the **case study authors**: Steve Blake, Jeff Clark, and Shelley Clark of Simcoe County School District, Canada; Jim Watterston and Jayne Johnston, ACT, Australia; Kim Newlove and Patricia Prowse, Saskatoon Public Schools, Canada; Jan McClure, Colin Esdale, and Lani Sharp from Ballarat Callendon College, Australia; Sharron Graham, Grande Prairie Public School District, Alberta, Canada; Bill Gartland, Catholic District School Board of Eastern Ontario, Canada; Tony Bracken and Don O'Brien, Diocese of Broken Bay, Australia; and Calvin Baker, Vail Unified School District, Arizona, USA.

Similarly, we salute the **authors of our narratives**: Linda Forsyth, Scotland; Gaye Williams and Deb Hodges, Alberta, Canada; Gordon Livingstone, Scotland, Joanne Pitman, Alberta, Canada; Pauline Ward, Scotland; Wendy McNaught, Scotland; Sheena Ness and Raechelle Goretsky, Alberta, Canada; and Jim Coutts, Ontario, Canada.

Finally, it is crucial to have a great publisher. Our sincere thanks to Arnis Burvikovs, senior editor at Corwin; Cassandra Seibel, project editor; Amy Marks, copy editor; and the rest of the crew at Corwin, who were always gracious, constructive, creative, and caring about our book that we affectionately and proudly call *FACES*.

ABOUT THE AUTHORS

 **Lyn Sharratt** is a professor at the Ontario Institute for Studies in Education at the University of Toronto, where she lectures and currently coordinates the twenty-five-student Learning and Leadership Ed. D. Cohort program. Lyn is the former superintendent of Curriculum & Instruction Services in the York Region District School Board, a large Canadian school district, where she and her curriculum team analyzed assessment data and developed a comprehensive literacy improvement program, which they launched with the cooperation of senior leadership, principals, and over 8,800 teachers. The continuously improving 14 parameter program resulted in increased achievement for a diverse, multicultural, and multilingual population of over 115,000 students, and the district became the top performing district in Ontario, where teaching positions became among the most sought-after in the nation. Lyn has been a curriculum consultant and administrator, and she has also taught all elementary grades and secondary-age students in inner-city and rural settings. Lyn has analyzed and commented on public policy for a provincial trustee organization, the Ontario Public School Boards' Association, has taught preservice education at York University, and led in-service professional learning in a provincial teachers' union head office. She is lead author, with Michael Fullan, of *Realization: The Change Imperative for Increasing District-Wide Reform* (Corwin, 2009). Currently, Lyn consults internationally, working with states, districts, administrators, curriculum consultants, and teachers in Chile, Australia, the United States, the United Kingdom, and Canada. Visit her website at www.lynsharratt.com.

Michael Fullan is former dean and professor emeritus at the Ontario Institute for Studies in Education at the University of Toronto. He is currently the special advisor to the premier and minister of education in Ontario, Canada. He holds three honorary doctoral degrees— from the University of Edinburgh in Scotland, Nipissing University in Ontario, and the University of Leicester in England.

He is recognized as an international authority on large-scale reform, leadership, and educational change. Michael is engaged in training, consulting, and advising governments around the world. His work is driven by the moral purpose of raising the bar and closing the gap for all students.

He is an innovative thinker who is sought-after by institutions, publishers, and international think-tanks to present, write, and focus the global educational community on what matters in education in the 21st century.

He is the author of many best-selling books, most recently *Moral Imperative Realized, Motion Leadership, The Challenge of Change, All Systems Go, Change Leader,* and *Stratosphere,* among many others. His books are published in many languages.

Visit his website at www.michaelfullan.ca.

CHAPTER ONE

From Information Glut to Well-Known FACES

Introduction

About a decade ago we came to the conclusion that what mattered most in accomplishing school success on a large scale was *focus*. Too many priorities were coming and going as systems became both fragmented and constantly overloaded. So we did begin to focus—on literacy and numeracy, for example, first in the York Region District School Board, then in Ontario as a whole system, and indeed in our work around the world. It paid off in results, as we shall see, but we discovered something even more important in the course of this work. To focus best, teachers need to combine *technical expertise* with a strong *emotional connection* to what they are looking at. The key is how to make important things personally important to the individual on both cognitive and affective grounds. This is what *FACES* is all about.

We all know that the sheer volume of information is becoming overwhelming. As Eli Paris (2011) puts it in *Filter Bubble*, "900,000 blog posts, 50 million tweets, more than 60 million Facebook status updates, and 210 billion e-mails are sent off into the electronic ether every day" (p. 11). All human communication, from the dawn of time to 2003, is replicated in volume every two days!

It is not that more information makes us smarter. Nicholas Carr (2010), an early technologist himself, tells us in his book *The Shallows*, "[W]hat the Net seems to be doing is chipping away my capacity for concentration and contemplation" (p. 6). In *Distracted*, Maggie Jackson (2009) argues that there is so much going on that we are losing our ability for "deep, sustained, perceptive attention"

(p. 13). The result is that we are attracted to what is flashy and instantly stimulating, literally not being inclined to pay attention to what is important.

Instant and ubiquitous access to everything further dulls one's emotions. The meaning, for example, of 10,000 people dying in a monsoon in Bangladesh doesn't register. Yet, show one up-close picture of a small girl being swept to her death in the larger tragedy, and we are stirred. We are wired to feel things for people, not for numbers.

Education, of course, is overloaded with programs and data. The growth of digital power has aided and abetted the spread of accountability-driven data—adequate yearly progress, test results for every child in every grade, common core standards, formative and summative assessments galore. Not to mention that around the corner will be the demands of two new assessment consortia in the United States—the Partnership for Assessment of Readiness for College and Careers, and the SMARTER Balanced Assessment Consortia—both of which will issue reports in 2015.

It is not just the sheer volume of information that is daunting. It is the form in which the data arrive—can you imagine a devoted teacher becoming excited about the latest electronic report that serves up scores of disaggregated statistics? Our colleagues Andy Hargreaves and Dennis Shirley (2006) say that teachers are "data-driven to distraction." They have data all right, but it comes in waves of indigestible, dehumanized information. We say, as do Hargreaves and Shirley, that teachers' actions need to be "evidence informed," but more than that—they must be moved and inspired by the data, and helped to pinpoint the action that will be effective. They need, in short, to be able to put FACES on the data, and to know what to do to help the individual children behind the statistical mask.

What matters to most teachers is their children, their humanity— what we have called their FACES and what lies behind them. We asked over 500 teachers and administrators, "Why should we put FACES on data?" One teacher said playfully, "Because they are so damned cute." True enough for kindergarten, but overall our answer is "because it is so damned important." You need to care for students, but you also need to help them get better in the one thing that can serve them for life—their day-to-day learning.

As well as the need to connect to students emotionally, teachers need to be able to diagnose and act on their students' learning needs. In other words, teachers need to be knowledgeable experts for each student. All of this is a tall and demanding order because effective teachers will need to combine emotion and cognition in equal measure. Weaken one of these links, and the learning possibilities collapse.

Toward Well-Known FACES

In this book, we distill what we have learned about getting to the human side of learning, while zeroing in on the knowledge base and expertise required for deep and widespread learning outcomes. What will be essential is not just to discover a passionate teacher here and there but rather how to generate emotional commitment and effective instruction on a very large scale—for whole systems. To do so you do need data, but you need to generate and use it in a way that makes the child come alive in the minds and actions of teachers. We and our colleagues have learned a great deal about how to do this.

We know that lessons may be learned from leaders who have created and sustained district-wide improvement, lessons about the importance of uncommon persistence in the face of competing priorities, unfailing attention to the details of implementation, hard-nosed decision-making regarding where best to allocate scarce resources, ego-free leadership, and ongoing attention to evidence about what is working and what needs to be modified. Leading educational reform in your state, district, school, or division is not for the faint-of-heart, the impatient, or those who are easily distracted. This book offers critical and detailed lessons for those aiming to help schools do a better job on behalf of their students, lessons learned from those who are achieving state, district, school, and student success.

Throughout each chapter, readers will find "Deliberate Pauses," which offer an opportunity to reflect on some of the questions that the chapter may raise. These questions and more are collected in Appendix H to use as a book study. In addition, we include in each chapter at least one "Narrative from the Field." These narratives are based on the stories that outstanding teachers and leaders have shared with us about an emotional connection or a cognitive insight they have gained in to a student's or a teacher's FACE. Finally, throughout the book we integrate case studies of real schools, districts, and a whole state that have achieved success.

Deliberate Pause

- How useful have your data been?
- Of all the data available, which are most critical?
- Which data are missing?
- Instead of using data, do players at every level "hope for" exceptional instructional practice within the mysterious black box known as the classroom?
- Give examples from your data that demonstrate you know that every child is learning at his or her maximum potential?

Since about 1990 a growing body of work has pointed to the use of data to inform decisions made by successful states, school districts, school administrators, teachers, and the broader community about the state of student achievement. However, one could say that a "faceless glut" of data is a both a political and a systemic pathological problem facing educators almost everywhere. With so much information available, can politicians and education leaders with the will to raise the common core state standards in their districts and schools find the right mix of simple-to-read data to overcome the inertia in their jurisdictions? Can they find a proven "how to" solution to drive achievement? If they find a solution, how can they ensure that every child learns, that every teacher teaches well, such that their systems and every school within their systems become high performers and therefore are accountable for the funding dollars they receive and for achieving their social-moral imperative? Let's see what's "out there" that might answer these questions.

Both of us are researchers and, as well, one of us (Sharratt) is a leader-practitioner-consultant and the other (Fullan) is an external leader—an international authority on change and leadership. We have worked in many different states and districts across North America and beyond on full implementation or what we are calling "collective capacity-building." We examine here what it means to "put the FACES on the data"—the powerful notion of how to go deeper within focused assessment, by harnessing the value of only relevant data that tell teachers what to teach next for each student, and by doing so in a way that connects the emotions and the intellect of teachers and students.

An example of getting the right data and using it to direct student achievement is that of Luis, a boy in eleventh grade—out of the classroom more often than in, due to highly disruptive behavior. Every week, often on a daily basis, he was suspended for rude, uncontrollable, aggressive behavior. He had been forced to change districts and schools many times. Not knowing what to do next, the vice principal at his latest school, in search of a deeper cause, recommended that Luis's literacy skills be tested. The results presented at an in-school case management meeting (see Chapter 4) showed that Luis was reading at a second-grade level. His teachers and his parents were shocked and disbelieving. His father said, "It's not true. Luis reads his texts every day in the car on the way to school." (Luis had been banned from riding the school bus.) Luis had been covering up and faking it for several years, acting out or withdrawing because he was being asked to read texts way beyond his level of competence.

After a lengthy case management meeting, it was decided that Luis would meet Miss Andrews, the high school's literacy coach, every day after school for a focused *word study* (see Glossary) and reading comprehension strategies lesson. Miss Andrews gradually built rapport and trust with Luis, and at the same time determined that Luis was attempting texts and recreational reading (such as *Harry Potter*) that were well beyond his skills and that he couldn't do his class work or homework. Being frustrated, Luis "acted out" belligerently, to the puzzlement of his teachers, who later began to avoid interacting with him. Over the next few months, after school, demonstrating patient work with Luis, Miss Andrews brought Luis to reading and writing, gradually increasing his competence and confidence. When Miss Andrews "chunked" high-interest, low-vocabulary texts with Luis, the words became sentences and the sentences in paragraphs had meaning for Luis. Now Luis reaches for a newspaper each morning, and not only does he look for the hockey scores, but he also reads the front page because he likes to learn about what's going on in the world. And in class? Luis's teachers learned to modify his written assessments, using simpler words that Luis could understand, and his scores rose gradually to grade level. Luis, and everyone around him, experienced much less frustration as a result. This is the story of a tragic situation in which a simple data-driven analysis and intervention resulted in a positive ending.

How many Luises and Vickys (see Narrative from the Field on page 6) fall through the cracks? It is not good enough to catch the

Narrative from the Field

Another positive story about caring and cognitive teaching, this time at the elementary school level, involves a teacher who didn't think her sixth-grade student Vicky could learn. After several weeks of working in cooperative learning groups and rotating roles within groups, Vicky, who has communication challenges and specific learning needs, was given the role of reporting to the class what her group had done. The teacher was quite anxious about Vicky's ability and how she would manage, so the teacher gave the groups the opportunity to pass the reporting to another child in their group if the child selected didn't want to do it. When it came to her group's turn, the group endorsed Vicky. She stood up and then clearly and confidently told the class what her group had done. After this, Vicky regularly shared her learning and ideas with her groups and her class. The story of Vicky challenged the teacher never to doubt a student's ability but to support each and to recognize each student's work and worth—and to become even better informed by "listening" to the data presented in the actions of other students.

—Linda Forsyth, deputy head teacher,
Perth and Kinross Council, Scotland

odd Luis and Vicky here and there. We must catch each and every student. FACES is about humanizing the teaching of each student and having the tools to do so systemically for all. This book helps you to reach all students without dehumanizing education in the process.

We begin by discussing the *14 parameters,* a district reform strategy that identifies the drivers and keys to implementation that has now been replicated in many jurisdictions worldwide. With the inclusion of a strong literacy-numeracy strategy, schools and districts that have deployed this strategy have reached and sustained success. We also speak about how the use of student achievement data is a powerful tool for improvement at every level—especially if improvement is noted and monitored on the basis of drilling down

Deliberate Pause

- How many students (in your state, school, and classroom) can read with fluency and *comprehension* (see Glossary) by the end of grade 1? How do you know?

into that data to individual student names and FACES in individual classrooms.

How the 14 Parameters Came to Be

In the book *Realization,* we discussed the 14 parameters, the key drivers that we have found to be important for schools, districts, and states to become places where high student achievement is expected and delivered year after year by energized staff teams of true professional educators. To summarize, in the late 1990s, when Bill Hogarth, director of education for the York Region District School Board, stated that all children will read by the end of grade 1, a literacy initiative was launched within the district's seventeen lowest performing schools, as determined by results of the Education Quality and Accountability Office (*EQAO*—see Glossary) standards-based test for grade 3.

We draw frequently in this book on EQAO data. It should be noted that the level 3 and 4 threshold represents a very high standard which includes higher-order thinking skills and requires a student to achieve a score of 70% in order to meet the standard.

Of 150 schools in York Region at that time, 17 found a small staffing allocation within their overall staffing allotment, sufficient to have half-time literacy coaches in each school. There were two caveats concerning the role and the professional learning provided by the district: (1) the literacy coach had to be a respected, valued teacher selected from the school staff; and (2) the principal and the literacy coach had to attend monthly district professional learning sessions together.

The initiative became known as the Literacy Collaborative. It was driven by the Literacy Steering Committee, which comprised the superintendent of curriculum (Sharratt), curriculum coordinators, an appointed system literacy principal, and selected principals from the field. The Literacy Advisory Committee—composed of the elected chair of the board, Bill Crothers; director of education Hogarth; two field superintendents; Sharratt; an elementary and secondary principal representative; and the literacy principal—strategically guided the initiative— similar to Barber's guiding coalition, discussed later in this chapter.

After one year, district scores began to improve with literacy as the priority; the scores from the seventeen Literacy Collaborative schools outperformed both state and district schools (Figures 1.1 and 1.2). In year 2, the seventeen schools again outperformed the others.

When we examined the seventeen schools more closely, we found that nine of the seventeen were able to align and sustain their work on improvement. We called these "high-focus schools." The figures show that in years 3, 4, and 5, the nine "high-focus" schools advanced their level of achievement. Scores for the eight "low-focus" schools were inconsistent because they could not maintain their focus on increasing all students' achievement. What factors differed between the high- and low-focus schools to affect scores as they did?

To determine why nine schools improved so dramatically while the other eight started well but failed to sustain their performance, we analyzed the annual reports from the seventeen schools and interviewed leaders of the initiative to learn which schools had incorporated the

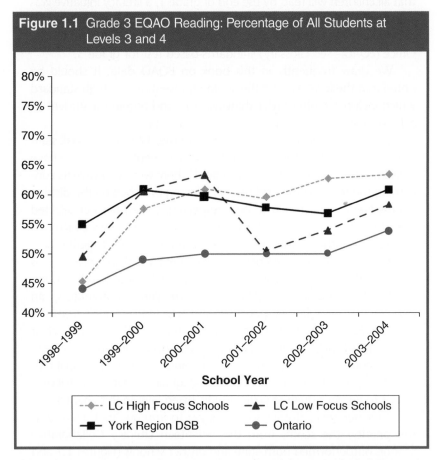

Figure 1.1 Grade 3 EQAO Reading: Percentage of All Students at Levels 3 and 4

Legend:
- LC High Focus Schools
- LC Low Focus Schools
- York Region DSB
- Ontario

Note: A Level 3 score means the student has met the minimum standard of 70%, and a Level 4 score means the student has exceeded the minimum standard.

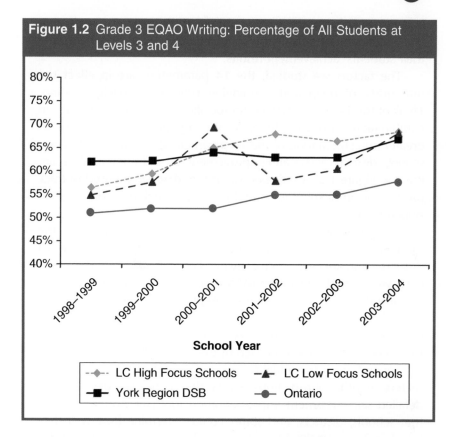

Figure 1.2 Grade 3 EQAO Writing: Percentage of All Students at Levels 3 and 4

literacy coach and professional learning monthly sessions more fully and how they had done it. The nine high-focus schools (see Figures 1.1 and 1.2) that did especially well were initially among the lowest performing schools in the district, yet they moved beyond the state and district averages in a relatively short time and sustained their achievement levels. The explanation for better performance in our view lies in more carefully focused attention to the details in each of 14 improvement areas, or what we call the 14 parameters (Sharratt & Fullan, 2009). It turned out, as we have found time and again, that it is not mere acceptance or endorsement of an idea or practice that counts but rather engaging in the actions that cause *implementation*.

Understanding the reasons for the gains, the district launched the parameter-based program broadly, K–12, by incrementally expanding the Literacy Collaborative. The low-focus schools refocused on increasing *all* students' achievement through intentional assessment and instructional practices. Over time, the remaining elementary and secondary schools in the district followed and began to raise their students' achievement results.

The factors we studied, the 14 parameters, are in effect the nitty-gritty of deep and sustainable collective capacity-building. Think of the 14 parameters as the specific reform strategies that—in combination (and over time, as the organization progresses to greater implementation of the 14 parameters)—"cause" classroom, school, district, and state improvement. The 14 parameters are listed in Figure 1.3. A self-assessment tool that can be used to track progressive implementation of the 14 parameters is provided in Appendix A.

We now know a great deal more about the 14 parameters—the fourteen drivers of reform and practice in successful school districts—and are even more convinced of their validity and efficacy. First, we learned and understood that effective change reform to increase student achievement involves precise planning and detailed work. We know that in order to improve student achievement individual school leaders must actively and diligently work to raise their school's assessment in each of the 14 parameters.

Second, from our initial results and further use of the 14 parameters in other jurisdictions across the globe, we developed a detailed self-assessment implementation tool (see Appendix A) so that schools, districts, and states could determine how well they "stack up" against the 14 parameters of successful schools and districts. The results of a district or school staff's self-assessment can become the outline of a purpose-built school improvement plan—specific to each school's needs and against which progress can be measured (see "Collaborative Inquiry," in Chapter 4).

Third, when we get some schools in a district to move ahead using the 14 parameters, we know we have the makings of a critical mass of instructional leaders who will lead to an almost inevitable tipping point toward system and school improvement for every school for every student in the district. We also know that reaching this point will cause some people in leadership positions to deviate from the plan—"too much work," "not my interest," "not my school"—being excuses and complaints they will use to distract motivation and remove resources from achieving the district's planned reform. With ongoing monitoring of all the assessments of

Figure 1.3 The 14 Parameters

1. Shared Beliefs and Understandings (adapted from Hill & Crévola, 1999)
   a. Each student can achieve high standards, given the right time and the right support.
   b. Each teacher can teach to high standards, given the right assistance.
   c. High expectations and early and ongoing intervention are essential.
   d. Teachers and administrators need to be able to articulate what they do and why they teach the way they do.
2. Embedded Literacy/Instructional Coaches
3. Daily, Sustained Focus on Literacy Instruction
4. Principal Leadership
5. Early and Ongoing Intervention
6. Case Management Approach: (a) Data Walls (b) Case by Case Meetings
7. Professional Learning at School Staff Meetings
8. In-School Grade/Subject Meetings
9. Centralized Resources
10. Commitment of District and School Budgets for Literacy Learning and Resources
11. Action Research/Collaborative Inquiry
12. Parental and Community Involvement
13. Cross-Curricular Connections
14. Shared Responsibility and Accountability

Source: Sharratt and Fullan (2005, 2006, 2009).

activity (see "Parallel Research" section) and listening throughout the system, leaders must ask key questions and confront factors that stand in the way of further implementation.

Fourth, the work can be and has been replicated successfully across contexts, as we illustrate throughout this book using case studies from several jurisdictions in which we are currently working. We know that learning how to succeed on every parameter is the ongoing work of education leaders. It is not surface beliefs that matter; it is focused commitment, making tough resource allocation decisions, drilling down to put FACES on the relevant data, and "staying the course" that matter, no matter what pressures or new concepts the unfocused might launch.

Finally, we learned that new strategies are needed to increase the specificity of teaching and the opportunity to learn. Although it is ideal to use student assessment data to tailor individual student learning, school performance data must also be used to define the precise and intensive support for instructional improvement that is needed in each school. In other words, not only must teachers differentiate student instruction by using various forms of student achievement data to inform the instruction, but system leaders and school administrators must also use student achievement data to differentiate support to teachers and administrators whose tracked student achievement scores represent needs for targeted professional learning sessions. Only a laser-like focus on student achievement data will enable us to put the FACES on the data so that we can improve instruction for all our students—our ultimate vision— our moral imperative. Not coincidentally, such an approach can improve our teachers' and administrators' professional lives, as well—as system leaders and administrators, we put the FACES on their data too.

Parallel Research

Sir Michael Barber's *Deliverology 101* (Barber, Moffit, & Kihn, 2011) speaks authoritatively to the *how* of making change occur in large public organizations, such as education. As chief adviser on delivery for U.K. prime minister Tony Blair, Sir Michael created sustained positive change resulting in increased performance and/or increased satisfaction levels as reported by users and voters across England.

Sir Michael's analysis of what worked in making the changes, and why the changes became so deeply embedded, in many ways parallels the specific elements described in the 14 parameters. We refer to *Deliverology* several times throughout our text, but here are a few instances of positive parallels with our findings and reform strategies:

1. Defining the organization's aspirations—what we call "shared beliefs and understandings" (parameter 1)

2. Defining the reform strategies—what we call the total concept of the 14 parameters, our drivers for reform—learning how to monitor and assess progress toward optimizing the organization's performance against the drivers that, when followed, will lead to increased student achievement

3. Creating and aligning the Delivery Unit with the drivers and bringing a relevant and influential leadership with authority over key resources onto the Delivery Unit—our matrix of scaffolded implementation of the 14 parameters (see Appendix A), from which we develop in this book specific assessment and instruction practices for schools, districts, or states

4. Ensuring an overarching guiding coalition of leaders (that is, the literacy steering and advisory committees) is in agreement, leading and continuously monitoring progress toward and detractors against the defined aspirations and the measurable trajectories and longer-term targets that represent those aspirations—our fourteenth parameter, "shared responsibility and accountability"—evident in "learning walks and talks" or the "learning fair" concept (see Chapter 5)

5. Training constantly for quality and to build organizational capacity to ensure sufficient understanding of and commitment toward continuing the program in spite of execution team changes at any level—our model of scaffolded leader and teacher professional learning from modeled to shared to guided to interdependent practice (see Appendix A)

6. Institutionalizing the solution through capacity building and by being so successful that the direction taken, and the many strategies on which it is based, become the new norm for the organization, replacing any and all previous conditions of mediocrity or worse—what we call "collective capacity-building" or "realization," such as in the way this book's case studies demonstrate how to incorporate perfected high-yield assessment and instruction strategies

As you can see, our work in reform implementation in education mirrors, in many ways, Barber's work in the Delivery Unit in England. In the discussion that follows, we speak more to our message of measuring and assessing how individual schools, districts, and states are performing and we speak to how we feel that putting the FACES on the data is a win-win strategy that creates changes in instruction and in achievement levels and that results in a culture of success for students and education professionals—a culture in which all stakeholders can be proud to participate.

We learned in our initial study, and subsequent work has reinforced the idea, of the overarching value of quality leadership at the school level. The successful schools in our research were led by principals, vice principals, and part-time literacy coaches who understood and were committed to the specifics. For example, in the schools we studied, we found the following:

1. School leaders clearly understood the model and, most important, lived the shared beliefs and understandings (parameter 1) in the design.

2. School leaders clearly understood that they needed to attend to the components of the 14 parameters.

3. School teams did constant self-evaluation, striving to align beliefs and understandings among the principal, literacy coach, Reading Recovery teacher, and special education resource teacher as the leadership team who worked with all staff. This involved *accountable talk* (see Glossary) and corresponding action, with each other and with teachers, in an ongoing way—during the school day.

4. School leaders did not let the "distracters" divert their energies and focus—they stayed the course toward literacy and student improvement—holding their nerve until improvement results were realized—no matter what!

We discuss further, in Chapter 5, the specifics of what it takes to put the FACES on the data as an instructional leader. At this point, let's put more flesh on the concept by considering a case study.

Simcoe County District School Board Case Study

Beginning in the 2010–2011 school year, Sharratt worked with Kathi Wallace, the director (chief superintendent) of Simcoe County District School Board, and her assistant superintendents. The Simcoe County District is a large school district in south-central Ontario, Canada, with approximately 50,000 students and 111 schools, covering about 1,800 square miles. The senior team of nine supervisory officers was interested in reflecting on their journey in adopting a deep literacy and numeracy direction to align and focus their work in increasing all students' achievement. Together, they looked to *Realization* (Sharratt & Fullan, 2009) and, specifically, the 14 parameters reform strategy as it provided a microscopic look into their practice and provided answers about how to improve. The work began with a collaboratively built plan of attack—crafted uniquely for the work in Simcoe County—honoring their context and ongoing work in assessment and instruction.

Scrutinizing the data as a team was a first step, specifically, moving from vague percentages to detail by putting the number of students on each set of results. Then they determined the professional learning needs of this supervisory officer team so that they could go deeper into the data with their principals. The work included a commitment to focused homework (replicating these sessions with selected school leadership teams) between sessions.

Results were inconsistent and sporadic but began to show a slight improvement trend. On closer inspection, leaders realized that the sheer numbers did not bring to life the actual students that they knew. It was agreed that the system needed to pay closer attention to who the FACES were and where they were—especially the FACES of real kids that the numbers of students below standard represented. They revisited resource allocation, to tighten it and to ensure that value was added from the same resource spending (such as having a 1.0 full-time equivalent teacher-librarian in each school take on the important role of literacy coach). They developed "expected high-yield practices" in all schools with a related communication-implementation plan. Together they determined collective questions to ask in monitoring principals' and leadership teams' work in each school, and after training with Sharratt, the learning team implemented "learning walks and talks" (Sharratt, 2011) to move beyond simply visiting schools to "looking for expected practices" in classrooms—sharing their findings and determining professional learning needed across the system.

(Continued)

(Continued)

One of the Simcoe senior team, Steve Blake, introduced his principals to *Realization* (Sharratt & Fullan, 2009), and it is with this introduction that the story of one school—one of many that we could choose in Simcoe County—begins. They recount their work to successfully put the FACES on the data by using the 14 parameters self-assessment tool as a lens for improvement.

> I'm not sure we would ever want to retreat . . . teaching and learning this way is too much fun!
>
> —Jeff Clark, principal

Brechin Public School has been using the 14 parameters approach to improvement since September 2009; it is a very positive "work in progress" with impressive initial results that demonstrate both the use of the 14 parameters as a self-assessment tool and how drilling down into the data puts the FACES on the data for everyone. Yes, it is a small school, but it does perfectly mirror any other school of its size within any district that has larger and smaller schools. The story here is "learning is the work" and how "assessment that drives instruction undertaken by every teacher in every class counts." Staff teams like those in Brechin and in the district believe that every child matters. And every example of good practice is worth a review.

Brechin Public School is a 200-student rural school located in Central Ontario, where at least 90 percent of students are transported by school bus every day. When Jeff Clark began as principal in September 2009, he was faced with very low 2008–2009 grade 3 and grade 6 EQAO reading, writing, and mathematics assessment scores; these scores had been inconsistent in previous years (Table 1.1). At a district principals' meeting, Jeff's colleague Shelley Clark (no relation, but everyone asks) reviewed *Realization* (Sharratt & Fullan, 2009), suggesting that the book's 14 parameters reform strategy framework would be the perfect starting point for rejuvenating a school in challenging circumstances. Jeff was sold on the evidence presented and began to work with Shelley on a strategy for improvement.

Beginning with the End in Mind

Why are we examining Brechin as an important case study? Did the work make a difference to all students at Brechin? Tables 1.1 and 1.2 show the scores of successive grade 3 and grade 6 classes. The year 2009–2010

Table 1.1 Percentage of Brechin Grade 3 and Grade 6 Students Scoring at EQAO Levels 3 and 4

Grade 3	Reading	Writing	Math	Number Assessed
2005–2006	59%	52%	52%	29
2006–2007	60	55	75	20
2007–2008	42	26	21	19
2008–2009	22	33	39	16*
2009–2010	*76*	*90*	*100*	*21*

*16 of 18 were tested in 2008–2009; in other years, all students were tested.

Grade 6	Reading	Writing	Math	Number Assessed
2005–2006	73	42	65	26
2006–2007	47	45	39	38
2007–2008	42	58	58	12
2008–2009	48	33	52	24*
2009–2010	*82*	*68*	*59*	*22*

*24 of 27 were assessed in 2008–2009; in other years, all students were assessed.

Source: Jeff Clark, principal.

results (in italics) are the first-year results of the new reform strategy at Brechin Public School.

Table 1.1 shows erratic, low performance from 2005–2006 to 2008–2009 by students assessed in both grades 3 and 6.

In Table 1.2, the actual number of students below standard in grades 3 and 6 from 2005–2006 to 2008–2009 is startling. In Tables 1.1 and 1.2, the year 2009–2010 results (in both percentages and actual numbers) show dramatic improvement. In our view, the percentage means nothing; the number of students—the actual number of FACES—is what matters. Every FACE counts to us!

Table 1.3 offers two interesting insights. First, in any discussion of successive class or cohort scores, there is often an issue with the perceived

(Continued)

(Continued)

Table 1.2 Number of Brechin Grade 3 and Grade 6 Students Scoring below EQAO Levels 3 and 4				
Grade 3	Reading	Writing	Math	Number Assessed
2005–2006	12	14	14	29
2006–2007	8	9	5	20
2007–2008	11	14	15	19
2008–2009	12	11	10	16*
2009–2010	5	2	0	21

*16 of 18 were tested in 2008–2009; in other years, all students were tested.

Grade 6	Reading	Writing	Math	Number Assessed
2005–2006	7	15	9	26
2006–2007	20	21	23	38
2007–2008	7	5	5	12
2008–2009	12	16	12	24*
2009–2010	4	7	9	22

*24 of 27 were assessed in 2008–2009; in other years, all students were assessed.

Source: Jeff Clark, principal.

academic strength of one class versus that of its predecessor or the following class. It is interesting in this case to follow the two cohorts available to us. Prior to the new Brechin Public School Improvement Plan, cohort 1 had EQAO reading and writing scores that dropped from grade 3 to grade 6, whereas it was able to hold its EQAO math score—while low, it was sustained. Cohort 2, which appears to be only slightly stronger in grade 3 reading and writing than cohort 1 but much stronger in math, does remarkably well with the strategies of the new plan focused on intentional instruction in reading and writing. The cohort does not appear to do as well in math, in fact dropping off from its grade 3 EQAO performance. The timing of consistent professional learning regarding math in the latter part of the 2009–2010 school year and what is clearly an erosion of skills acquisition in grades 4 and 5, are explanations offered for cohort 2's math scores.

Table 1.3 Brechin Same-Student Scores in Grades 3 and 6			
Cohort 1	Reading	Writing	Math
Grade 3 (2005–2006)	59	52	52
Grade 6 (2008–2009)	48	33	52
Cohort 2	Reading	Writing	Math
Grade 3 (2006–2007)	60	55	75
Grade 6 (2009–2010)	82	68	59

Source: Jeff Clark, principal.

Of course, the school and the district are keen to know if the progress was sustained into the 2010–2011 school year, and if the next same-student cohort enjoyed success like cohort 2. Pretests this year indicate that students are on a very positive trajectory. Having just written that, the most recent EQAO results are now available for the 2010–2011 school year. Grade 3 reading increased 23 percent and grade 6 writing increased 20 percent above 2009–2010 results. Amazing? Not really, when you read the case study and examine the whole-school approach to intentionality and consistency of instructional practice. Table 1.4 summarizes the astounding improvement that the cohort of students who were in grade 3 in 2007–2008 made when they were in grade 6 (in 2010–2011) in reaching the target of all students attaining Levels 3 and 4.

Table 1.4 Improvement of Same Cohort of Students in Reaching Levels 3 and 4 on EQAO Provincial Assessments, 2010–2011			
EQAO Area Assessed	Grade 3 (2007–2008)	Grade 6 (2010–2011)	Percentage-Point Increase in Achievement of Levels 3 and 4
Reading	42%	75%	33%
Writing	26	80	54
Math	21	42	21

(Continued)

(Continued)

What Was the Starting Point for Improvement?

Beginning in 2009–2010, staff members and Jeff held difficult discussions about the previous year's results and shared their beliefs and understandings about engaging all learners to their maximum achievement. They collectively agreed they didn't want to be at the "bottom" but weren't sure what to do—so they decided to learn together, to take responsibility and to be accountable for the poor results, and to make a positive difference for their kids. Scrutinizing the EQAO results coupled with knowing their learners, the staff team chose literacy learning—in the area of reading, first, as the focus for 2009–2010. So their new School Improvement Plan stated:

> All students will be able to respond to and reflect on a variety of texts by making inferences, extending understanding, analyzing, identifying, and extending points of view. Students will make connections when they are responding by using schema, questioning for deeper thinking, understanding the message of the story, internalizing what their thoughts are and how their thinking has changed, and thinking about other people's point of view.

Instructional Reform Strategies

The action plan was to build-in an increase in the teaching capacity of staff by aligning every aspect of the school's work with essential practices in assessment and instruction. Staff deconstructed the District Improvement Plan for Student Achievement in order to develop common understandings of the needs assessment and data analyses required to align their own school plan. Then, using the 14 parameters self-assessment tool (Appendix A), staff completed the assessment, identified needs, and formulated action plans to use 10 of the 14 parameters and proceeded to integrate these into the School Improvement Plan.

Going deeper, they then collaborated on divisional literacy planning documents (K–2 Primary, 3–6 Junior, and 7–8 Intermediate) that outlined clustered curriculum expectations to be addressed, reading strategies, writing forms, content units, assessment dates, and a timeline for teacher reflections on progress. It was a focused, whole-school approach to improvement. To equip students to make meaning in reading, they collectively agreed to common teaching targets. They agreed that they *must*

- Reach 100-percent consistency in the use of proven high-yield reading comprehension strategies

- Practice shared, modeled, guided, and independent reading, explicitly teaching skills and providing authentic, relevant, and engaging student tasks
- Base instruction on the clustered expectations (learning goals) of the Ontario Curriculum for all language strands (see Chapter 3)
- Develop and implement comparable learning experience across like grades and a continuum of knowledge and skills between grades
- Use common terminology from kindergarten to grade 8, taken from *A Guide to Effective Instruction in Reading* (Ontario Ministry of Education, 2003)

What Was Strategic?

Timetables were changed. The staff scheduled in a structured daily 100-minute uninterrupted literacy block at every grade level, with effective balanced literacy (see Chapter 4) as the instructional framework for teaching language.

All teachers were expected to deliver a program of modeled, shared, guided, and independent reading and writing based on *assessment for, as,* and *of learning* (see Glossary). The part-time literacy coach provided ongoing dialogue and support, articulating and demonstrating proven practices and identifying and providing resources.

A data wall (see Chapter 3) was used to visually update student achievement so that teachers could readily identify which students required strategy intervention and which needed in-class extended activities. Strategies were shared and implemented. Case management meetings (see Chapter 4), based on students' *developmental learner profiles* (see Glossary), including student work samples, were embedded and provided rich, ongoing discussion, with interventions consistently planned, implemented, monitored, and assessed. *Leveled books* and *mentor texts* (see Glossary) were purchased. The use of assistive technology for students identified with special needs became a priority focus to help differentiate or support curriculum content and assessment.

Teacher Buy-in Led to Engagement

Just as Jeff and the teachers focused on using the available student achievement data to inform instruction, he used data and the School Improvement Plan to inform professional learning. Professional learning was created for all, where universally valuable, and for individuals where

(Continued)

(Continued)

specifically needed; it was prioritized and timetabled. Also, he amended schedules to provide required time and support for staff to study and implement *Guides to Effective Instruction* (Ontario Ministry of Education, 2003) together.

Staff meetings quickly shifted focus from administrative items to literacy professional learning. Essential strategies were broken down to promote clarity and successful implementation in all classrooms, with staff sharing their own *big ideas* (see Glossary) and common understandings, and discovering new big ideas through the use of professional resources such as literacy webcasts (see, for example, www.edu.gov.on.ca).

They also planned weekly 35-minute demonstrations of the teaching-learning cycle (see Appendix D) during instructional time, with outstanding teacher leadership provided by staff members who had had previous professional learning in the pathway process. These pathways were informed by student achievement data and planned based on curriculum expectations and *learning goals* (see Glossary). Teaching strategies were determined by *teacher moderation* (see Glossary), and pre-assessments and post-assessments were analyzed to determine growth of individual students and the success of the specific strategies implemented.

All teachers were involved in visiting literacy demonstration sites early in the year, numeracy sites during the third term, and collaboratively focusing on improvement strategies after each visit by continuing to co-plan and co-teach (see Chapter 4). All teachers also participated in monthly half-day professional learning sessions with the literacy coach to build capacity in essential literacy and numeracy practices and in how this work in literacy and numeracy intersected—language being the common denominator. Joy Nelson, the school's literacy coach, consistently supported teacher efforts in classrooms and during staff meetings. Through scheduling and additional support and funding from the district superintendent, Steve Blake, and the provincial program staff, staff members felt supported

- In the implementation of specific literacy strategies by the literacy coach (see Chapter 4)
- With additional targeted text resources in a centralized book room (see Appendix A, parameter 9)
- In the effective use of learning goals and success criteria (see Chapter 3)

Triage Worked: Evidence of Success

The staff team together set targets that could be monitored and measured using the focused assessment tools available—the 2009–2010 EQAO results, PM Benchmarks (assessing reading comprehension, decoding, and fluency) for K–3, and CASI (assessing comprehension, attitudes, strategies, and interests) for junior–intermediate classes (grades 4–8).

The EQAO grade 3 and grade 6 standard assessments were beginning to show improvement. But this was not enough for the staff. Triangulating the data from the other two assessments with the EQAO assessment data gave the staff a richer view of how each student (FACE) was doing. There were gains in achievement levels in PM Benchmarks for primary reading (Table 1.5) and in CASI results for junior and intermediate students (Table 1.6).

Table 1.5	Percentage of Students in Grades 1–3 at or above Level 3 (Standard) on PM Benchmarks			
	Fall 2009	*Spring 2010*	*Fall 2010*	*Spring 2011*
Grade 1	35%	54%	63%	63%
Grade 2	74	79	42	50
Grade 3	55	65	68	84

Source: Jeff Clark, principal.

Table 1.5 shows that during the 2009–2010 school year, 64 students in grades 1–3 moved 491 benchmark levels, and during the 2010–2011 school year, 61 students in grades 1–3 moved 439 benchmark levels.

Table 1.6	Number of Students in Grades 4–8 at Each Level of Learning on the CASI Assessment			
	Fall 2009	*Spring 2010*	*Fall 2010*	*Spring 2011*
Level 1 (lowest)	15	2	8	4
Level 2 (below standard)	35	29	41	40
Level 3 (at standard)	20	39	40	48
Level 4 (above standard)	3	4	6	10

Source: Jeff Clark, principal.

(Continued)

(Continued)

Table 1.6 shows that 22 of 35 Level 2 students successfully moved to Level 3 (at standard) in 2009–2010, and 15 of 41 Level 2 students successfully moved to Level 3 (at standard) thus far in 2010–2011.

Anecdotally, at the beginning of the next school year of intense work, 2010–2011, teachers reported that students began their new grades being able to demonstrate the following:

- *Prior knowledge* of terminology, concepts, and reading strategies (see Glossary)
- The use of language and images in rich and varied forms to read, write, listen, view, and represent
- More critical thinking about big ideas

Most important, because all teachers learned to use the same terminology and to implement strong instruction with support, they could clearly express their excitement in sharing these precise observations about students' improvement. In other words, teachers could name the students' improvement with specificity—putting the FACES on the improvement data. These teachers and Jeff proudly write:

We have been successful in aligning instructional strategies and assessment for, as, and of learning to support all students. We have tried to "hasten slowly," ensuring that student and staff learning is *scaffolded,* with *learning goals* and *success criteria* [emphasis added; see Glossary] achieved before moving to the next stage of development. During principal literacy walks and supervision, much small-group, modeled, and shared reading and writing and guided reading have been noted. There is an ever-increasing use of technology in our classrooms to support accessing the curriculum and providing *differentiated instruction* [emphasis added; see Glossary]. Learning Goals and Success Criteria, generated by both teacher and students, engage teachers and students. There is a lot of evidence of observation leading to conferencing, whether teacher with student or peer to peer. Student achievement data are being regularly collected to inform practice, and essential instructional and assessment strategies are being utilized effectively.

Four Key Reflections

The successful improvement strategies identified by staff were as follows:

1. A focus on *balanced literacy* (see Glossary) gave the staff a clear vision and a shared sense of purpose. It helped "unclutter" their work and clarified their communication with colleagues, students, and parents.

2. Networking with a like-partner school, Rama Central Public School with principal Shelley Clark, was integral to developing and revising a comprehensive literacy plan based on *Realization* (Sharratt & Fullan, 2009), while networking with other principals regarding evidence-proven practices offered a constant stream of new thoughts.

3. Literacy coach (see Chapter 4) support of teachers and having the literacy coach as a coleader on the school leadership team contributed significantly to the school's success in the first year and catapulted their ability to continue through year 2. "The professional learning and collective capacity-building that occurred was amazing, as essential instructional practices were illustrated and implemented," emphasized one teacher.

4. Success breeds success. Being able to share increased targeted student achievement results on the 2009–2010 primary and junior EQAO assessments was an enormous boost to the staff and community—a valuable validation of the staff's conscientious commitment to "doing something positive" for all students.

"The entire school community knew we were on the right track!" Hand in hand with success was willingness—the very real willingness of the staff to take a risk with the new principal in attacking the problem together and to put into very public practice the idea that learning is the work (Sharratt & Fullan, 2009, p. 12).

Where from Here?

The School Improvement Plan, 2011–2012, is staying the course and will become even more closely aligned with the Simcoe County District Improvement Plan, in which the "Reach Every Student" goal states that "all students will have access to differentiated instruction and assessment

(Continued)

(Continued)

that is responsive to the unique needs of the learner to support students' high achievement and learning for life." The "Close the Gap" goal "ensures that achievement trend data will be analyzed to inform classroom instruction and specific interventions for all students." The "Assessment" goal states that all students will participate in instruction that is informed by *assessment for, as,* and *of learning* (see Glossary). Steve, Jeff, and Shelley as leaders, continue to commit to the process:

> We will continue to personalize our comprehensive literacy plans as adapted from *Realization,* working to deepen our implementation strategies on each of the 14 parameters. This work will continue to guide and support our staff, students, and school community. Specifically, we will continue to build collective capacity in teacher practice in the implementation of the Ontario Curriculum, in assessment for and as learning, and in the gradual release of responsibility in our comprehensive literacy program. We will continue to set high expectations for teacher and student learning, and we will ensure engagement of staff in a focus on the teaching-learning cycle. There will continue to be timely and tiered interventions delivered in a team approach, and data will continue to be used to inform instruction to improve student achievement.

Sustainability

Jeff reports that it seems relatively easy to envision sustainability of the progress made as a staff and as a school but notes that their dedication to the moral imperative—the focus on literacy learning, and the shared beliefs and understandings with colleagues—has been and will continue to be tested. It certainly appears that patience, endurance, compassion, and continuing to put the FACES on the data will all be needed to stay the course.

However, the school has made significant progress in embedding the 14 parameters in its classroom practice and school culture. It has experienced increased use and explicit teaching of literacy strategies that benefit all students, and a supportive and collaborative staff model that shares responsibility and accountability for all students. A huge shift has occurred in instruction, from rote learning and recall to developing the *big ideas* in ensuring conceptual understanding (see Glossary), making connections, reorganizing information, thinking critically, and engaging in a *critical literacy* stance (see Glossary) that compels social action. The staff has also seen a shift from a singular summative evaluation to multiple and varied opportunities for all learners to demonstrate the full range of what they know and can do.

At the district level, Simcoe County results from the 2010–2011 EQAO reveal that the focused intervention has made a difference at the grade 3 level. In grade 3, reading scores have increased by 3 percent and writing, by 5 percent. These are impressive results in a large school district. The district's focused work to put FACES on the data continues at every grade level.

Sources: Steve Blake, superintendent of education; Jeff Clark, principal; and Shelley Clark, principal, Simcoe County District School Board, Ontario, Canada.

Deliberate Pause

- What is your plan for improvement—how do all staff commit?
- What resources do you have available to implement this focused work?
- Are your instructional coaches offering added value to the professional learning of administrators *and* teachers?
- What lessons learned at Brechin Public School apply to your context?

Narrative from the Field

An audible silence struck the conference room. He had just shown the assembled school district administrators and principals the standard testing data they knew so well, but with a twist that changed their comfort level. He translated the cold district data showing the percentage of students falling into the "below standard" and "meets minimum standard"—data each member of the audience could repeat by rote—into very challenging new school performance data highlighting the precise number of student FACES each year who failed to reach the minimum standard. They could see the number of students who failed in their group of schools and they could see how many failed in their own schools.

(Continued)

(Continued)

She picked up the pieces. She showed how first one school district, then another, had used the 14 parameter strategy, and how they adopted the concerted, determined but inclusive leadership style that focuses on managing available resources to transform student achievement results. She showed them that this combined process—implementation strategy and leadership style—built "capacity" in the process. This collective capacity-building was successful because it improved student achievement results and also produced higher classroom teacher satisfaction measures—Realization was occurring. The conference room silence was broken by the buzz of very real and keen interest. They got to work.

So far we have had only a taste of what it means to move from a page of statistics to the flesh, blood, and destiny of individual children. And we have shown that it can be done for all students in a school and in a district. In Chapter 2 we go deeper to demonstrate the power of putting FACES on the data. Then in the rest of the book we work through the heart of our model—the integration of assessment, instruction, leadership, and ownership.

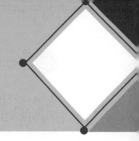

CHAPTER TWO

The Power of Putting FACES on the Data

All large-scale reform faces a dilemma. How do you get coherence in an otherwise fragmented system? It's all well and good to say, "Let's start with shared beliefs and understandings," but operationalizing those beliefs and understandings requires definitions of each that result in goals, and we need structures through which we accomplish our work toward those goals. Deeper than the question, Did we get to our goals? is an underlying need for organizations and for everyone in them to know what they have to do to achieve the goals and then, at the end of the day, to know how they performed in moving toward the goals.

In schools and within education systems, we know that moving toward the goals defined in our shared beliefs and understandings starts with structured plans that are based on shared specificity and consistency of good practice across all classrooms—without imposing it (which we know doesn't work). But which practices are so effective that they become nonnegotiable, that is, the expected operating norms in every classroom? And how do we ensure these practices are in fact delivered in every classroom? For example, if we believe that every child can learn and has the right to learn, then we need to determine not just if every child has learned, but to optimize classroom teacher effectiveness, we need to know on an ongoing basis that every child is learning by making ongoing assessments and by incorporating that information about each child's learning into daily instruction—a nonnegotiable practice. All teachers can teach if supported with the right resources. We need to offer them rich, easy-to-use inputs, including putting the FACES on the data, so that they can do what it takes to reach the goal of every student learning. Doing so is the system's responsibility to the students and it is necessary to guarantee every teachers' right to teach well.

Genesis of the Dialogue with Educators

We know from research and experience that understanding student performance enables teachers to present or to ask more appropriate questions, but there are so many forms of information, so many types of data available, and so many students in our classes that sometimes our teachers become bewildered, facing what they perceive as an "information glut," that sense that if only they knew what information was important, and how to cut through all that "stuff," they would know what to do in their classrooms and with each of their students. "If only I could put FACES on the data" is a comment we have heard dozens of times in working on system-wide reform projects and on projects to improve student achievement.

We started with this notion of the faceless glut, and in 2011 we approached hundreds of professional educators with whom we were working in the United States, Canada, the United Kingdom, and Australia for their views on three questions and to gather examples or stories we could share. These are the questions we asked:

1. Why do we put FACES on the data?

2. How do we put FACES on the data?

3. What are the top three leadership skills needed to put FACES on the data?

When and How We Asked the Research Questions

In group sessions we had the cooperation of and received input from 507 educators from across the globe. We used a Placemat format to gather the data (see Appendix B) and gave the participants time to provide open-ended responses to the first two questions and to reach consensus on the third question. Participants included directors of systems, superintendents of regions within systems, principals, vice principals, curriculum consultants, literacy or instructional coaches, support teachers, and many classroom teachers.

We were delighted with the response—not one of the 507 respondents lacked for definite opinions on this critical subject! We discuss and display the general findings from the three questions in this chapter. The details from question 1 follow in this chapter. Question 2 is answered in depth in Chapter 3 (on assessment) and Chapter 4 (on instruction). Leadership, a review of what practitioners defined as the top three leadership skills, is examined in Chapter 5.

In reviewing the answers received from respondents, we noted a number of broad generalizations that have implications for us in communicating the importance of using data correctly and vigilantly at varying levels within an organization. In sum, messages must be target specific—which sounds parallel to the importance of understanding student data, doesn't it?

Table 2.1 displays the number of responses received to each question. These are the generalizations we noted from the data:

1. The questions received very different numbers of responses.

2. Respondents understand and report a broad range of reasons for putting FACES on the data.

3. Respondents often used the 14 parameters (Sharratt & Fullan, 2009) or other common language that clustered readily.

4. Respondent groups provided approximately 2.2 responses per person for question 1, showing their interest in the "humanity" aspects of putting FACES on the data.

5. Respondent groups provided approximately the same number of responses per person for question 2 as for question 1, showing they had definite opinions about and viable experiences in putting FACES on the data.

6. Participants (placed into small groups, usually of four) were asked to reach consensus on the top three leadership skills before responding to question 3; as a result, the overall number of responses to question 3 is many less than for questions 1 and 2.

Table 2.1 Number of Responses Received for Each of the Three Questions Asked

Question	Question Asked	Number of Responses	Percentage of Responses
1	Why do we put FACES on the data?	1,102	43%
2	How do we put FACES on the data?	1,095	43
3	What are the top three leadership skills needed to put FACES on the data?	369	14
Total		2,566	100

Research Findings: Question 1

Research question 1 (Why do we put FACES on the data?) had 1,102 individually crafted responses, which, when clustered, fell into four categories: human-emotional, instruction, assessment, and ownership. Figure 2.1 demonstrates that 46 percent of responses focused on the human-emotional connection to the question, 29 percent of the responses focused on the connection to instruction, 13 percent focused on the ownership connection as the reason for putting FACES on the data, and 12 percent focused on the assessment connection for putting FACES on the data. The pattern of these responses confirms the theme of this book—putting FACES on the data. What excites and motivates humans, teachers all the more so, is emotional connections to other humans with respect to current life situations. In fact, when you take this connection and incorporate "instruction"—both values on the human condition—fully 75 percent of respondents identified with this core moral purpose.

The responses grouped into each of the four clusters are shown in Table 2.2. Each identified cluster may have had dozens of unique responses, which have been reduced to exemplars of thinking and expression. We believe that most educators and parents will not only understand these clustered responses, but most will relate to them.

Figure 2.1 Question 1: Why Do We Put FACES on the Data—
Clustered Responses by Percent

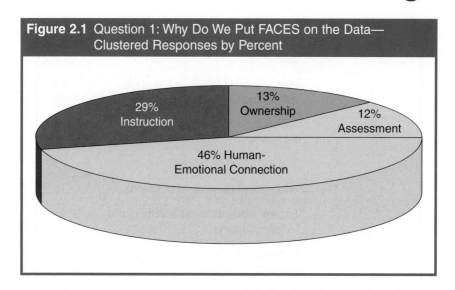

13% Ownership

12% Assessment

29% Instruction

46% Human-Emotional Connection

Table 2.2 Question 1: Why Do We Put FACES on the
Data?—Items in Clustered Responses

Cluster	Responses	Rank
Human-Emotional	Adds a personal, human, emotional element	1
	Encourages all system, school members to make the work personal, motivating, meaningful	3
	Identify areas of need for individual students	4
	Make our work about the real students	5
	Know all your students	6
	Be engaged with, make connection to learners	11
	Support individual growth	14
Instruction	Align teaching strategies	2
	Specify strategies required for improvement	6

(Continued)

(Continued)

Cluster	Responses	Rank
	Ensure success for all—no one gets left behind	12
	Base teaching on student aptitudes and interest	13
	Support effective teaching practices	15
	Bring moral purpose to our work	16
	Engage students in the teaching and learning process	18
	Inform curriculum decisions and resource allocation	21
	Set goals for future instruction	26
Ownership	Promote shared responsibility for student success, collective responsibility, commitment	8
	Promote accountability	9
	Make a connection with the parents	23
	Use the research to guide the practice	25
Assessment	Understand if the processes and strategies we are using are having an impact	10
	Identify students who are struggling and require additional supports	16
	Find, measure, and celebrate success	19
	Target those students who may require special strategies to achieve curricular learning goals	20
	Identify possible groupings of students with like needs	22
	Look for trends (e.g., socioeconomic, cultural, family circumstances, English language learners)	24

Table 2.2 displays the summary phrases for clustered responses collected for question 1. Once listed summary phrase items were totaled within the clusters, they were ranked by the number of "mentions" underlying each. The ranking appears in the right-hand column and is for the entire collection of items, as opposed to representing rankings within each cluster. Line items with similar ranking were scored as ties with the subsequent ranked line item skipping one numbering position to accommodate the tie.

The human-emotional connection was the highest overall ranked cluster. Five of its seven line items fall into the top ten of all mentioned responses. Instruction and ownership each have two in the top ten, whereas assessment has one in the top ten, and that is number 10.

Responses from the 507 respondents indicate that putting FACES on the data helps them to

- Know the students (personal, human-emotional element; encourage colleagues to make the work personal; make our work about the real students; know your students)
- Plan for them (align teaching strategies, specify strategies required for improvement)
- Ensure everyone knows they are responsible or "own" all students (all are our students, promote accountability)
- Assess progress widely and for individuals (understand if the processes and strategies we are using are having an impact)

Figure 2.2 represents graphically the item distribution in response to question 2: How do we put FACES on the data? Table 2.3 summarizes the 1,095 individual responses from the 507 respondents. Gathered into three clusters, the data set is a collection of 19 topics that themselves are compilations of like-responses. The uses of data fall into three clear categories that we would call assessment oriented, instruction oriented, and learner-identity oriented. If, as a teacher, you combine these three orientations, you come pretty close to becoming a teacher of choice, one who can effectively help all children to learn.

As seen in Figure 2.2, the overall split of responses among assessment, instruction, and knowing the learner were 36 percent, 39 percent, and 25 percent, respectively. Respondents provided the largest number of responses for the first item—assessment "for"

Figure 2.2 Question 2: How Do We Put FACES on the Data—Clustered Responses by Percent

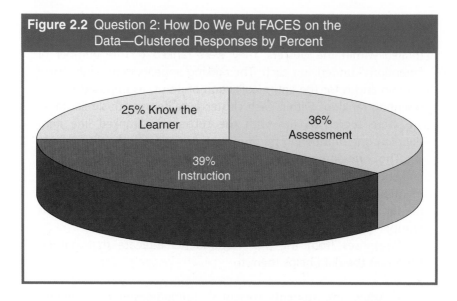

Table 2.3 Question 2: How Do We Put FACES on the Data?—Items in Clustered Responses

Cluster	Responses	Rank
Assessment	Assessment of learning and to determine next steps in learning—tracking walls	1
	Collect, monitor data to track students' progress on intervention program over the year	5
	Goal setting—clear, identified goals for individuals and classrooms for a period of time	9
	Assessment results used to identify groups of like abilities, and specific learning strategies	10
	Assessment to develop profiles of need for individual students	16
	Data analysis to determine trends, patterns among students, classes, and groups in the school	19
Instruction	Collaborative use of evidence gathered for group input	2

Cluster	Responses	Rank
	Discussion of specific student work at school teams to discover new strategies with teacher	3
	Adapt styles of teaching to match styles of learning as evidenced in data	6
	Identify target students for interventions—usually bottom three students in the class	10
	Identify marker students whose work is brought regularly to grade or team meetings	12
	Celebrate successes at every stage of learning; assume all students will have some success	15
Know the Learner	Engage students (e.g., in making decisions about what to learn and mode of assessment)	4
	Build meaningful relationships using information about the learner to build trust, confidence	7
	Get to know each student's learning style and interests to capture their attention	8
	Have all of a student's teachers look at the student's full-work portfolio to understand whole student	13
	Use photos everywhere; ensure no student name goes unknown; highlight all who need help	14
	Believe in parameter 1—all students can learn if all teachers understand the data-driven strategies	17
	Engage parents in dialogue early, often; be sincere in offering them ideas, asking their help	18

learning and assessment "as" learning to determine the next steps in learning—over 220 responses. Respondents were the next most responsive in the instruction category—collaborative use of evidence gathered for group input, those opportunities taken when teachers bring all their evidence of student work to grade meetings, co-teaching meetings, or to special group meetings designed specifically to discuss instructional challenges (see discussion of case management meetings and co-teaching in Chapter 4).

Balancing the two notions of assessment to lead instruction and data that can enlighten a group about a student's performance is the notion that data can inform the teacher and other staff about a student sufficiently that they can begin to form a working relationship with that student by putting a FACE on the data. Respondents feel that the more a teacher can know about each learner, the greater the opportunity to break through, to create trust, and to show the teacher's respect for every student.

Within the assessment cluster, responses included the following:

- To *set goals so that teachers can prepare lessons* and break lessons into learning style segments to match what their class data sets say
- To *identify trends in learning or low levels of learning* coming from other grades or classes, or from communities within classes

Within the instruction cluster, responses included the following:

- To *identify and target students early for interventions* and for potential ongoing monitoring by others
- To be able to *adapt teaching styles to learning styles* as noted in the various forms of assessment done in class during the early part of the year, and in an ongoing manner

Knowing the learner responses can be divided evenly among the following:

- Learning everything a teacher can about every student in order to *build a positive environment* for all children
- Using technologies like digital photography and video to "*name the student*"—so that as many staff as possible can know as many students as possible, especially those in their divisions or in classrooms next door, again, to provide a positive learning environment for all FACES
- *Knowing the parents* and having them *become learning-teaching partners* with the student and the teacher, as their influence can be (should be) very powerful and positive

As shown in Figure 2.3 and Table 2.4, the respondents clearly identified three critical leadership skills. Responses were spread more evenly across these clusters than they were for questions 1 and 2. This even spread of importance may have been due to the collaborative manner in which the small (usually four-person) groups produced their lists of the top three leadership skills. Respondents talked to key elements of leadership theory: vision, leader-learner, and preparation of and participation in a sustainable, enjoyable working environment or culture. They want someone who

- Will know what to do (*knowledge and understanding of best practices, professional; is an effective manager of resources, the structure, time, human resources available; is a teacher but is leading, as lead learner, modeling continuous improvement*)
- Is visible and gets people moving in the same direction (*involved in meetings, with the data, in professional learning sessions—leading and learning, consistent messages communicated well in words and follow-through actions, someone who everyone sees because he or she is around*)
- Leads for the long term (*builds and sustains strong relationships to foster trust, positive environment of trust, is a committed advocate for the learner, and shares responsibility for each child's progress*)

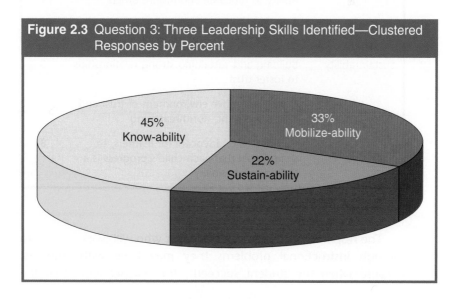

Figure 2.3 Question 3: Three Leadership Skills Identified—Clustered Responses by Percent

Table 2.4 Question 3: Three Leadership Skills Identified—Items in Clustered Responses

Cluster	Responses—Skill Items Defined	Rank
Know-ability	Knowledge and understanding of best practices, professional	1
	Having a strong, compelling message	4
	Effective management of resources, structure, lead organization to gather data, meetings, accountability	6
	Effective management of human resources; looks after well-being of the team	9
	Capacity building for collaboration, empowering through shared leadership, recognizes contributions	10
	Leader as "lead learner," why this, why now, modeling continuous learning	11
Mobilize-ability	Instills collaborative culture focused on shared values	2
	Effective communication skills, delivering clear consistent messages	3
	Ability to motivate and inspire others	11
	Being involved and visible—in meetings, with the data, in professional learning	11
Sustain-ability	Building and sustaining strong relationships to foster trust	5
	Creating positive environment of trust and encouragement, nonthreatening	7
	Committed to advocate for learners, to shared goal that each child's progress is a shared responsibility	8

The respondents clearly value a leader who will work with them through instructional problems they may have with students, because when the student succeeds, the teacher and often the whole staff will have learned new skills together to apply at another time. Using data to lead, modeling collective capacity for collaboration, and empowering through shared leadership were other key skills that respondents noted (discussed in more detail in Chapter 5).

All of these findings corroborate what we know about effective leaders (for example, principals). Above all, they *participate as learners* in helping teachers figure out how to make instructional improvements. Leaders who participate do learn. Their "know-ability," "mobilize-ability," and "sustain-ability" get stronger as they learn. They become more effective and more appreciated for being so.

Clustering the Parameters

The graphs in Figures 2.1, 2.2, and 2.3 show how the research data allow us to cluster the 14 parameters from our previous work in *Realization* (Sharratt & Fullan, 2009) into four big ideas that we call improvement drivers. To zero in on putting FACES on the data, these are the things that great leaders do. These four drivers are underpinned with our foundational belief in parameter 1—the answer to question 1: all students can learn and all students have a right to learn, as discussed in this chapter. Table 2.5 organizes our thinking about how we take the research data, weave in our previous research work with the 14 parameters, and unfold the story in the remaining chapters in this book. We are now in a position to answer clearly the question, why do we put FACES on the data?

Why Do We Put FACES on the Data?

> In every block of marble I see a statue as plain as though it stood before me, shaped and perfect in attitude and action. I have only to hew away the rough walls that imprison the lovely apparition to reveal it to the other eyes as mine see it.
>
> —Michelangelo, 1475–1564

Revealing "the lovely apparition" is our work. Adding a human-emotional element to our work is what makes teaching "the

Table 2.5 Four Drivers Answer Our Questions

Research Question	Drivers	Clustered Parameters	Chapter
1. Why do we put FACES on the data?	Our moral imperative: All students can learn and have the right to learn.	Parameter 1: Shared Beliefs and Understandings: • All students can learn • All teachers can teach • Early intervention and high expectations are critical • Teachers, leaders can articulate why they do what they do	2
2. How do we put FACES on the data? Part 1	1. Assessment	Parameter 5: Early Intervention Parameter 6: Case Management Approach (a) Data Walls Parameter 8: Grade/ Subject Meetings	3
2. How do we put FACES on the data? Part 2	2. Instruction	Parameter 3: Timetabled Literacy Block Parameter 2: Embedded Coaches Parameter 6: Case Management (b) Meetings Parameter 9: Centralized Resources Parameter 13: Cross-Curricular Connections Parameter 11: Collaborative Inquiry	4

Research Question	Drivers	Clustered Parameters	Chapter
3. What leadership skills are needed?	3. Leadership	Parameter 4: Principal Leadership	5
		Parameter 7: Professional Learning at Staff Meetings	
		Parameter 10: Budget Allocation to Strategic Resources	
4. Where does this happen?	4. Ownership	Parameter 12: Parent and Community Involvement	6
		Parameter 14: Shared Responsibility and Accountability	

noblest of all professions"—and also the most complex yet motivating and meaningful. Feedback from teachers and leaders across the world defined our work as making connections with learners to find FACES in the data and then to make "statues of exquisite beauty appear from sometimes rough-hewn stone." Not only in the answers to question 1 but also in the answers to questions 2 and 3, the common theme of knowing learners as real students with real-life stories emerges. Comments such as "know the child—grow the child" call us to place students at the center of what we do in teaching and learning, making data today become instruction tomorrow for each one. In considering leadership skills needed to do just that, respondents mentioned the importance of tying leadership decisions to the instructional core and monitoring that moral purpose in every school, believing that every child has the right to be known and literate. This book is about finding "the lovely apparition" and being the best we can be to carve and create real people.

Of course, Michelangelo was being disingenuous. He had to bring out the best in the marble. He had to carefully chisel it to display its magnificence. This is what teachers do. They unleash and stimulate what students are capable of becoming.

Similarly, Sir Ken Robinson (2009) writes about a teacher finding Gillian Lynne's lovely apparition,

> someone looked deep into her eyes—someone who had seen children like her before and knew how to read the signs. Someone else might have put her on medication and told her to calm down. But Gillian wasn't a problem child. She didn't need to go away to a special school. She just needed to be who she really was. (p. 4)

How Do We Drill Down to Find "the Lovely Apparition"?

When first faced with a mass of student achievement data or state-provided information on populations related to school districts, most of us would rather look for something else to do. Our shared beliefs and understandings are based on a simple foundational beginning—all children can learn—and the capstone, our realization that we are all accountable for the learning of each and every student in our system or school. So how do we make the right choice—get the coffee or break down the data?

Some educators are really good at breaking down the data, but most are not trained or experienced at chipping away the marble in their system reports—they haven't been shown how to imagine there might be a "statue" in there. What follows is a look at how some of the more complicated information provided, such as by state or district authorities, may be chipped away to provide a glimpse at what is happening in the district or system, or the network, or even at the school level.

We have been privileged through our consulting at every level in nations, states, systems, and individual schools to meet and learn from some exceptionally fine state and system analysts—often incredible teachers who have become quite expert in data use because early on in their careers they really wanted to know what they needed to do to understand how to help "all our kids learn." What follows then is our look at some tables, adapted from various systems with which we have worked, that provide a glimpse of the "statue" from different vantage points around it.

To Be, or Not to Be (Good):
That Is the Question

We will not become involved in the debates over whether standards-based testing is good or bad, or whether or not the data posted on websites are too detailed or invasive. Our only interest here is in what the data sources say about the students in a system or in a system's schools and how these data can best be used (1) to stimulate further improvement and (2) to satisfy the public that the system is in strong working order.

We are interested in numbers related to scoring levels, particularly at minimum standard or below minimum standard to reveal the statues (that is, the FACES) in our midst. Our interest arises from the fact that a student who starts in grade 1 at a minimum standard with a minimal literacy level will likely never recover from that start throughout his or her entire education. Students who start below minimum standard in their first assessments will likely continue to barely pass throughout elementary school and will most likely not graduate from secondary school—all because they did not learn to read with fluency and comprehension by the end of grade 1.

We work here with some charts from various jurisdictions. Beginning with Table 2.6 are the standard assessment results for a group of schools we call Bear Paw Schools, a group of schools within a district that we call Small System. The results are for four assessment years (grades). The values shown for our Bear Paw Schools are the percentages of the population of year 3 students who were at or below minimum standard. The trend is for these values to increase: the percentage of students across testing years 3, 5, 7, and 9 reaches its highest point in year 9. The percentage of students performing at the lowest two bands (that is, at or below minimum standard) increases each year. Compared to other schools in Small System, Bear Paw Schools actually performed about the same in years 3, 5, and 7; in year 9, they performed better than other schools in the system, with fewer students in the bottom two bands.

Now let's put some FACES on these bits of data!

Table 2.7 causes us to take more notice, given that these data are the actual numbers of students who were at or below minimum standard. Notice that the number of students in the bottom two bands increases from year 3 to year 9. We learned that there is a

Table 2.6 Percentage of Students in Bottom Two Bands at Bear Paw Schools

| | Percentage of Students in Bottom Two Bands | | | | |
	Reading	Writing	Spelling	Grammar and Punctuation	Math
Year 3 Bear Paw Schools	**11%**	**5%**	**15%**	**14%**	**12%**
Year 3 System	12.7	6.3	14.9	14	12
Year 5 Bear Paw Schools	**18**	**16**	**21**	**18**	**16**
Year 5 System	17.9	15.4	22.3	17.6	16.3
Year 7 Bear Paw Schools	**13**	**18**	**18**	**20**	**12**
Year 7 System	15.4	20.2	20.6	18.7	17
Year 9 Bear Paw Schools	**20**	**34**	**21**	**19**	**17**
Year 9 System	26.6	35.7	24.4	25	22.9

slightly anomalous dip in year 7 due to changes in student enrollment; however, the trend is unmistakable. Students started slow in year 3, and because they had not learned to read proficiently in year 1, the values continued downward to year 9. The trend continues across all domains assessed.

Is the fact that 120 students are underperforming in reading in year 9 all that bad? Table 2.8 shows that the 120 students came from a pool of only 593 who were assessed from Bear Paw Schools. To Small System and to Bear Paw Schools, the number of FACES underperforming was deemed to be unacceptable. And they have done something about it.

More graphically, if staff from Bear Paw Schools were not engaged in a major reform initiative that called for intervention using assessment data and specific instruction for all students, we could say that their results would probably not improve over the

Table 2.7 Number of Students in Bottom Two Bands at Bear Paw Schools

	Number of Students in Bottom Two Bands				
	Reading	Writing	Spelling	Grammar and Punctuation	Math
Year 3 Bear Paw Schools	**78**	**37**	**106**	**100**	**84**
Year 3 System	302	151	354	333	286
Year 5 Bear Paw Schools	**112**	**107**	**144**	**120**	**105**
Year 5 System	416	360	523	413	379
Year 7 Bear Paw Schools	**87**	**121**	**121**	**134**	**80**
Year 7 System	330	438	446	405	370
Year 9 Bear Paw Schools	**120**	**201**	**125**	**112**	**99**
Year 9 System	554	750	511	523	475

Table 2.8 Number of Students Assessed in Bear Paw Schools in the Years Shown

	Number of Students Assessed				
	Reading	Writing	Spelling	G and P	Numeracy
Year 3 Bear Paw Schools	722	719	724	724	725
Year 5 Bear Paw Schools	678	678	674	674	668
Year 7 Bear Paw Schools	666	671	671	671	666
Year 9 Bear Paw Schools	593	599	596	596	592

years to come. If that were the case, we could assume that a mythical cohort made up of the test year classes in years 3, 5, 7, and 9 could represent an actual class traveling through Bear Paw Schools (Table 2.9). Looking at proficiency, we can see how the numbers of those who are assessed as doing well would dwindle—again, all things being equal and with no interventions occurring.

Another way to portray and use data from a specific grade or year over time is simply to stack them, year over year in order. Tables 2.9 and 2.10 are from a single district in Ontario, Canada. You can stack the years across the whole district or just in one school in order to read the trends. The EQAO standard is for 75 percent of students in any grade assessed to be at Level 3 or Level 4. The percentages shown below refer to the percentages of students who had reached Levels 3 and 4.

The grade 3 scores in Table 2.9 are not good—in any domain assessed—75 percent of students at Levels 3 and 4 is the expectation. There has been a slow improvement trend. However, scores were well below state averages in every year shown—at no point did Ontario County as a whole reach standard. Now look at Table 2.10.

Table 2.9 Percentage of Ontario County Grade 3 Students at EQAO Levels 3 and 4, 2000–2009

| | EQAO Assessment | | |
School Year	Reading	Writing	Math
1999–2000	50%	48%	49%
2000–2001	50	52	58
2001–2002	50	54	58
2002–2003	49	60	54
2003–2004	49	58	52
2004–2005	52	65	62
2005–2006	58	70	66
2006–2007	64	70	69
2007–2008	65	71	68
2008–2009	62	70	70

Table 2.10 Percentage of Ontario County Grade 6 Students at EQAO Levels 3 and 4, 2000–2009

School Year	EQAO Assessment		
	Reading	Writing	Math
1999–2000	50%	48%	49%
2000–2001	53	53	50
2001–2002	55	55	52
2002–2003	55	57	50
2003–2004	57	58	54
2004–2005	65	63	58
2005–2006	67	67	61
2006–2007	67	67	58
2007–2008	70	72	62
2008–2009	72	72	65

Table 2.10 shows improvement in Grade 6 since assessment began. However, although the grade 3 and grade 6 reading scores were almost identical in 2000, the grade 6 reading scores climbed much more rapidly and steadily toward standard than did the grade 3 scores. In fact, Ontario County started its own internal improvement program for literacy in 2007, followed by outside consulting in 2009. In some districts, reviewing these two simple charts would lead to questions about the quality of instruction and the quality of the "new" internal intervention program in the primary grades (years 1–3). Is it possible that senior leadership did not pay attention to the potential for improvement? Were there shared common beliefs and understandings? Did anyone "own" the need to increase student achievement? Yet, there was some notice of the need for improvement, at least by the junior-grade (4–6) teachers, that created the positive variance in grade improvement over the primary improvement. Why the difference at the junior level?

One way to project future performance is to review same-student assessment results across the full spectrum of years assessed. Where assessment has not been in place long enough to do this, you might look at all the years and domains assessed and assume that the results could represent a mythical cohort moving through all assessment years. You might assume that you can project future results, but that, of course, would be a mistake. Planned interventions to rectify what you have seen and other unplanned factors will make differences, too. The exercise, however, does add a sense of urgency. Would the declining assessment results in Figure 2.4 be an accurate prediction of what would happen in a larger system? Can this downward spiral in assessment results be stopped? Can it be corrected?

Whereas Figure 2.4 represents a mythical cohort, what follows in Table 2.11 is a longer-term look at a large system's actual assessment data to see if a downward spiraling might be accurate for a larger system, too. And, if it is accurate, are there ways to halt the downward trend?

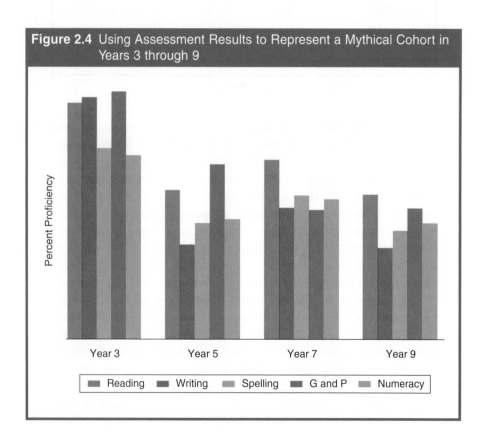

Figure 2.4 Using Assessment Results to Represent a Mythical Cohort in Years 3 through 9

In Table 2.11, the Ontario County student data have been arranged into a cohort report to show the percentage of students who meet EQAO standard (75 percent is the expectation) and the actual number of students who *do not meet* the standard. Now the trend data of Tables 2.9 and 2.10 are really apparent and screaming out for interpretation and action by the district's senior leaders. The average population of the grade 3 and grade 6 classes across Ontario County during the years shown for cohorts was 5,000 students in grade 3 and 6,000 in grade 6. This is not, strictly speaking, accurate; however, it is close enough to illustrate the power of showing class progress, from which some strong conclusions can be drawn for planning purposes.

Table 2.11 shows the progression of the same students in six cohorts with several interesting differences between grade 3 and grade 6 assessments in reading, writing, and math:

- In every cohort the difference between grade 3 and grade 6 reading scores is at least +7 points, with the greatest difference being +18 points. This represents increasing scores by the same students, which can be attributed only to strong junior school instruction.
- Grade 3 reading results increased very slowly after the introduction of the EQAO assessments, such that by the sixth year of EQAO assessments only 58 percent of students met standard, whereas the grade 6 teachers managed to increase the percentage of reading scores at Levels 3 and 4 from 57 percent to 72 percent in the sixth year of assessment. Why would it have taken so many years to improve grade 3 reading levels? Ontario County argues that, because of high immigration, it is impossible to have higher primary scores. Many districts worldwide refuse to accept the argument and apply high-yield classroom teaching practices and matching strong intervention programs to have had at least 80 percent of their grade 3 students achieving at or above expectation (that is, at Levels 3 and 4).
- Writing scores improved in both grade 3 and grade 6; however, grade 6 continues to outperform grade 3. Again, the same children are learning more in grades 4, 5, and 6, while neither grade 3 or grade 6 assessment results are at state standard (75 percent) at this point.

Table 2.11 Ontario County Same-Student Cohort Performance

	Percentage of Students below Standard (Not at Levels 3 and 4)				Number of Students below Standard (Not at Levels 3 and 4)		
Cohort 1 in		Reading	Writing	Math		Reading	Writing	Math
Grade 3	2000–2001	50%	52%	58%	Grade 3 2000–2001	2,500	2,400	2,100
Grade 6	2003–2004	57	58	54	Grade 6 2003–2004	2,580	2,520	2,760
Cohort 2 in		Reading	Writing	Math	Cohort 2 in	Reading	Writing	Math
Grade 3	2001–2002	50	54	58	Grade 3 2001–2002	2,500	2,300	2,100
Grade 6	2004–2005	65	63	58	Grade 6 2004–2005	2,100	2,220	2,520
Cohort 3 in		Reading	Writing	Math	Cohort 3 in	Reading	Writing	Math
Grade 3	2002–2003	49	60	54	Grade 3 2002–2003	2,550	2,000	2,300
Grade 6	2005–2006	67	67	61	Grade 6 2005–2006	1,980	1,980	2,340
Cohort 4 in		Reading	Writing	Math	Cohort 4 in	Reading	Writing	Math
Grade 3	2003–2004	49	58	52	Grade 3 2003–2004	2,550	2,100	2,400
Grade 6	2006–2007	67	67	58	Grade 6 2006–2007	1,980	1,980	2,520
Cohort 5 in		Reading	Writing	Math	Cohort 5 in	Reading	Writing	Math
Grade 3	2004–2005	52	65	62	Grade 3 2004–2005	2,400	2,100	1,900
Grade 6	2007–2008	70	72	62	Grade 6 2007–2008	1,800	1,980	2,280
Cohort 6 in		Reading	Writing	Math	Cohort 6 in	Reading	Writing	Math
Grade 3	2005–2006	58	70	66	Grade 3 2005–2006	2,100	1,750	1,700
Grade 6	2008–2009	72	72	65	Grade 6 2008–2009	1,680	1,680	2,100

- Math results started low for both grades 3 and 6 and have improved only slowly at grade 3, with a similar slow and small improvement in grade 6. It is not just language literacy that requires attention, but mathematical literacy, as well. Note: Math results continue to disappoint on the grade 9 assessment for those students selecting applied rather than academic math, with only 40 percent of students in applied math achieving standard.

Let's look again at the mythical cohort. The answer to the question posed—will low test results continue to decline as the cohort advances through school—is no, provided there is focused assessment and instruction beginning in kindergarten and early primary to identify the FACES who require early support.

In Bear Paw Schools, senior leadership has engaged powerfully and involved everyone in the system, developed an agreed-upon set of principles (beliefs and understandings), supported everyone in ongoing professional learning, engaged the emotional connection of FACES across the system, and shared cognitive insights of teaching and learning across the system. Their ongoing cohort results will move ahead rapidly toward all students achieving. Bear Paw Schools will not be satisfied with mediocrity—all FACES will count.

FACES at High School

Once you establish the habit of seeing behind the statistics, powerful new strategies come naturally. A case in point is Ontario's Student Success Strategy. By using a personal, focused approach on a large scale, Ontario had been able to increase its high school graduation rate from 68 percent to 81 percent in six years across the 900 secondary schools in its school system. The basis of the program is the strategy whereby each of the 900 schools has on staff a "student success teacher" whose job it is to help the school identify students who are on the margins (at-risk and vulnerable) and to take action with each student. We have written elsewhere about the details of this program (Fullan, 2010b; Levin, 2009), but here we wish to report a recent spinoff.

As the schools and the system got in the habit of paying personal attention to students, one of the central leaders thought to identify on a system level how many students entered grade 11 but did not graduate two years later. They identified 7,000 students who got as far as grade 11 but dropped out before graduating. A simple and direct program—let's call it FACES—was developed quickly. The central leaders contacted the seventy-two school districts in the Ontario system and gave them the lists of dropouts for each school. They then provided a small amount of money to each school and suggested that the schools hire recently retired guidance counselors to track down each student and figure out what it would take to invite them back to complete their program. Of the 7,000 students, 3,500 returned, most of whom will graduate. Our point is that personalization programs—FACES, for short—do not occur spontaneously, but the effects of a simple realization about the numbers of FACES, even on a large scale, can be dramatic. In his new book on high school reform, Ben Levin (2012) points out that making contact on a personal basis for even 20 minutes a day can make the difference in whether a student drops out or stays in school. As Levin concludes, it is essential to know your students. Statistics can and must be converted to strategies that are founded on the human touch. This can be done on a pinpointed basis, but it also can and must be done on a large scale.

We examine in this chapter the Community Schools Case Study, in which system and school leaders plan how they will put FACES on

Narrative from the Field

I worked with a class teacher who was making some negative comments about new approaches and workload. I went into her class to demonstrate cooperative learning techniques—she was very skeptical, but through discussion, we set up cooperative learning groups and began a program to develop social skills within the class. During the first lesson, she sat at the back of the class and marked some other work. I persevered and did weekly sessions with her class. By week 3, she was participating in the lessons, talking to the children. We evaluated each lesson: what went well, what could be improved, and our next steps. At week 6, she was giving me ideas about our lessons and what she wanted the children to learn. After eight weeks, she asked me when she could go to a cooperative learning academy so that she could learn how do it by herself. *Festina lente:* Make haste slowly!

—Linda Forsyth, deputy head teacher,
Perth and Kinross Council, Scotland

their data and make a difference for the students in their ten schools in most challenging circumstances.

Community Schools Case Study

Since 2004, Saskatoon Public Schools, a large urban school district in Western Canada comprised of 45 elementary schools and 10 high schools has targeted students' literacy learning outcomes through a priority focus called Literacy for Life (L4L). The program's clear goal is for "all students, K–12, [to be] reading at or above grade level." In 2007, with disaggregated data available to the school district, it became apparent that, on average, L4L had made a significant difference for students, but the data also highlighted an achievement gap between the district's K–8 suburban schools and its ten K–8 urban community schools.

The district responded through a major initiative led by superintendents of education Kim Newlove and Patricia Prowse, who commissioned a literature review on high-performing, high-poverty schools in order to understand how other jurisdictions had succeeded where schools were located in neighborhoods of need. In the Saskatoon Public Schools, this meant neighborhoods with high levels of social concerns, high levels of student-family poverty, and students marginalized by ethnic or cultural backgrounds. (Over 50 percent of the First Nations, Inuit, and Métis students in Saskatoon Public Schools attend the ten community schools.)

The report pointed to making an adjustment in the improvement plan underpinning L4L to enable all schools' students to achieve the goal. The district established a strategy committee (what is called the guiding coalition) that led to the creation of an action plan to raise the literacy achievement bar. Newlove and Prowse engaged Sharratt to advise the district on the community schools' improvement plan as the literature review and action plan paralleled the recommendations in *Realization* (Sharratt & Fullan, 2009).

The initial gathering of over 100 staff from the 10 K–8 community schools with Sharratt was motivational and purpose-setting. Principals, teachers, and district staff reaffirmed their own beliefs and understandings (parameter 1) and the district's reading goal. Then they began the process of putting FACES on their school-based data. Now, every community school meeting and workshop begins with a restatement of the beliefs and understandings and a recommitment to make plans for their schools and individual students, in a manner that is culturally responsive to their students and families.

(Continued)

(Continued)

The Plan

The adapted L4L action plan for community schools now embeds all 14 parameters. Key drivers among the strengthened and re-resourced activities are as follows:

- Formation of school data teams led by the principal and consisting of teachers, community school coordinators, a literacy coach, the vice principal, and the school's learning resource teacher. They meet on a regular basis to study their students' literacy achievement levels and attendance data, intervening as soon as they assess a need.
- Locking in on the goal of all students reading at or above grade level (parameter 5) and being "culturally responsive."
- Assignment of incremental staffing resources by the district in the form of a literacy coach (parameter 2) to each community school to analyze data, to support assessment for learning practices, and to model instruction by co-teaching in classrooms.
- Protection of instructional time and honoring the literacy block as cornerstones (parameter 3).
- Regularly scheduled meetings (parameter 8) to support each other and working as instructional leaders in teams of two to "walk" in each other's schools, having been trained by L. Sharratt (2011) in "learning walks and talks," in order to serve as critical friends to one another.
- Professional learning (focused on perfecting literacy instruction) in centralized workshop days and in school-based collaborative inquiry days (parameter 11).
- Addition of books to classroom libraries so that each will attain a goal of 300–500 books, with an appropriate variety of reading levels and genres, including fiction and nonfiction, in every classroom (parameter 9).
- Learning how to achieve SMART goals (specific, measurable, attainable, results-based, time-bound) by creating action research/collaborative inquiry questions (parameter 11) that can be answered using specific school data and, then, sharing the answers and how the answers-turned-learning-strategies made a difference to student achievement, at the culminating event (parameter 14), the June end-of-year Literacy Learning Fair.
- Actively engaging parents and school councils (parameter 12) in creating a culture of readers by

  o Promoting and participating in the district's Just Read initiative

- Hosting reading events such as Bannock and a Book, or Book and a Bagel
- Reviewing school-based data on students' volume reading (that is, library circulation data and students' self-reporting data on books they have read independently)
- Engaging in the annual Literacy for Life Conference for students and adults—sessions featuring internationally known authors, illustrators, and journalists (*Note:* In the first four years, over 30,000 student and adult conference delegates have participated.)
- Making *cross-curricular literacy* connections (see Glossary)

Results

Figure 2.5 shows the comparative results for K–4 students continuously enrolled in community schools before L4L, and then following its introduction in 2007. Even prior to the new community schools initiative, the stanine scores shifted higher due to L4L. The latest scores, for the 2010–2011 school year, demonstrate an even greater shift in scores as a result of the community schools initiative with Sharratt, Newlove, and Prowse and the adaptations to the L4L program.

Figure 2.5 Results Before and During Literacy for Life Implementation

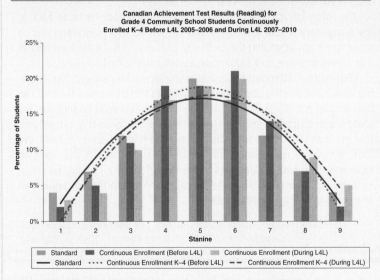

Source: Kim Newlove and Patricia Prowse, superintendents of education, Saskatoon Public School Division, Saskatchewan, Canada.

Deliberate Pause

- What data sets are most helpful to you in humanizing the FACES in your class, school, and system?
- How does knowing the data have an impact on what students learn?
- How do you ensure that each FACE counts and is accounted for?
- How do teachers know what data sets matter?
- Do teachers know what data sets look like for the whole school and system—beyond their class and school? In other words, do they get to see the big picture, too?

Narrative from the Field

Kevin is a boy who came to me after being suspended from another school. He had experienced many in- and out-of-school suspensions while at our school due to at-risk behaviors and previous attitudes he had developed toward school. He rarely, if ever, completed any tasks or assignments given to him by his teachers. I worked with him to support his math and literacy skills from grades 7 to 9. At the end of his grade 9 year, he admitted that he learned a lot from the help I had given him. He moved on to high school, and I often wondered about how he was doing.

The Friday he was graduating from secondary school, he came back to the elementary school to find me and tell me he was graduating and to make sure I was attending the ceremony. Unfortunately, I wasn't working at that school anymore, so I didn't meet up with him as he had planned.

That night, I attended the graduation ceremonies without him knowing that I was coming. Before the ceremonies began, he saw me and ran over to give me a big hug and tell me that he had tried to find me. He said he was so glad to see me. He thanked me for "believing in him" and told me that I was the one teacher that made him believe in himself. We took pictures of us together, and when he walked across the stage to receive his diploma, I had tears in my eyes—I knew all along, he could succeed . . . he just needed someone to "push" him in the right direction and show him that somebody cared!

—Deb Hodges, intervention teacher, I. V. Macklin Public School,
Grande Prairie Public School District, Alberta, Canada

It is time to pull out our four big improvement drivers. When assessment, instruction, leadership, and ownership synergize on a wide scale, you know that you have made every FACE count. We recommend starting with assessment.

CHAPTER THREE

Making It Work in Practice—Assessment

Beginning with the end in mind is just good assessment practice. We model that approach here by beginning with a case study from Australia that demonstrates brilliantly our beliefs in the centrality of assessment literacy. You have to start where the student is—and put FACES on the data.

Assessment Case Study

Ballarat Clarendon College (BCC) is an independent regional school in Victoria, Australia, with 110 teachers and 1,200 students from 3 to 18 years old. The school's approach to improvement is progressive. In 2009, the school leaders, David Shepherd and Jan McClure, appointed two teachers as primary-level mathematics specialists who co-teach (see Chapter 4) and open their classrooms to demonstrate to other staff how to assess in an ongoing way and integrate their data immediately into instruction. The teachers, Lani Sharp and Colin Esdale, share a belief

in the importance of developmental learning, so our work focuses on ways to effectively differentiate instruction using assessment data. Hence, we need current, high-quality, clear, unambiguous information on student learning that will allow us to make informed decisions about how to use our time most efficiently at the class, group, and individual levels in order to maximize learning. We know that this, in turn, relies on well-designed, accurate, and objective assessment instruments.

(Continued)

(Continued)

Assessment forms an integral part of the teaching and learning process at both formal and informal levels. By informal, we mean the information that teachers gather during lessons, to adjust the pitch, pace, and direction of current and successive lessons. Formal assessment refers to information that is collected to provide an objective and detailed picture of what students do or do not understand at a point in time. Both informal and formal assessment have been a major focus at BCC, providing the staff with the powerful data their decision-making demands.

As they began their assessment journey, the BCC staff had to overcome three major problems:

- How to create assessments that needed to cater to many achievement levels and that allowed for several years' worth of student variation in order to provide a valid representation of each student's understanding
- How to ensure consistency from year to year so that data could be compared by teacher teams and between teacher teams when the program was replicated or became an across-grade program
- How to ensure their data scrutiny was accurate and could provide detailed information on which to base future teaching (assessment items for each level needed to be numerous, fine grained, and easily tracked)

Initial endeavors to solve these problems resulted in "tests" that became increasingly lengthy, as students worked through items either inappropriately easy or difficult, wasting their time and motivation, while Lani and Colin sought more detailed data.

The solution was to significantly expand assessments for each unit of mathematics to cover students' developmental paths. Common assessment tasks were developed and organized into sections so that, although the instrument itself was very long, each student would see only the appropriate levels, not the levels the teacher already knew the student could achieve, nor the levels well beyond the student's current understanding.

The data from each assessment was recorded on a spreadsheet that spans level 1 to level 9, approximately the first seven years of mathematics learning. Figure 3.1 is an excerpt from one such spreadsheet.

The developmental nature of their program has made pretesting unnecessary, as data are always available to show how students achieved in this unit previously, whether during the last term or last year. What they have found useful is a midunit assessment allowing for

Figure 3.1 Putting FACES on Mathematics Data at BCC

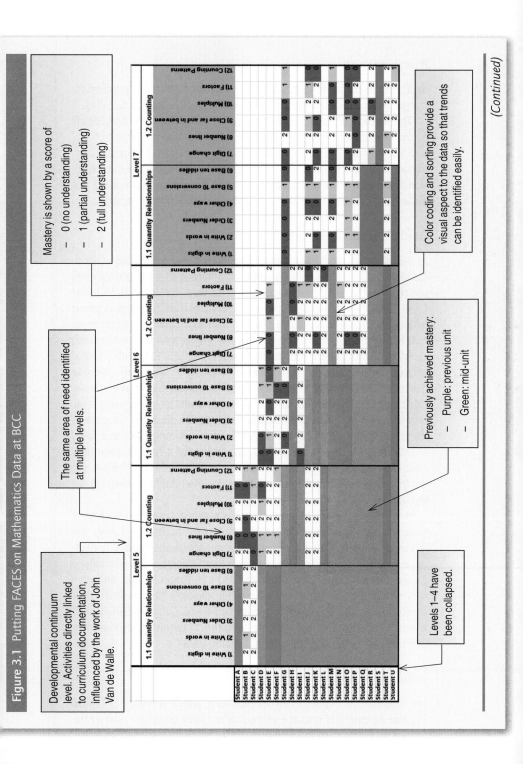

(Continued)

(Continued)

midcourse adjustments to instruction. This allows them to keep their data current and to check that informal observations are accurate as recorded.

The structure of the BCC mathematics co-teaching program rests heavily on the belief that assessments should be formative—that is assessment "for" and "as" learning. The purpose of assessment is to guide the student's learning and to inform the teacher's instruction. Assessment, even at the conclusion of the year, is not an endpoint, but rather, for teacher and student, it is evidence of progress made and a map of where and how to proceed.

Guiding Student Learning

At BCC, teachers work hard to develop a focused learning culture in which students are aware of what they know and still need to learn, and they can use this information to take responsibility for their own learning. Lani and Colin realize that students' self-monitoring enables them to become lifelong learners. Scores on tests are not provided. Instead, students are encouraged to take a deeper look at their assessment and analyze their responses to each question. To facilitate self-monitoring, students highlight their mathematical achievements on *success criteria* cards (see Glossary). These are rubric-like documents from their *developmental learner profile* (see Glossary) that make explicit what they need to be able to demonstrate to master each level. Students, who are learning developmentally and are given the resources to identify their strengths and weaknesses, become self-competitive and savvy at *self-assessment* (see Glossary), always striving for a new personal best. They have learned at BCC that, not only do teachers need to be able to see the individual FACES in the data, but also it is essential for students to see themselves.

As students become more aware of their learning needs and can track their progress and as tasks are pitched more accurately (using the modeled–shared–guided–independent approach, or the gradual-release-of-responsibility model; see Sharratt & Fullan, 2009, pp. 22–62), behavior management issues are minimized and motivation is high. Although it is challenging to plan for and manage multiple tasks with student choice of learning arrangements, from Lani's and Colin's experiences, it is worth the effort because it creates a culture of entrusted responsibility and is based on factual, current, and shared data.

Informing Teacher Planning

The Common Assessment Task spreadsheets, shown in Figure 3.1, have become an essential resource without which they no longer plan at the lesson level. Without this critical information, decisions made regarding activity selection, pitch level, lesson structure, or student groupings would be blind guesses.

The data can be used at whole-class, small-group, and individual planning levels. Generally, classes have a data range of three to four continuum levels (minimized because they regroup for instruction between same year-level classes). Knowledge of the group spread or clustering is valuable for defining instructional starting points and identifying general needs and misconceptions that can be addressed in a whole-group situation. Although lessons tend to begin and end with a whole-group session, the structure during a lesson does not follow a formula. The most efficient and effective method of differentiated delivery is dictated by the shape, nature, and spread of the data. Class structures include

- Whole class instruction, with differentiation at the task level for groups or individuals
- Focus group or "pullout group" teaching within the classroom
- Flexible like-need groupings (*not* fixed-ability groups)
- Mixed-ability groups
- Open-ended tasks that allow for varying levels of sophistication
- Peer instruction and peer and self-assessment approaches

Choices regarding methods of grouping and delivery, task selection, and task modification are made based on data that show the learning needs of the students, as a group and as individuals.

The effectiveness of the program is due largely to the fact that their curriculum documentation and assessment tools have been created collaboratively. The mathematics team has developed a common language and understanding that enables team members to align practice and to maximize their ability to move all students' learning forward. Assessment construction also provides opportunities for collaborative reflection on the effectiveness of the team's practice. This reflection is a crucial part of ongoing *action research/collaborative inquiry* (parameter 11; see Glossary) as teachers (see Chapter 4). The journey is by no means complete; however, the mathematics team members believe they are moving ever closer to teaching, learning, and assessing in a developmental way—a true co-planning, co-teaching, co-debriefing, and co-reflecting approach (see Chapter 4).

Sources: Jan McClure, deputy principal, and Lani Sharp and Colin Esdale, co-teachers, Ballarat Clarendon College, Ballarat, Victoria, Australia.

This case study defines in practice what many assessment books and articles in theory have focused on: how to capture the impact that we all believe effective assessment practices have on student learning. Dylan Wiliam (2011) defines what Lani and Colin are achieving when he writes:

> An assessment functions to the extent that evidence about student achievement is elicited, interpreted, and used by teachers, learners, or their peers to make decisions about the next steps in instruction that are likely to be better or better founded, than the decisions they would have made in the absence of that evidence. (p. 43)

The Ontario Ministry of Education (2010a) reinforces Wiliam's stance and the co-teachers' practice at BCC by reminding us that assessment, evaluation, and reporting practices and procedures are *fair, transparent,* and *equitable* for *all* students.

What Have We Learned about Assessment from This Case Study?

This case study from BCC is a strong example of powerful assessment practice. Lani and Colin, as co-teachers, know and care passionately about improving the learning for all of their students—beginning and ending their work by putting FACES on the data—every day in every way. We've used what we have learned from this case study as an advanced organizer for the assessment discussion that follows.

Through this case study, we have learned to

1. Begin by knowing the learners

2. Co-plan using student diagnostic data

3. Make learning goals (from the curriculum expectations) and success criteria visible

4. Use continuous informal assessment during teaching

5. Deliver ongoing formative assessment and reflect on mid-course corrections through formal assessment

6. Provide students with oral and written descriptive feedback

7. Create opportunities for peer- and self-assessments

8. Ensure that summative assessment informs next steps for students and parents

9. Use the data wall process to see the big picture and the detail—the FACES—so that teachers self-assess and reflect on their teaching

10. Share learning with whole-school collaborative marking of student work

In the sections that follow, we elaborate on each of these ten components of high-yield assessment practice.

1. Knowing the Learner

Around 1987, Donald Graves asked an audience to draw three columns on a piece of paper. In the first column, we were to record the names of all the students in our class. Graves scolded us for forgetting even one name and said that the one (or more) that we forgot were not being acknowledged as humans and asked us to consider what that lack of acknowledgement might do to their self-esteem. In the middle column, we were to write ten things that we knew about each student in our class, and he said that if we couldn't, we were failing these students. Finally, in the last column, we were to put a check mark beside the name of each student who knew that we, as teachers, knew those ten things about them. His point was that if we could not perform these tasks, we should get busy knowing our learners inside and beyond the walls of the classroom. One could not forget the impact of those exercise questions—even after many years. In our terms now, Graves was asking if we knew the whole child in order to put a FACE to the learning data—could we humanize him or her fully and be reminded that we were talking about real kids with real hopes and dreams.

Good teachers spend time getting to know their learners—academically and socially-emotionally. According to Cornelius-White (2007), "the power of positive teacher-student relationships is critical for learning to occur. This relationship involves showing students that the teacher cares for their learning as students, can see their perspective, and communicate it back to them so they have valuable feedback to self-assess, feel safe, and learn to understand others and the content with the same interest and concern" (p. 123).

In the BCC case study, teachers Lani and Colin modeled for us that they knew their students well—what they could do, what they couldn't do, and what they would be able to do with their continuing explicit instruction. They developed a developmental learner profile for each student, including the student's individual data, samples of current student work, their completed success criteria cards, and their anecdotal notes and written observations. They also developed an at-a-glance class profile that they brought to each of their daily planning meetings.

2. Co-Plan Using Student Diagnostic Data

When starting a new year with a new class or launching a new major topic, a teacher can review previous assessments and carry out any *diagnostic assessments* (see Glossary) needed to further clarify what students already know, to determine instructional starting points if uncertain, and to group students with like needs. Simply, the concept is to avoid having students sitting through classes where the instruction is about what they already know. How often does that happen? As Dufour and Marzano (2011) point out, "The longstanding practice in American education has been for individual teachers to use assessment to provide a student with the opportunity to demonstrate his or her learning at the appointed time. The standard pattern has been, 'Teach, test, hope for the best, assign a grade and move on to the next unit.' Assessment has been used as a tool for sorting students into 'our A Students, our B students,' and so on" (p. 139). Lani and Colin discuss that their assessments are ongoing and continue to be developmental, doing away with the need to test what they already know about their students, which is a waste of instructional time. This is precision teaching. A deeper discussion of the power of the co-planning, co-teaching, co-debriefing, and co-reflecting model is found in Chapter 4.

3. Make Learning Goals and Success Criteria Visible

If the *learning goals* (see Glossary) from state standards or curriculum expectations of what is to be taught, and teacher and student co-constructed success criteria are clear, visible in classrooms, and easily understood by students, students are more likely to be successful and hence engaged more readily. Success breeds success. When teachers incorporate evidence-proven teaching practices, such as visible learning goals and co-constructed success criteria, all students' achievement will improve. Thus, teachers are able to enjoy their professional practice more as specificity breeds success for teachers, too—that is, teacher and student engagement occurs.

For example, here is a learning goal from the Ontario Language Arts Curriculum (Ontario Ministry of Education, 2010b):

[A]ll students will be able to develop questions and answers that reflect higher order thinking skills. [See Appendix F.]

During their learning together about Higher Order Thinking Skills, teachers and students at Waterloo, Ontario's Park Manor Senior Public School (see discussion of data walls, later in this chapter) co-constructed and displayed the following *anchor charts* (see Glossary) in their classroom. The anchor charts help students to be clear about the task and the expectations to complete it. This reflects moving from state standards or curriculum expectations to transparency for students in what they will learn and what they need to be able to do in order to be successful.

Figure 3.2 shows three sample anchor charts that detail what students are expected to know and to do in using "thick" answers in their work—that is, higher order answers that demonstrate the use of critical thinking skills and *big ideas* (see Glossary). The anchor charts support students at work, and students and teachers review them often.

We have moved away from developing rubrics (using scales ranging, for example, from "unacceptable" to "outstanding") to focusing on co-constructed success criteria in all classrooms. This occurred to us when one of us (Sharratt), who teaches, discovered that students said that they only wanted to know how to achieve outstanding work—and what that work looked like. We were determined then to be very clear about what success criteria looked like by providing strong and weak examples of real students' work. Students tell us that this is the specificity that they need to excel.

Figure 3.2 Sample Classroom Anchor Charts for "Thick" Thinking

"Thick" Answers Use G.W.A.

Givens

- What I know

Working it out

- Show attempted solutions (try different strategies)
- Use symbols, numbers, words, pictures, tables

Answer

- Explanation of solution
- Written summary

Students and teachers then co-developed success criteria for thick questions and thick answers, shown below. These anchor charts were displayed in the classroom for students' easy reference while completing their work.

SUCCESS CRITERIA for THICK QUESTIONS

Students can

- Have more than one answer
- Invite different opinions
- Encourage rich discussion (higher-order thinking)
- Encourage speculation, prediction, connection, and inference about an issue or idea

SUCCESS CRITERIA for THICK ANSWERS

Students can answer

- Using interesting, attention-grabbing, thought-provoking ideas
- Beginning with a clear statement
- Organizing in a clear, concise way
- Using evidence (proof) from the text, self, or world
- Restating opinion using similar words at the end of answer

4. Use Continuous Informal Formative Assessment during Teaching

Throughout the teaching-learning cycle (see Appendix D), teachers use formative assessment—currently well-known in the research literature as assessment "for" and "as" learning. Formative assessment enables the teacher to position learners for individual attention or for group strategies within the content and concepts being taught. BCC teachers Lani and Colin informally reflected on their pitch, pace, and direction of the lesson throughout their teaching and referred to this as the informal assessment that they did on an ongoing basis—keeping the FACES of their student foremost in their minds. Whatever it is called, we say that assessment in real time is necessary to determine how it's going and to be able to throw out the lesson if it is not working in order to try a different, more relevant approach. The students' FACES are the gauges in getting them to a conceptual understanding of what is being taught—intuition becomes action. Teachers must be flexible and adaptable by changing directions if students are not getting it.

5. Deliver Ongoing Formative Assessment during Teaching and Reflect on Formative Assessments as Part of Midcourse Corrections

Since 2004, we have been working to intentionally embed assessment into practice as Wiliam describes. We discussed it in *Realization* (Sharratt & Fullan, 2009, p. 47) as guided assessment practices that lead to teachers' interdependent practice and students' ownership of their learning. We haven't changed our minds. For us, deliberate assessment looks like teachers who do the following:

- Understand that pieces of student work are data *so that* they use student work as evidence to move each student forward
- Develop ongoing formative assessments *so that* these assessments are used daily in classrooms to inform instruction
- Develop a repertoire of assessment and instructional strategies *so that* they can access them, immediately, matching strategies to students' needs identified by the formative data
- Develop a common language *so that* teachers and students use the same appropriate, common language
- Develop a deep understanding of curriculum expectations, develop student-friendly learning goals, post them in the classroom for all to see and discuss, and then co-construct success criteria with the students *so that* students develop an

understanding of what is expected of them and how they will achieve success—no secrets!

- Develop an understanding of core standards and how to construct rich tasks based on them *so that* students receive meaningful, timely descriptive feedback (see next section) and can articulate clearly what they need to do to improve
- Develop and effectively use common assessments and mark students' work collaboratively (see Section 10 on p. 85) to reach consensus *so that* there is consistency of practice across the same grades within and across schools
- Encourage students to self-assess and to set their own learning goals from explicit descriptive feedback received *so that* students' voices are heard in classrooms and they begin to own their successes as well as their unique personal needs and improvement strategies

Deliberate Pause

- How am I impacting the learning for all students and teachers?
- How do I know?
- Do I start with knowledge of the learners?
- How do I select what is to be taught?
- How do I make the learning goal easily understood to all students?
- Do teachers co-construct success criteria with the students?
- Are all students and teachers improving?
- If not, why not?
- Do I give descriptive feedback that is factual and objective and outlines how to improve?
- Where can I go for help?

6. Provide Students with Descriptive Feedback

At Armadale Public School (Sharratt & Fullan, 2009, pp. 85–90), teachers' professional learning this year is focused on giving clear descriptive feedback. Figure 3.3 shows their staffroom "learning bulletin board," which is focused on what they have discovered about the critical importance of giving students and each other descriptive feedback.

Beyond the positive value of very clear learning goals, classroom anchor charts, and success criteria, we know that students' understanding is furthered when they engage in *accountable talk* (see Glossary) in classrooms. This often occurs when they give or receive descriptive feedback—a

Figure 3.3 Armadale Public School Staffroom Learning Bulletin Board

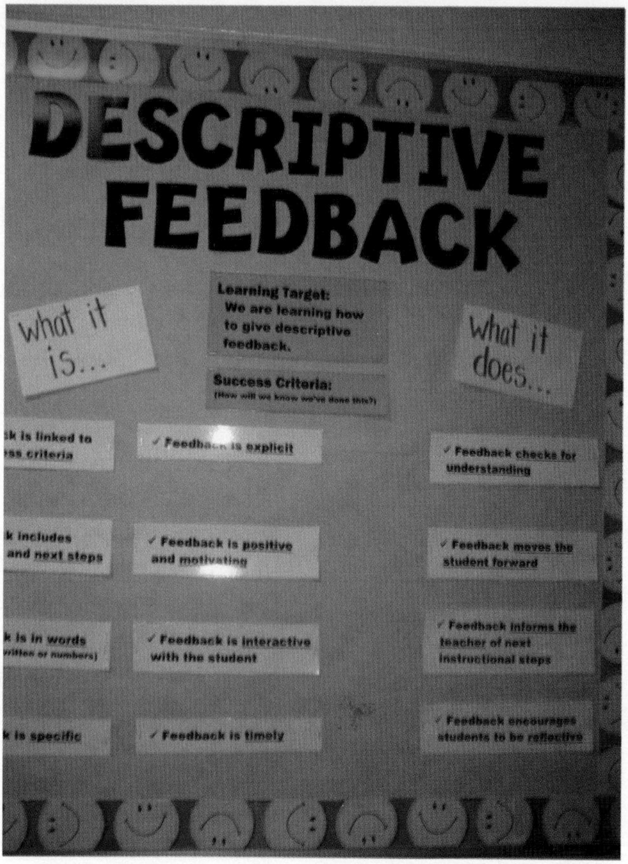

Source: Jill Maar, principal, Armadale Public School.

critical component of formative assessment. Teachers and students can learn to give specific feedback that initiates the next level of learning. Descriptive feedback provides students with practical, direct, and useful insights that outline how they can use the success criteria in order to achieve the intended learning goal. Such feedback comes from the classroom teacher or a student peer (once he or she is taught the components), and it has an impact when it

- Focuses on the intended learning (learning goal) and the success criteria

- Is timely
- Identifies specific strengths
- Points to areas needing improvement
- Suggests a pathway that students can take to close the gap between where they are now and where they need to be
- Chunks the amount of corrective feedback the student can handle at one time
- Models the kind of thinking in which students will engage when they self-assess
- Allows teachers to take immediate action in a daily effort to improve student work
- Offers students information about their work, product, or performance relative to simply stated learning goals
- Avoids marks, grades, or comments that judge the level of achievement

Deliberate Pause

Do students

- Set their own individual goals and monitor progress toward achieving them?
- Seek clarification or assistance when needed?
- Assess and reflect critically on their own strengths, needs, and interests?
- Identify learning opportunities, choices, and strategies to meet personal needs and achieve goals?
- Persevere and make an effort when responding to challenges?

—Ontario Ministry of Education, 2010a

Descriptive feedback can be either oral or written. Most important, descriptive feedback must be tracked by teachers so that they know what students are working on. Once students show that they can apply a skill (from their descriptive feedback), teachers must have tracked the feedback well enough so that they do not accept any other work in which that skill is lacking. Tracking the descriptive feedback is a critical part of the teaching-learning cycle (see Appendix D).

Explicit descriptive feedback is the key element in assessment that improves instruction, and it is best used by students when they articulate what next steps they will take to improve their learning prior to a summative point in their learning.

To reinforce what is expected, teachers at Armadale Public School also post strong and weak examples of work so that students are surrounded with support for their learning. Figure 3.4 is an excellent example of a teacher's explicit teaching—showing the learning goal (from the curriculum), co-constructed success criteria, a strong example of a retell (co-constructed by students and teacher), and a yes/no classroom anchor chart constructed cooperatively to further reinforce what the teacher is looking for (and not looking for) in students' work.

Figure 3.4 Sample Learning Goal, Success Criteria, and Anchor Charts at Armadale Public School

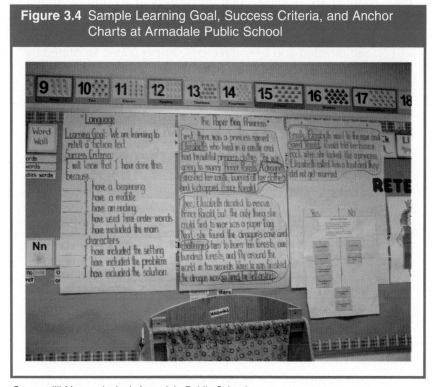

Source: Jill Maar, principal, Armadale Public School.

7. Create Opportunities for Peer- and Self-Assessments

Remember from the BCC case study that a key point was that "not only do teachers need to be able to see the individual FACES in the data, but also it is essential for students to see themselves." The ability to peer- and self-assess is the ultimate goal in teaching. Teachers must ask, "Can the student apply what has been learned to new situations?" This occurs only when students reread their work on their own volition to improve or when they use the teacher's descriptive feedback to self-assess and improve their work, thereby becoming independent learners—taking ownership of their learning. When formal, summative evaluation takes place (discussed in the next section), students are part of the process and there are no surprises because they know how they have done. Peers can influence learning by helping, tutoring, providing friendship, giving feedback, and making class and school a place students want to come to each day (Wilkinson et al., 2002, p. 61, cited in Hattie, 2012). Self-directed and peer-directed learning (albeit facilitated by the teacher) is pedagogy at its powerful best. Dufour and Marzano (2011, p. 131) concur, suggesting that student-generated assessments are probably the most powerful and revolutionary form of assessments made available by performance scales. Here students approach the teacher and propose what they will do to demonstrate they have achieved a particular status on a proficiency scale. As Greenan (2011a) writes,

> By recognizing the relationship between understanding the curriculum expectations [state standards]; communicating what is expected to students; constructing success criteria with students in language that they understand and connecting it to their work; creating meaningful and rich tasks; and using student-based assessment in the classroom that allows all student work to be honored and viable learning targets to be established by peers and self, all students will forge successfully into the 21st Century. (p. 13)

A "test" of how we are doing is whether students in every classroom can answer the five questions shown in Figure 3.5. We ask students these questions when we purposefully walk in classrooms (see Chapter 5).

The answers are revealing. When students can answer these questions confidently and accurately, then we know that self-assessment has taken place—because teachers have been explicit in making their expectations for successful learning transparent to their

---

Figure 3.5 Five Key Questions for Students

- What are you learning?
- How are you doing?
- How do you know?
- How can you improve?
- Where do you go for help?

---

students. Hattie (2012) agrees with our laser-like focus, saying "if the learning intentions [goals] and success criteria are transparent, then there is a higher likelihood that students will become engaged in reducing the gap between where they started and where we would like them to finish." Hattie and Timperley (2007) both agree that

> [W]hen students have the metacognitive skills of self-assessment, they can evaluate their levels of understanding, their effort and strategies used on tasks, their attributions and opinions of others about their performance, and their improvement in relation to their goals and expectations. They can also assess their performance relative to others' goals and the global aspects of their performance. As students become more experienced at self-assessment, multiple dimensions of performance can be assessed. (p. 94)

Most important, students know how and when to seek and receive feedback from others. The following story illustrates how one teacher has captured the essence of peer-assessment at the high school level.

Narrative from the Field

This short story is about "students helping students achieve," or an individualized approach to progress monitoring through peer mentoring. Year 3 secondary school students have weekly meetings with trained

(Continued)

(Continued)

year 6 students to discuss their progress in school. After each meeting, next steps are agreed upon by both parties involved—and these are reviewed at the beginning of next week's meeting. The focused discussions form an artifact of progress and cover a wide range of areas (subject specific or not) as determined by the year 3 secondary student. A teacher gets an overview of the meetings and can offer suggestions, but the agenda is always student driven. The meetings offer a chance to look at particular subject problems or more general issues. They provide a chance to celebrate success and for each student to "be heard." The careful planning and arranging is well worth the effort as both year 3 and year 6 students are becoming more confident learners and very articulate problem-solvers.

—Gordon Livingstone, pupil support teacher,
Renfrew High School, Renfrewshire Council, Scotland

8. Ensure That Summative Assessment Informs Next Steps for Students and Parents

Hattie (2012) distinguishes between formative and summative assessments by referring to the time at which a "test" is administered and, more important, by the nature of the interpretations made from the test. If the interpretations from the test are used to modify instruction while it is ongoing, then the assessment is formative. If the interpretations are used to sum up the learning at the end of the teaching, then it is summative. Thus, summative evaluation (what have students learned?) concludes the teaching-learning cycle (see Appendix D) when a judgment is made as to how well a student has learned the materials, concepts, and content. Clearly, too, at this point, teachers like Lani and Colin reflect on the outcomes for the class and for the individual students, adapting new insights into teacher planning for the next time a concept is taught or for the next topic with the student and the class. Steve Stake (cited in Hattie, 2012) uses an apt analogy: "[W]hen the cook tastes the soup it is formative and when the guests taste the soup it is summative." Whereas summative assessment has traditionally been an examination, it now often includes creative opportunities to demonstrate student learning, such as learning fairs, symposia, a congress, and many other processes through which students can showcase their learning.

A summative assessment opportunity that significantly increases student and family ownership of the learning is the student-led conference, during which parents can play an important role in student's learning. Student-led conferencing (Millar-Grant, Heffler, & Mereweather, 1995) is a summative assessment process that validates the important role that families play in putting FACES on the data. When children present a significant piece of work and take control of a planned meeting to report on what they have learned and to review their progress during the term, magic happens!

Students are in charge of the meeting (and their own assessment of their learning). The teacher is present only as a guide, if necessary. Self-reflection is the key to the success of student-led conferencing. It begins to occur when students select pieces of work to be presented, continues with rehearsing for the meeting with their parents, and ends with students conducting the presentations or meetings. Teachers are in the background as guides, when needed. When students can clearly articulate their own learning (a culminating event, but also a goal in any classroom), they have taken ownership of their learning.

The benefits of student-led conferencing are many:

- Leadership is evident.
- Confidence is strengthened.
- The student's voice is heard.
- Parents discuss student work and better understand student performance.
- The student's communication and thinking skills are increased.
- Parents are partners—as evidenced in the stories below (from principals in a district in which we work).

The following two snippets illustrate the power of students directing their own learning as they interact with their parents:

Student-led conferencing provides parents with an opportunity to become active participants in their child's education. Parents have an opportunity to see what their child has accomplished and what he or she wants to achieve. Parents are involved in reviewing the work with their child, and through their comments, suggestions, and classroom visits, they are able to promote their child's learning. Portfolios offer tangible evidence of a student's work and, as such, provide an excellent basis for discussing student achievement during conferences. Parents are prompted to make encouraging comments, help their child set realistic goals, and make a plan to reach those goals.

—Shannon McDougald, principal,
St. Peter Catholic School, Cornwall, Canada

We believe that students will achieve more consistently when students, parents, and teachers set specific and individual learning targets together and focus harmoniously on meeting them. Parents and their children discussed and celebrated samples of their work in their "browsing boxes" and then set goals for the next term. Teachers were encouraged and at times surprised at how engaged and focused every parent was while working with his or her child. Every teacher can confidently say that the student-led conference evening was an overwhelming success and paved the way for future learning on the part of both the student and the parent.

—Donna Nielsen, principal, Immaculate
Conception Catholic School, Cornwall, Canada

These are clear examples of how parents are critical learning partners through conversation with students and often powerful influencers on the teaching-learning cycle (see Appendix D).

9. Create Data Walls for Teachers' Self-Assessment and Reflection to See the "Big Picture" and the FACES!

Data walls create visuals of all students' progress and provide a forum for rich conversation among teachers. Finding a confidential place to display the data is as important as finding time to stand and discuss those FACES on the wall. The process of finding a common assessment tool on which to evaluate and level students' work is a high-yield first step (see the discussion of collaborative marking of student work in the next section). Once a common assessment task is agreed upon and the levels of achievement determined, the next step is to place those FACES on sticky notes. Each student's name, photo (optional), and assessment ranking are placed on the data wall above the assessment scores. When students are leveled on the wall—as being below, within, or beyond their grade level—teachers can see who is lagging, who is stuck, and who is succeeding. Teachers discuss with each other what is needed to move all—each and every student—forward. The focused conversation then becomes how can *we* move all our students forward? How can *we* extend the thinking of these high-achieving students? Once all students are placed in their levels on the data wall, and the overlaps of plummeting, staying still, and soaring students are noted, teachers stop saying *I* because it becomes a *we* challenge—teachers own all the FACES. When we have done this in our own work globally, leaders have noted that a sharing of ideas, strategies, and concepts starts almost immediately when they stand together with their teachers in front of the completed data wall. Leaders and teachers together make emotional connections to each FACE and also capture cognitive insights about each and every student regarding what instructional actions to take.

Figure 3.6 is an example of a data wall that puts student FACES on the wall. The data wall, at Park Manor Senior Public School in Waterloo, Canada, has all 280 students from grades 6–8 on it, including the nine students in the special needs class. Blue sticky notes identify boys and pink notes identify girls. The school staff members are concerned about performance differences between girls and boys, and they want to be able to monitor the variance in an obvious manner. Each student's sticky note also carries a photograph (see an example in Figure 3.7).

But this data wall carries a lot of decision-making information. The principal, James Bond, writes about the key points that help his staff to individualize their support for all students:

Our data wall is in a confidential location we call the Staff Learning Center. It's a small room that we set up in order to come together to discuss issues like how to increase all students' achievement. Our learning goal for this year, arising from our data and connected to the Ontario Curriculum, has been to improve the written communication for all students, paying particular attention to boys.

Figure 3.6 A Data Wall That Does More Than Just Put the FACES on the Data

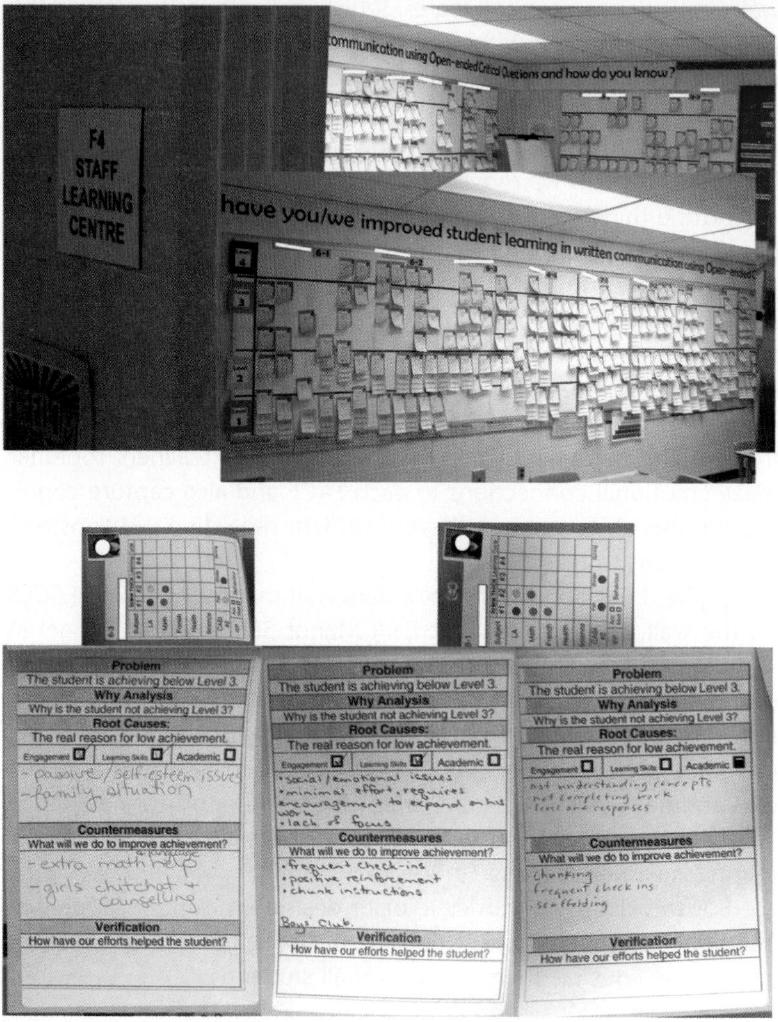

Source: James Bond, principal, Park Manor PS.

For our teachers, the success criteria have been the teaching tool to make their expectations explicit. An example of this is a learning goal from the Ontario Curriculum Expectations: "students can create and answer open-ended critical questions to a high degree." This year we are focusing on open-ended critical thinking questions, which we called "thick" questions—most of my teachers are teaching at least four Thick Learning Cycles (TLCs)—each based on fewer than three clustered curriculum expectations. Once the teachers have completed their TLC, they place colored dots, based on their common assessment of thick questions and answers, on each student's sticky. Teachers can choose from four different colors—red for Level 1 (well below standard), yellow for Level 2 (below standard), blue for Level 3 (at standard), and green for Level 4 (above standard), corresponding to EQAO expectations [see Figure 3.7]. Therefore, a student could have "dots" for math, language arts, science, French, and health, each taught by a different teacher. We do this to help teachers understand how well students are achieving across all subject areas.

Based on a student's lowest, most recent "thick" achievement, he or she is placed at the appropriate level on the data wall. This allows teachers to focus on the specific subject area in which a student struggled. If a student is achieving below Level 3, teachers complete a yellow sticky to determine the "root causes" and develop "countermeasures" [intervention strategies]. The pink strips along the bottom of the data wall are support for teachers [anchor charts], reminding them of the high-yield strategies they are working on to get higher-order responses from students.

Figure 3.7 shows in close-up detail how a student has done in each subject area when the expectation for all students is that they can create open-ended questions and answers that demand higher-order thinking.

Principal Bond wrote the following explanation of this work to his staff:

- We use Thick Learning Cycle (TLC) scores to help identify students who are not achieving the expected Level 3 with respect to communicating their higher-order thinking in writing, to clarify why they aren't achieving, and to provide a focus for our discussions to help them get there. The TLC scores on the wall will track our progress towards our school's SMART (specific, measureable, attainable, results-oriented, time-bound) goals in our School Improvement Plan.

Figure 3.7 Close-Up of a Blue Data Wall Sticky for a Boy

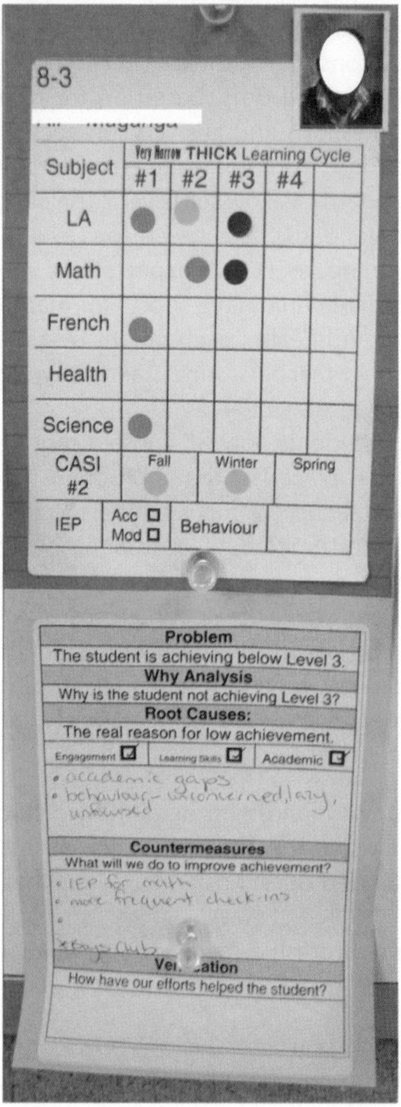

- I will help you post your dots, but I need you to use your collaboration periods to get all of the current information on your students, so we can then place the FACES in the correct level.

- Once you place a dot, move the student's sticky to the appropriate level. There should be some interesting discussions when the level isn't clear, and I'm looking forward to it.
- Once we have identified who is achieving at Levels 1 and 2 (below standard), as in Figure 3.8, we can then add the yellow problem-solving sticky notes (Figure 3.9). These sticky notes should be the springboard for all our discussions during our collaboration time, staff meetings, and teacher release days.

Figure 3.8 Example of Dots on Data Wall to "See" All Students' Achievement

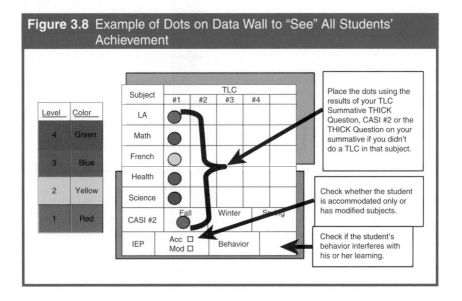

Principal Bond surveyed his staff regarding the value-added learning from developing the data wall and their comments follow:

- We were able to see student growth with respect to open-ended critical thinking (thick) responses over the year.
- It was very clear to see the FACES of who was struggling and who to focus on.
- We were able to see the subjects in which students were successful and the subjects in which the same students struggled—which posed lots of questions for us.
- The yellow stickies highlighted initial variances in assessment practices between teachers and led to greater collaboration,

Figure 3.9 Two Views of Problem-Solving Sticky Notes on a Data Wall That Make Student Needs and Interventions Visible

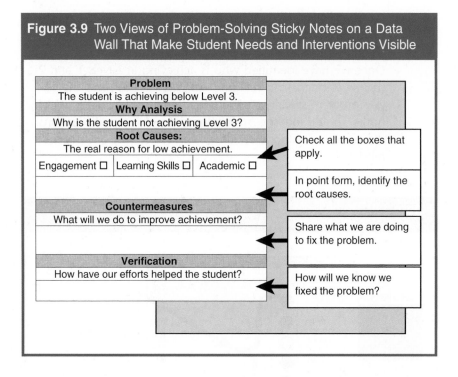

co-constructed success criteria, and subsequently greater consistency in assessing higher-order responses.

- The use of the stickies led to a student survey and a focus on more caring connections for specific students with certain teachers—resulting in teachers making emotional connections and gaining cognitive insights about all students.
- The yellow stickies allowed us to narrow our focus and to pinpoint the root causes of poor student achievement—and to take action immediately.

Principal Bond concluded that the data wall enabled teachers to see their efficacy with respect to students' using open-ended, higher-order, critical thinking questions and answers. The data wall was visible to all teachers, so it made teachers aware and accountable to each other for the success of all students. By analyzing the root causes of poor achievement, Bond and his staff were able to narrow their focus to the key areas for effective countermeasures, or instructional interventions, and then to verify all students' improvement through the data.

This is an outstanding example of the use of a data wall to see all students' performance and the interventions needed and acted upon. It also helped Bond and his teachers to determine which students they needed to bring forward for case management meetings (see Chapter 4) to evaluate the best instructional strategies for those students—and for whom they individually had no answers for improvement. Engagement abounded—both teachers and students were engaged in these worthwhile activities: making students' achievement visible by putting FACES on the data and supporting teachers in seeing where alternative instructional strategies were needed. We think that this data wall is alive—with precision and endless possibilities!

10. Use Collaborative Marking of Student Work as Critical Data

For BCC teachers Lani and Colin, student work is housed in developmental learner and class profiles, which are brought to all planning and improvement team meetings—since evidence of student work must be at the forefront of all meetings at the school. For example, weekly after-school meetings, by division or department, may focus on literacy achievement of individual students by using common assessment tools and exemplars so that same-grade or same-course teachers can reach common understandings of the expected standards of students' work across a grade level or subject area. This collaborative examination of students' work, by administrators and teachers, promotes consistency, ideally across classes within schools and across schools in a district. This will ultimately eliminate variation between classrooms, which is a very real problem for so many parents. Our goal here is a consistent, high-quality education for all.

To our point, Reeves (2011, p. 116) cites Gerald Bracey (2005), Mike Schmoker (2005, 2006), William Sanders (1998), and Linda Darling-Hammond and Gary Sykes (1999), confirming our thoughts that the most significant variation is not from one school system to another or even from one school to another, but rather from one classroom to another. Meetings in which teachers come together to develop a common assessment and mark it together provide places where teachers can learn and share new assessment and instructional approaches and, importantly, where they can develop a common, consistent language of practice. Collaborative marking of student work is a powerful process. Reeves (2011, p. 51) concurs that perhaps one of the best and most practical ways to improve accuracy is the collaborative scoring of student work. This is also a superb professional learning experience, allowing teachers to improve the quality, consistency, and timeliness of their feedback to students. Sometimes collaborative scoring occurs informally, when a teacher asks a colleague for help: "I'm on the fence about this particular project, how would you evaluate it?" In more formalized collaborative marking, sometimes called teacher moderation, teachers come together at a scheduled time to examine a common work sample from students and, by sharing beliefs and understandings, to reach consensus about the levels the students have achieved and why a certain level is the appropriate one.

Ben Levin (2012) believes that collaborative marking provides a great impetus for secondary school teachers to work together on the student achievement agenda. The Alberta Teachers' Association, in their recent teacher survey, notes that 76 percent of teachers surveyed expressed considerable or high interest in "examining student work." "When teachers work with each other to examine student work and develop curricula, resources and plans, they all benefit from the collective experience, regardless of their career stage" (Alberta Teachers' Association, 2010).

As Lani and Colin showed us in the BCC case study and Harlen (2006) concludes:

Using the terms "formative assessment" and "summative assessment" can give the impression that these are different kinds of assessment or are linked to different methods of gathering evidence. This is not the case; *what matters is how the information is used.* It is for this reason that the terms "assessment for learning" and "assessment of learning" are sometimes preferred. The essential distinction is that assessment "for" and "as" learning is used in making decisions that affect teaching and learning in the short term future, whereas assessment of learning is used to record and report what has been learned in the past." (p. 104; emphasis added)

We close with a quote from the Ontario Ministry of Education (2010a) *Growing Success* document, which puts our urgent work in perspective: "Fairness in assessment and evaluation is grounded in the belief that all students should be able to demonstrate their learning regardless of their socio-economic status, ethnicity, gender, geographic location, learning style, and/or need for special services" (p. 34, citing Volante).

As Reeves (2011, p. 28) says, the best coaches give direction in a way that will influence the action at precisely the right time. As well as change agents, we believe that teachers and administrators are coaches who act as "knowledgeable others" for each other on the field and in the classroom (Sharratt, Ostinelli, & Cattaneo, 2010).

Grande Prairie Case Study

Grande Prairie Public School District is within a city of 55,000 people in northern Alberta, Canada, north of the 55th parallel. The main industries are oil, gas, farming, and forestry. The district has 14 schools: one high school, five elementary/junior high schools, seven elementary schools, and one outreach school.

In 2009 the Grande Prairie District received provincial (state) funding to begin Cycle IV of the school improvement program focusing on literacy from grades 1 to 12. With the funding, they implemented Reading Recovery in schools in the most challenging circumstances, balanced literacy in grades 1–6, and reading comprehension programs across all content areas for grades 7–12, along with a key new component for 2010—improving teacher instructional practice, in grades K–12. The central office senior executive team and the board of trustees supported using the 14 parameters as a self-assessment tool for the district, and Sharratt was contracted to work with the district in aligning the district's plan through the 14 parameters. Because the goal was to increase *all* students' literacy achievement across the district, the district asked Sharratt to do the following:

- Become a critical friend for the improvement of the overall district leadership improvement plan

(Continued)

(Continued)

- Provide collective capacity-building professional learning sessions to deepen the district-wide reform

Before the collaborative initiative began, the 14 schools operated in isolation. It was determined that they needed to become "one district of 14 schools" and to adopt the collective view that "*all* students are *our* students." Within each school the goal was to have 90 percent of the teachers consistently and collaboratively scoring student work. This is reflective of all the work on FACES, which involves personalizing the data, on the one hand, and clarifying collective capacity and commitment, on the other.

The key message sent consistently was that everyone was responsible for increasing students' literacy skills by having literacy become an essential component in every part of the school day in every classroom. Resources from the state program made it possible to bring leaders and teacher representatives to the group professional learning sessions.

Sharratt reviewed district data, and school teams reviewed their own data. Together they developed a plan to concentrate on three parameters plus develop an action research question for each school that was relevant to the school's own data. The district chose that all schools would focus on parameter 1—shared beliefs and understandings. A non-negotiable outcome of each professional learning session was that each team would take back what they learned to their staff meetings, where modeled–shared–guided–interdependent practices were implemented. Each school selected three at-risk students, putting FACES on their data, and the Marie Clay statement (personal communication with Sharratt, 2004) "It is never the child's fault!" became a mantra. In previous years, the list of excuses for mediocre performance included the high teacher transition rate, the high rate of student transience during the year, or comments like, "some parents don't seem to care about education." No longer would these excuses work!

To the district's credit, it realized early on that the majority of teachers in the district had minimal literacy training. As a result, the district followed the *festina lente* model of "going fast slowly" to allow time to increase the skills of all teachers. Because sustainability was a key factor in future student success, Sharratt and the leadership team reviewed progress, modeled new assessment and instructional strategies, and tactically brought more teachers into the work with the school teams. Sharratt modeled scaffolded learning, pressing forward with the twin notions in parameter 1—that *all* students can learn and *all* teachers can teach, given time and support. Learning coaches were added as part of the aligned district-wide focus to guide student progress, to help facilitate change, to work alongside teachers on their identified instructional needs, and to work closely with the leadership teams to examine data and help close the gaps. Principals and district leaders lived the notion that the ability of leaders to develop other leaders is *key* to increasing student achievement . . . this call to strategic leadership did not absolve them as individual leaders from personal responsibility for doing what they could to bring about meaningful change in all their schools.

Results of these intense efforts demonstrated a new collective commitment, led to meaningful skill development, and included several key areas of continued focus:

- Moving from a collection of individuals to teachers and leaders helping each other across the district, as reflected in the overheard comment, "These are *our* students in *our* district."
- Gaining a deeper understanding about which evidence-proven instructional strategies are required for student learning.
- Acting on Sharratt's mantra, "Data today is instruction tomorrow."
- Relearning instructional techniques, such as
  - Descriptive feedback,
  - Student self-assessment, and
  - Standards-based reporting.
- Shifting from the supervision of teaching to the supervision of learning.
- Realizing that "learning is hard work" but well worth it.
- Articulating where each student is and being able to address all students' improvement needs.
- Increasing teacher and administrator instructional capacity through instructional coaches.
- Setting an example that blaming is not an option—teachers hold themselves accountable.
- Opening classroom doors to peers within the school and across the district, to establish trust at all levels.
- Speaking a common language and focusing on student achievement in all schools.
- Celebrating our successes at the end-of-year with the learning fair.

(Continued)

(Continued)

Did It Work?

Part and parcel with developing capacity for quality instruction is the idea of "buy-in" to the concepts of improving all students' outcomes and, specifically, ensuring that all students are reading at grade level. Such buy-in is as much a result of successful experiences as it is a cause of them. At the learning fair, every school in the Grande Prairie District presented its action research findings and made reflective comments on the nature of the year's work. What follows are excerpts from several of the school reports:

> The positive commitment to literacy improvement that was set last August, and that has been developed throughout the year, is unlike any other. The commitment that everyone is a teacher of reading has resulted in a learning environment where all teachers feel supported. Monthly staff professional learning and the three-step peer coaching process are becoming entrenched in the professional culture at Crystal Park School.

> We found, when dealing with literacy across the curriculum, agreeing as a staff to focus on only a few strategies at first is helpful. For example, by focusing on before, during, and after reading, we were able to try these strategies without a lot of pressure and the students were seeing the same teaching pedagogy integrating literacy in all their classes.

The following comments relate to the district's next steps to continue on its current trajectory toward its goal:

> Believing that all students can learn and that all teachers can teach is a critically important first step.

> Continuing to foster a common literacy environment within the school and bringing our parents together to see the importance of literacy in all of their student's work is a big part of how we move forward together. As well, teachers will continue to improve their skill in including literacy and comprehension strategies within their lessons. We will continue to come together collaboratively to share resources central office has given us and the resources which are available through our further readings.

Through our journey, I think the most rewarding thing has been to see a secondary school culture begin to take shape. Literacy is seen in our halls, in our classrooms, and heard in the words of our students. Teachers feel united in common strategies and in the fact that literacy has become a daily part of lessons and activities. This culture can only grow stronger and more viable as we witness soaring student achievement.

The ultimate result is that the Grande Prairie District has become closer and is operating as a unit of 14 schools—no longer with each school in isolation.

Figure 3.10 shows the beginning of the district thinking as a unified entity. In most categories, Grande Prairie has moved its ratings upward, toward a much better score. On the chart, blue is excellent or improved significantly; green is good or improved; yellow is acceptable, intermediate, or maintained; and orange is an issue or low. In key areas that show concern for students, such as school improvement, levels on the Provincial Achievement Test (PAT), high school completion rate, drop-out rate, and program of studies, the district has improved. With the total team focused on the FACES, the district is now accelerating its work toward consistent, overall high academic achievement in every school. And—they have only just begun!

Source: Sharron Graham, assistant superintendent of education, Grande Prairie, Alberta, Canada.

Figure 3.10 Alberta Government Accountability Pillar Overall Summary—Grande Prairie District

Accountability Pillar Overall Summary
3-Year Plan - May 2011
Authority: 3240 Grande Prairie School District No. 2357

Government of Alberta ■ Education

Measure Category	Measure Category Evaluation	Measure	Grande Prairie School District			Alberta			Measure Evaluation		
			Current Result	Prev Year Result	Prev 3 yr Average	Current Result	Prev Year Result	Prev 3 Yr Average	Achievement	Improvement	Overall
Safe and Caring Schools	Good	Safe and Caring	64.0	63.6	62.7	88.1	87.6	86.6	Intermediate	Improved	Good
Student Learning Opportunities	Good	Program of Studies	81.4	79.9	80.1	80.9	80.5	80.1	High	Maintained	Good
		Education Quality	87.5	87.6	86.6	89.4	89.2	88.9	High	Maintained	Good
		Drop Out Rate	5.4	5.9	8.3	4.3	4.3	4.7	Intermediate	Improved Significantly	Good
		High School Completion Rate (3 yr)	65.3	64.7	64.2	72.6	71.5	71.1	Intermediate	Improved Significantly	Good
Student Learning Achievement (Grades K-9)	Good	PAT: Acceptable	78.3	76.3	74.8	79.1	78.3	77.2	Low	Improved Significantly	Good
		PAT: Excellence	13.9	13.2	12.5	19.4	18.3	18.2	Intermediate	Improved	Good
Student Learning Achievement (Grades 10-12)	Acceptable	Diploma: Acceptable	81.9	84.2	81.9	83.4	84.3	84.3	Low	Maintained	Issue
		Diploma: Excellence	11.7	14.4	13.1	19.6	18.6	19.2	Low	Maintained	Issue
		Diploma Exam Participation Rate (4+ Exams)	44.2	36.9	36.9	54.9	53.5	53.5	Intermediate	Improved Significantly	Good
		Rutherford Scholarship Eligibility Rate (Revised)	46.6	38.7	40.1	59.6	56.9	57.0	Low	Improved Significantly	Good
Preparation for Lifelong Learning, World of Work, Citizenship	Acceptable	Transition Rate (6 yr)	45.6	49.1	46.5	59.3	59.5	59.1	Low	Maintained	Issue
		Work Preparation	76.6	73.1	73.0	80.1	79.9	79.9	Intermediate	Improved	Good
		Citizenship	75.1	74.4	73.4	81.9	81.4	79.9	Intermediate	Improved	Good
Parental Involvement	Acceptable	Parental Involvement	75.2	76.0	75.1	79.9	80.0	79.4	Intermediate	Maintained	Acceptable
Continuous Improvement	Excellent	School Improvement	82.2	76.0	76.4	80.1	79.9	78.6	Very High	Improved Significantly	Excellent

Narrative from the Field

What if you knew precisely how your students were performing on an exercise or assignment in real time? Or you could track student's internet search movements during assigned class tasks at the end of class so that you could adapt your questions or change your direction the next day? What if you could track the entire class against their own "personal best" working patterns and know their levels of engagement and what factors motivated them during any given part of the lesson?

"That's fanciful! You're dreaming," you may say. But these capabilities may not be so far off in the future.

The Australians, who have more international sports success per person than most populations, are not only focused on winning. Their coaches are intentional about winning and getting the best possible performances from their athletes in competitions and in training sessions. Like coaches and teachers everywhere, they know that performance bests come only after periods of high-performance training with intense descriptive feedback that the athletes can use to adjust their tempo and their body movements to get the very best performance in competitive situations.

Sound familiar?

A good teacher knows that assignments that begin at the students' current capability and stretch them forward—combined with descriptive feedback—provide students with the greatest opportunity to develop optimally in order to perform best on assessments and in future situations, depending on the foundation skill being taught or practiced. Feedback from instantly available data is the basis of ongoing formative assessment interpreted by the teacher who has put FACES on the data, and who will therefore know how to offer precisely the unique messaging a student needs (at his or her own performance level, using motivational and instructional phrases that will work for him or her).

Unbelievable? Next century, maybe? No, now!

GPSports in Australia offers GPS equipment that enables coaches to determine what players are doing in training sessions and during games. Real-time heart rate monitoring tells coaches how hard players are working, enabling the coaches to know when to let athletes rest or when to provide an urgent statement that further intensity is needed. Accelerometer technology measures all accelerations and decelerations, reporting g-forces the athlete's body has endured, because too many g-forces above a certain level lead to excessive muscle damage, resulting in delayed recovery time. On the bench, through the use of other medical technologies, immediate blood oxygen levels can demonstrate that on-field training or playing has been at peak, or less. Postgame analysis of the GPSports on-field tracking can show if athletes have been in the correct on-field playing positions relative to the ball and team mates.

In comparison, some new online and digital media learning tools offer such immediate tracking and progress reporting and capture formative assessments of content learned. After-class analysis of these data can inform the teacher of next steps—and, in many cases, during-the-lesson analysis by the student can lead to immediate feedback, leading to better learning. As the BCC math teachers showed in their case study, they can be more effective teachers for a range of students in a class, because of the various real-time assessments *for* and *as* learning that they provided.

"Not for me," you say?

Who uses this system to improve sport performance? Only the "who's who" of high-performance premier league teams in soccer—Manchester United, Real Madrid, AC Milan; in NRL Australian Rules Football—St. George, Manly Sea Eagles; and many more. But dozens of second-tier teams (for example, the North Ballarat Roosters), several sports research centers, and many university and school teams use it, too.

The question that should be asked is, who in field sports *doesn't* use it? Only the real fact of domed stadiums, with retractable roof structures that preclude GPS functioning, stops U.S. National Football League teams from using this technology during games and practices.

Who uses real-time measurement in the classroom or during homework sessions? Teachers like Colin and Lani use ongoing real-time tools that can summarize and show individual student performance.

Whatever our positions within education, there are tools that permit ongoing performance assessment—we can know and must know what we are looking for in good performance, in great performance, and in unacceptably low performance—and we must know how to follow "seeing it" by offering feedback that optimizes the performance immediately. Not for us, the administrators and teachers, but for the benefit of the FACES—our students.

Source: J. Coutts, with reference to GPSports, www.gpsports.com, Adrian Faccioni, president.

All the assessment information we have covered in this chapter (not to mention the next three "improvement driver" chapters) sounds like a lot of work. Well, it is and it isn't. First, when lots of people are doing it, in coordination, it is in fact less work. Second, if you get it right from the beginning, it saves considerable time later. Third, student labor, so to speak, becomes a free resource as they engage in self and peer assessment. We turn now to Chapter 4, where we discuss how assessment in practice is accomplished with will, perseverance, and galvanizing forces around our second powerful driver: instruction.

CHAPTER FOUR

Making It Work in Practice—Instruction

Schooling has moved away from a one-size-fits-all mentality and now places the goals, aspirations, and context for each student's learning at the heart of the matter—to ensure that every student matters! But little is known about how to do this in systems, schools, and classrooms. Assessment that drives instruction is complex, even though we strive for what we call credible "simplexity." The simple part is that you need to focus on just a small number of things; the complex part is how to make it jell. The chemistry of change is a precise, fine craft. Professionals must develop increasing intentionality and finite precision in their instruction.

Analyses of student achievement data provide us as system leaders and classroom teachers with rich sources of information but often do not tell a complete story until available data sources are scrutinized more carefully so that we can put FACES on the information.

For us, there are three tiers of instruction (Figure 4.1)—each of which is informed by student data and each of which provides further student data:

Tier 1—Good First Teaching and Classroom Practice—is specific, intentional assessment used to design instructional strategies in every classroom.

Tier 2—Case Management—is a systematic, scheduled forum to discuss and debate internal intervention. It is an internal support mechanism for teachers focused on instruction—a place in which to plan the implementation of alternative or new strategies.

Tier 3—Early Intervention—is escalation for support of students with the use of intensive instruction that directly serves the most struggling young learners.

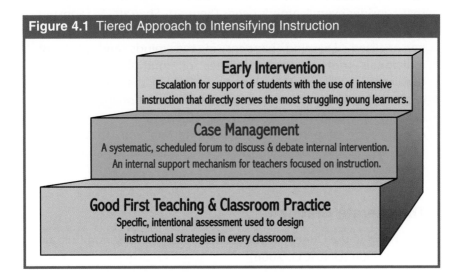

Figure 4.1 Tiered Approach to Intensifying Instruction

Early Intervention
Escalation for support of students with the use of intensive instruction that directly serves the most struggling young learners.

Case Management
A systematic, scheduled forum to discuss & debate internal intervention. An internal support mechanism for teachers focused on instruction.

Good First Teaching & Classroom Practice
Specific, intentional assessment used to design instructional strategies in every classroom.

Tier 1–Good First Teaching and Classroom Practice

There are so many good texts. Indeed, libraries are full of texts and resource banks on what comprises good teaching and classroom practice. Our intent here is not to repeat but rather, within a brief summary, explain how assessment—when used correctly—more fully engages every student and positively impacts instruction, enabling teachers to teach optimally. In Chapter 3 we discussed assessment, including knowing the learner, understanding the value of using assessment to drive differentiated classroom instruction, and having high expectations for all students.

As Hattie (2009) says, "[I]t is teachers using particular teaching methods, teachers with high expectations for all students, and teachers who have created positive student-teacher relationships that are more likely to have above average effects on student achievement" (p. 129). Instruction is the strongest predictor of student achievement. That is, poor instruction predicts poor student achievement (although some students excel in spite of us), and strong instruction promotes high student achievement.

However, any chapter on effective instruction must begin with a caveat. No single instructional strategy is guaranteed to result in high levels of student learning. *Instructional intelligence* (see Glossary) occurs when teachers combine high-yield strategies that consider every learner's needs (Bennett, Sharratt, & Sangster, 2001). Curriculum (content + assessment + instruction) must be personalized. Learning happens in the minds and souls of individuals—not in the databases of multiple-choice tests (Robinson, 2009, p. 248). Putting FACES on the data happens easily and naturally when assessment and instructional approaches are aligned—following one after the other every day in a never-ending cycle of perfecting practice. Starting with that end in mind, we discuss what our vision is for all graduating students—the literate graduate.

The Literate Graduate

According to the United Nations Educational, Scientific and Cultural Organization (UNESCO, 2006),

> The United Nations Literacy Decade (2003–2012) was launched because "literacy for all is at the heart of basic education for all . . . [and] creating literate environments and societies is essential for achieving the goals of eradicating poverty, reducing child mortality, curbing population growth, achieving gender equality and ensuring sustainable development, peace and democracy."

A good literacy program for 21st-century learners continues to comprise three components: making meaning, language study, and *inquiry-based learning* (see Glossary; Harste, 2003). Literacy instruction is our theory of action, not only in the international K–12 reform agenda, but also here—to narrow our focus on evidence-proven instructional strategies that benefit all students. As many others, we believe that literacy is freedom.

Assessment reminds us to begin with the end in mind (see Chapter 3), and we did just that. We asked what literacy skills our high school graduates need so that they can be contributing world citizens (adapted from York Region District School Board, 2004). We found that literate graduates embrace multiple forms of *multi-literacies* (see Glossary)—often simultaneously—and therefore must be able to do the following:

- Write with purpose and clarity
- Communicate effectively using a variety of text forms
- Read for purpose and pleasure
- Think critically
- Locate and access information from a variety of sources
- Use oral communication appropriate to purpose and audience
- "Read" and interpret multiple text forms
- Articulate a point of view
- Question and respond using higher-order thinking skills (see Appendix F)
- Problem solve

After identifying the all-encompassing skills that a literate graduate needs, it is easy to chunk our discussion of instruction into manageable pieces. We begin with literacy in kindergarten; continue with support for strong classroom instruction, including an effective literacy approach and cross-curricular literacy; and conclude with collaborative inquiry. Clearly, for the 21st-century learner, these skills represent the new "basic" foundational skills required to work and learn with ever-evolving new technologies.

The Literate Graduate Begins in Kindergarten

Children do learn to read and write in kindergarten. Don't let anyone tell you that they can't or that they aren't ready developmentally. What happens in kindergarten predicts high school graduation rates (Hanson & Farrell, 1995). If children don't begin to learn to read, write, and do math, in an engaging kindergarten learning environment, high school graduation rates will reflect the poor and late start.

Temple, Reynolds, and Miedel (1998) report, in their study of the Chicago Child Parent Center (CPC) program in preschool through third grade, that "probit regressions indicate that family and student characteristics measured in the early school years predict high school dropouts. Simple regressions from that large urban sample indicate that variation in the probability of school dropout can be explained in the participation in the CPC program . . . evidence of this kind is rare" (p. 21).

It is virtually impossible for grade 1 teachers to get students to read at the expected levels (16–22, using the *PM Benchmark assessment tool kit*—see Glossary) by year end, if they enter unprepared, at Level 0. We continue to work diligently with kindergarten teachers, as well as child care providers, to provide the professional learning needed so that the teachers know how to use a balance of whole-group, small-group, and independent approaches as part of the gradual-release-of-responsibility teaching model. This approach will ensure that teacher teams can scaffold and support learning in responsive ways.

Time for focused talk and opportunities to be exposed to print in meaningful ways need to occur. The 100-minute literacy block in kindergarten provides a deliberate structure so that the teacher can scaffold the learning intentionally as well as throughout the rest of the day. Again, assessment for learning (Chapter3) begins in kindergarten in order to determine literacy instructional starting points for each child. As we have said, high school graduation depends on a strong literacy focus in kindergarten.

As Schleicher (2011) demonstrates, 2009 Programme for International Student Assessment (*PISA;* see Glossary) results show that, in general, students who attended preprimary education [kindergarten] performed better in reading at the age of 15 than students who did not. In 32 Organisation for Economic Co-operation and Development (OECD) countries, students who attended preprimary education for more than one year outperformed students who had not done so—in many countries by the equivalent of well over a school year. This finding held in most countries, even after accounting for students' socioeconomic backgrounds. However, across countries, considerable variation existed in the impact of attendance in preprimary education and reading performance at age 15 years. Among OECD countries, in Israel, Belgium, Italy, and France, students who attended preprimary education for more than one year performed at least 64 score points higher in reading than those who did not, which corresponds to the equivalent of roughly one-and-a-half school-years. Again and notably, this was the case even after accounting for students' socioeconomic backgrounds. These results underline the importance of preprimary education.

On the other hand, in Estonia, Finland, the United States, and Korea, no marked difference in reading scores was found between those who attended preprimary school for more than one year and those who did not attend at all, after accounting for students' socio-economic backgrounds. In his presentation, Schleicher (2011) notes, as we do, that the one factor that might explain the variations in the impact of preprimary education on later school performance is the quality of the preprimary education.

This hypothesis is supported by the fact that the impact tends to be greater in education systems in which preprimary education is of longer duration, has smaller pupil-to-teacher ratios, or benefits from higher public expenditure per pupil. When this impact is compared according to socioeconomic background, in most OECD countries, there is no significant difference in the impact between students from socioeconomically disadvantaged and advantaged backgrounds. Students benefit equally from attending preprimary school in 31 OECD countries, including Japan and 25 partner countries and economies. The United States is the only OECD country for which PISA results show most significantly that disadvantaged students benefit more from preprimary education than do other students.

We also believe that the rigor of schooling (starting in pre-school) must be examined with an expectation that high-yield literacy practices are givens. For example, in the 2006 internal Cohort Tracking Study, the York Region District School Board showed that the end-of-year PM Benchmark minimum standards (16, 20, and 22 in grades 1, 2, and 3) were too low and a good predictor of NOT attaining the provincial (state) standard on the grade 3 EQAO reading assessment (grade 1, 57 percent; grade 2, 52 percent, and grade 3, 49 percent). To have an 80-percent probability of achieving Level 3 on the grade 3 EQAO assessment, student performance on the PM Benchmark assessment would need to be at levels 21, 25, and 28, respectively, in grades 1, 2, and 3. In addition, the tracking study indicated that international data below show that, at the end of grade 1,

- Level 16 is the 31st percentile (that is, only 31 percent of students will meet EQAO standard)
- Level 18 is the 53rd percentile
- Level 21 is the 73rd percentile

Based on those data sources, York Region District School Board set higher targets (Table 4.1). Statistics show that, in the York Region

District School Board, grade 1 students have moved impressively from 59 percent (1999) to 92 percent (2010) of students reading at the end of grade 1, using the new higher reading expectations. To support achieving the higher standards, teachers were provided with relevant professional learning and intentional literacy instruction began in the kindergarten/preprimary years. These remarkable results have been achieved by a nonnegotiable focus and precision with respect to the specific instruction that would lead to increased learning for ALL students.

Table 4.1 Year-End K–3 Reading Expectations Using the PM Benchmark Assessment Tool		
Grade	*Minimum Standard (Level)*	*Target Standard (Level)*
SK	3	6
1	16	21
2	21	25
3	25	28

Figure 4.2 demonstrates what is possible in a kindergarten classroom. Shared/interactive writing is a focus in a kindergarten classroom at Armadale Public School, Canada, where literacy is taught in an engaging, purposeful way. Careful consideration has been given here to setting up the classroom learning environment, using materials and resources wisely, developing the common language of instruction and supporting teachers in identifying students' instructional starting points.

The bottom line is that kindergarten students can learn to read and write! Accept no less.

Deliberate Pause

- Are your expectations for all students high enough?
- Is there planned and purposeful literacy learning in kindergarten?
- How is *oral language* (see Glossary) the foundation of all kindergarten programs?
- How do teachers model, share, and guide reading and writing beginning in kindergarten?

Figure 4.2 Writing in Kindergarten

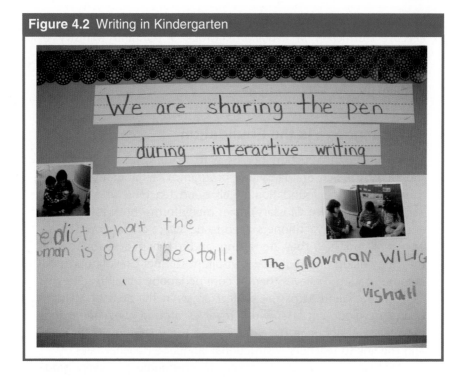

Components of an Effective Literacy Program

Not only does literacy learning begin in kindergarten, but it continues throughout students' school experience. Successful instruction comes from using the gradual-release-of-responsibility model discussed here (see Appendix A) as a modeled, shared, guided, and independent approach to teaching the balanced literacy strategies, visible over the course of a day or week in all classrooms:

- Modeled (teacher does; student watches)
- Shared (teacher does; student shares)
- Guided (student does; teacher guides)
- Independent (student does; teacher observes)

The eight essential components of a balanced literacy approach are modeled reading/think aloud, shared reading, guided reading, independent reading, modeled writing, shared/interactive writing, guided writing, and independent writing. These components are powerfully connected when teachers use the gradual-release model in teaching these components—and they are detailed in *A Guide to Effective Instruction in Reading: K–Grade 3* (Ontario Ministry of Education, 2003). This approach to teaching results in the "gradual acceptance of responsibility" by all students for their own learning—our ultimate goal for all the FACES.

Oral Language Is the Foundation

Strong literacy instruction begins with reading and writing, surrounded by a rich oral language program. Oral language in K–12 classrooms is the foundation of all good teaching and learning. *Accountable talk* (see Glossary) takes many forms, both for students and the teacher. Practitioners need to be aware of classroom talk— who is talking, how they are talking, and to whom and about what they are talking. International consultant Carmel Crevola (personal communication) believes there is core pedagogy for all teachers, of all year levels and across all subject areas, in the area of oral language development. Her work revolves around the connections between the language development of every student in the class and the link to teachers' instructional language (teacher talk).

Oral language should permeate the environment at every grade level as talk supports the thinking process and talk develops the reader and writer before beginning each of those learning processes. As eight-year-old Elizabeth said in *Book Talk* (Chambers, 1985), "I don't know what I think about a book until I've talked to someone about it!" (p. 138). The same is true for writing. Oral rehearsal in writing is a necessary prerequisite for thoughtful writing pieces. Thus, the critical part of literacy block planning is the intentional integration of teaching of oral language skills that weave reading and writing skills together. Just as reading and writing are taught intentionally, so must speaking and listening skills be taught. Lucy McCormick Calkins (2001) puts it this way, "In schools, talk is sometimes valued and sometimes avoided, but . . . and this is surprising—talk is rarely taught. . . . Yet talk, like reading and writing, is a major motor—I could even say the major motor—of intellectual development" (p. 226).

The Literacy Block

During the uninterrupted literacy block, the time begins with a teacher-directed whole-group mini-lesson. The teacher then circulates among the working groups to guide and support students' learning—taking one or two guided reading groups, as appropriate—while students are working on relevant literacy activities or reading or writing independently. Finally, the teacher concludes by facilitating a sharing time, which involves reflecting on and consolidating learning with the whole group. An example of a detailed weekly literacy block planner is found in Appendix E (M. Sharratt, 2011).

Common core principles of an effective literacy program include the following:

- Reading, writing, viewing, representing, media, and oral language
- Modeled, shared, guided, and independent instruction and student practice
- Flexible groupings (homogeneous, heterogeneous, large group, small group, and one-to-one)
- Intentional, powerful texts using a variety of media
- Nonfiction and fiction writing
- High-yield, differentiated instructional strategies
- Daily and varied assessment strategies
- Higher-order-thinking questions and answers

A comprehensive resource for teaching each of these core literacy components is found in *A Guide to Effective Instruction in Reading: Kindergarten to Grade 3* (Ontario Ministry of Education, 2003). A similar guide to instruction is available for grades 4–6, as well.

Differentiated Instruction

What am I teaching? Why am I teaching it? How will I teach it? How will I know when the students have it? What then? These five focusing questions must be at the top of all teachers' minds when they are planning for instruction. When teachers begin their planning for instruction, they keep the end in mind—what do the state standards or curriculum expectations say

> **Deliberate Pause**
>
> - What am I teaching?
> - Why am I teaching it?
> - How will I teach it?
> - How will I know when all students have learned it?
> - What then?

that I am teaching? Which can be clustered together? How can ongoing formative assessments (see Chapter 3) help me to group together students with similar needs? Differentiating the instruction throughout the teaching-learning cycle (see Appendix D) becomes critically connected to improving learning. Differentiated instruction provides for the diverse needs in each classroom. Students are engaged when the instruction is differentiated and students are in flexible groupings to meet their individual needs at that moment. Instructional strategies, such as the gradual-release-of-responsibility model (see Appendix A); effective group work; and *graphic organizers* (see Glossary) become powerful enforcers and enhancers of democratic learning environments where students' voices are heard often.

Hattie (2012) reminds us that teachers must have a clear reason for differentiation of instruction, relating what they do differently to where the student is located on the progression from novice to capable, relative to the learning goals and success criteria (see Chapter 3). Hattie warns, however, that even though classrooms are structured in groups or pairs, most activity is still individual or whole class instruction.

We believe that differentiation of instruction is more than flexible groupings. We add the importance of the gradual-release/acceptance-of-responsibility model when teachers scaffold the level of learning for each student through modeling, questioning, clarifying, chunking, sharing, rehearsing, guiding, and making their thinking visible through words, pictures, and symbols—all to make meaning of their world. In differentiating instruction, teachers create instructional processes at the level where students are (using ongoing assessments) to bring each of them to the next level of instruction—one size doesn't fit all. In this *intentional* teaching, teachers must know what comes before and after the skills being taught, how long to teach a skill and in what depth—definitely an art and a science! In short, they need to put FACES onto their instructional tactics, skills, and strategies selected.

Rich Authentic Tasks

According to Bereiter (2002):

> Educating is more than teaching people to think—it is also about teaching people things that are worth learning and [teaching them] to be able to discern what is worth learning.

Good teaching involves constructing explanations, criticizing, drawing out inferences, finding applications . . . if the students are not doing enough thinking, something is seriously wrong with the instruction. (cited in Hattie, 2012)

Research tells us that students become involved in *authentic learning* (see Glossary) when tasks enable them to answer their own questions and explore their own interests . . . teachers report that students "come alive when they realize they are writing to real people for real reasons or reading real-life texts for their own purposes" (Duke & Duke, 2006). Willms, Friesen, and Milton (2009) report that effective teaching is characterized by the thoughtful design of learning tasks that do the following:

- Require and instill deep thinking
- Immerse the student in disciplinary inquiry
- Are connected to the world outside the classroom
- Have intellectual rigor
- Involve substantive conversation

These characteristics can often be captured in effective group work situations—group situations that differ incredibly from just putting students into groups without structure and thoughtful intent. We call this instructional intelligence (Bennett, Sharratt, & Sangster, 2001), which enhances the learning of both the individual and the group. Instructional intelligence includes five elements: positive interdependence, face-to-face interactions, individual accountability, some structured activity and social skills, and team-building and group processing skills (Bennett & Rolheiser, 2001). All the elements are woven carefully into rich, meaningful learning tasks for students and teams. For example, refer to Figure 3.2, regarding thick questions and answers. Such questions could be: In your opinion, is homework a good or bad idea? or Do you think biking is a sport? Why or why not? Ultimately, we are striving to develop students who can capture the *big ideas* (see Glossary) in texts, novels, or curriculum units to raise their level of thinking and to be able to articulate a critical stance (Greenan, 2011b).

City, Elmore, Flarman, and Teitel (2009) state that the instructional task is the actual work that students are asked to do in the process of instruction—not what teachers think they are asking students to do, or what the curriculum says that students are asked to

Deliberate Pause

- How are students required to use old and new ways to think about and solve problems?
- How are tasks designed to be relevant to and authentic for students?
- Do disciplines come together, and can they be explored in the tasks?
- How does the task prompt thinking and creativity and stimulate curiosity?
- Do students need to confer, consult, and communicate with others?
- How is students' thinking visible?
- When are students required to write down and reflect on their thoughts?
- If we were to watch you teach over a two-month period, what would we see that would increase the learning and life chances of your students?

do, but *what they are actually asked to do.* A rich authentic task requires higher-order thinking, involves student inquiry as a way of constructing knowledge, relates to the broad categories of achievement and expectations outlined in the curriculum, makes connections across subject areas, and relates classroom learning to the world beyond the classroom (Ontario Ministry of Education, 2004).

Questions and Student Inquiry

Teachers must continually ask reflective questions about their own practice in order to promote higher-order thinking (see Appendix F) on behalf of all their students. Questions are also good for students' reflection, as in the example shown in Figure 4.3, which is a classroom co-constructed *anchor chart* (see Glossary) of how students think they should ask and answer questions.

Figure 4.3 demonstrates how teachers involve students in thinking through the success criteria needed and in making their thinking visible.

At all levels, in all classrooms, higher-order questions beget higher-order thinking, and answers—when married with teachers' skilled competence (instructional intelligence) in providing wait time, checks for understanding, descriptive feedback (see Chapter 3), and scaffolded learning so that students can find new meaning. Moss and Brookhart (2009, p. 122) write that engaging students in generating effective questions helps them to perceive themselves as

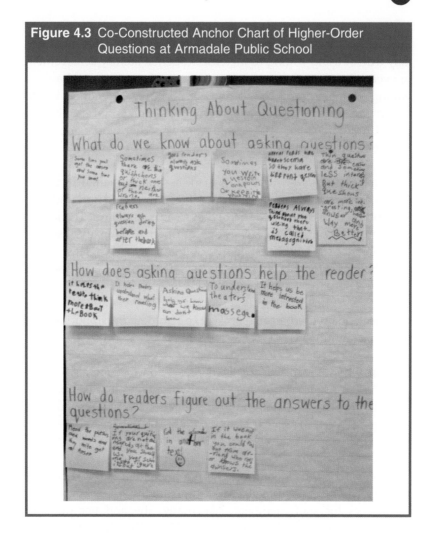

Figure 4.3 Co-Constructed Anchor Chart of Higher-Order Questions at Armadale Public School

autonomous and independent learners, producers of knowledge, and generators of important lines of inquiry.

The Power of Writing

In *Realization* (Sharratt & Fullan, 2009, pp. 38–40), we said that at the classroom level, successful elementary and secondary teachers use the progression of modeled, shared, and guided practice in all of their teaching approaches to ensure that students experience scaffolded learning to gradually accept responsibility to become independent learners—and owners of their learning. This is particularly true in using writing to increase students' literacy achievement in every discipline. From our experience, an increased emphasis on writing, in many forms for all kinds of purposes, is a critical key to improving student learning. Internationally recognized literacy expert Margaret Meek (1991) did not mince her words about the power and magic of writing:

> Literacy begins with writing. A mark, a scratch even, a picture or a sign made by one person which is interpreted and understood by others may be regarded as a form of writing. The idea is simple enough. Once we have grasped it, even the hieroglyphics of the Egyptians seem, if not familiar, then at least part of the same world as our word processors. To me, writing seems to be a perpetual and recurrent miracle. (p. 18)

Meek again used a broader view to reinforce the importance of writing, stating:

> Those who study the history of writing are convinced that it is one of the most momentous of all human inventions. It makes possible the use of language beyond speech. It makes us conscious of language itself in ways that affect both our public and private lives. It creates what is to read, and, therefore, readers. (p. 23)

We watched the literacy coach from one of our highly successful Ontario schools guide practice by demonstrating nonfiction writing techniques for staff members. Like many, she and her principal believe that when students are engaged in authentic writing tasks, requiring higher-order and critical thinking, significant improvement is evidenced in both reading and writing provincial assessment scores. We know we can bring all students successfully to reading through individually crafted, authentic, nonfiction writing tasks.

Allen (2003) concurred:

> As a nation we can barely begin to imagine how powerful K–12 education might be if writing were put in its proper focus. Facility with writing opens students up to the pleasure of exercising their minds in ways that grinding on facts, details, and

information never will. More than a way of knowing, writing is an act of discovery. (p.1)

Now we are saying it again. As writers ourselves, we know the higher-order and metacognitive skills involved in writing that we are trying to express above in rich authentic tasks, in connecting cross-curricular content, and in emphasizing higher-order thinking skills that students must have to become 21st-century thinkers and problem solvers. At every turn, we model the moral imperative of establishing writing as the hallmark of not only a literate graduate but of a literate society. Reeves (2010) strengthens our thinking by saying,

Consider the case of nonfiction writing, a powerful cross-disciplinary strategy that has consistently been linked to improved student achievement in reading comprehension, mathematics, science, and social studies. . . . It is an established fact that a majority of students in the United States need improved writing skills and that our failure to respond to this evidence causes employers, and colleges to spend billions of dollars to address writing deficiencies. Where has that overwhelming quantitative case led? Kiuhara, Graham, and Hawken (2009) conducted a national study on the teaching of writing to high school students and found that evidenced-based teaching practices to support writing were insufficiently used with any degree of frequency and depth. The teachers in the study claimed that they had not been sufficiently trained to teach writing, with the percentage of teachers believing that they were ill prepared in this subject directly related to their failure to apply writing strategies in the classroom. In other words, teachers do not do what they do not know. (pp. 73–74)

This leads us to reflect on the very serious shortfall in teacher preparation and teacher quality if we expect them to prepare the next generation of learners-leaders for the 21st century and beyond.

Student Inquiry and the 21st-Century Learner

We believe that rich authentic tasks, such as nonfiction writing, lead to higher-order thinking needed by all children and youth in order to forge into and contribute to the next century—beyond the

21st century. ITL Research project director Maria Langworthy (personal communication, June 2011) concurs and sets the record straight when she writes that "the evidence is converging on a simple truth: expanding and deepening student learning is directly related to the *content and quality of teaching.* Technology can and often does support high quality teaching. However, to strongly impact student learning, technology must be integrated with learning goals and combined with fundamental pedagogical capacity-building. In parallel, teachers and school leaders must be empowered to use this capacity through the modernization and alignment of learning objectives and assessments across all system levels."

Volumes have been written about the 21st-century learner. Hundreds of speakers have engaged millions of listeners on the topic. Is there really a different way of learning, a different way of teaching, a different way of thinking required to work with the 21st-century learner?

Some educators wax eloquently about the need for new outcomes for 21st-century learners in a digital world. We both agree that the term *21st-century learning* is "over-used and vague." Beyond the majority of students gaining proficiency, we feel that we should be aiming for the vast majority of students to be able to engage in higher-order thinking. Advanced proficiency is the new norm. The key is for learners to demonstrate the appropriate application of higher-order thinking skills to a wide range of learning and life tasks.

We argue that the same successful twentieth-century methodology—assessment that informs instruction—is valid today and will be valid tomorrow. We believe that if sufficiently high performance or achievement standards are expected of learners and if sufficiently high-quality training is available and demanded of teachers, then 21st-century learners will excel.

The essential skill for successful teaching from the first step has always been to teach in a manner that appeals to the learner—begging the questions, What do I know about the learner that can get her interested beyond just playing back to me what she memorized, wrote, or determined from the internet? and What FACE can I put on that learner from the assessments and information I have?

Sure, some background understanding of the technologies is important, but more important than knowing how to run them is knowing how to ask the same questions about what the student is learning based on the way those FACES learn and what they have already learned and now, too, based on the level of technology the student is using. The key questions for us remain, Can students move beyond simple comprehension to in-depth inquiry (see Appendix F)? and Can teachers use emotional connections and cognitive insights to put FACES on results?

In *The Rise of Generation C*, Friedrich, Peterson, and Koster (2011) describe how the "Connected Generation" will change the consumer and business landscape—and, we add, the learning landscape. They write that 21st-century learners have

> grown up under the influence of Harry Potter, Barack Obama, and i-Everything—iPods, iTunes, iPhones. Technology is so intimately woven into their lives that the baby boomer concept of "early adopters" is essentially meaningless. . . . This is the first generation that has never known any other reality than that defined and enabled by the Internet, mobile devices and social networking. (p. 56)

This is a global phenomenon, not a western-world happening. The answer to the riddle of how to deal with these kids is to know what they know by assessing and leading them to finding out more through inquiry—using whatever tools and technologies are available and appropriate to them—keeping up with their investigations through ongoing assessment (see Chapter 3).

Our most important gift to students will be to teach them how to continually learn and think critically as they go through five to eight different careers. Since the late 1990s, the Galileo Project, sponsored by TELUS in Alberta, Canada, has conducted research on learning with technologies. Their *Evidence of Learning in the 21st Century Classroom* (Galileo Educational Network, 2008) was created to guide leadership for learning with technology. This continuum identifies the low to high ranges of the following elements: tasks, assessments, learning environments conducive to learning when learning is engaging, self-direction, relationships in a learning community, role of the teacher from guide to learning designer, teacher strengths, and teacher as learner. The language is strong, purposeful, and very much the language of intentional instruction and focused self-assessment that must be reflected in current administrator and teacher professional learning. For further information, see www.galileo.org/research.html.

So, is learning different for the 21st-century student? Absolutely! At its best it is both entertaining and deeply engaging. It is about well-defined high standards, assessment, and instruction and may be more professionally demanding and commensurately more rewarding, too, because higher-order thinking is central (Fullan & Watson, 2011). But it is also radically more relevant and interactive. We ourselves are involved in creating a new experience for students and teachers in our ML/MadCap initiative, which creates innovative digital curriculum content integrated with ongoing assessment strategies, focusing on the big ideas in higher-order thinking (project planning document for Gates Foundation; Fullan, Devine, Sharratt, Cuttress, Butler, & Mozer, 2011). We both believe emphatically that skill in higher-order, critical thinking is the new basic for 21st-century teachers and students—the additional foundational literacy skill that accompanies the ability to read, write, speak, listen, view, and represent.

The role of technology in society is incredibly complex, given that it is both sophisticated and dangerous. Technology is essential to achieving success on both the micro and macro levels. One of us is examining the whole technology phenomenon in a separate book (*Stratosphere: Integrating Technology, Pedagogy, and Change Knowledge* [Fullan, in press]).

Cross-Curricular Literacy Connections

This new 21st-century basic skill, higher-order thinking, engages students in inquiry, rich authentic tasks, and an exploration of the big ideas. It is achieved when teachers cluster state standards or curriculum expectations across the disciplines, assess students' strengths and needs, and plan to embed literacy competencies in instruction in all subject areas. For example, for students to make sense of their world, teachers can make cross-curricular connections in the following ways:

- Modeling reading from the current history theme (using a think aloud to model what good readers are thinking as they read)
- Writing different genres in science (teaching procedural writing)

- Making thinking visible in a mathematical problem-solving lesson (using pictures, words, and symbols to explain the thinking)
- Using a graphic organizer in a geography lesson (locating the main idea)
- Building a word wall in health and nutrition (strengthening understanding of the language of the subject area)

It is critical for teachers (especially in middle and high schools) to find time to discuss and to demonstrate to each other what cross-curricular literacy instruction looks like and then to implement teaching the language of the disciplines and the literacy skills in the content areas across all grades and subject areas. Because the integration of literacy in all subject areas is central, cross-curricular connections must be valued and utilized in support of literacy instruction at all grade levels.

According to PISA statistics (Schleicher, 2011), although 15-year-olds who read fiction are more likely to achieve high scores, it is students who read a wide variety of materials who perform particularly well in reading. To consolidate understanding and embrace metacognition, students need multiple opportunities in multiple ways to share their understanding. We know, for example, that weakness in reading or writing skills provides barriers to success in mathematical problem solving. Thus, teachers must explicitly embed at least one literacy instructional strategy in every content lesson. To do that, all teachers need to know and be able to use strategies to develop vocabulary and comprehension skills—strategies that good readers do naturally. Struggling readers, by contrast, need explicit strategies to help them negotiate texts. Some concrete examples we have seen, at district learning fairs (see Chapter 5), include the following:

- Word walls to build the vocabulary of the subject area
- Making text-to-text, text-to-self, and text-to-world connections using sticky notes or using highlighters to mark the main ideas
- Putting concepts in students' own words while reading the text
- Reading comprehension strategies explicitly taught at all levels using the subject text to model think alouds, inferring, predicting, visualizing, and finding the main idea
- Graphic organizers to organize the essential ideas in a text

- Strategies to read and navigate the variety of formats used in electronic or printed texts, which can be dense or confusingly busy
- Supplementary sources with easier or simplified content if students can't read the level of the materials used (raising the key question of whether teachers are able to determine the appropriate readability of the printed or electronic resources that they use)

For additional cross-curricular literacy strategies, ideas, and support, see www.curriculum.org/thinkliteracy/library.html. Additionally, Appendix G is an impressive handout prepared by the school district that we highlight in the case study at the end of this chapter. It displays explicit cross-curricular literacy indicators for successful teaching of literacy in all content areas at the middle and high school levels.

Data Chart Tells an Improvement Story

We are zeroing in on the connections made between the FACES seen in assessment and the FACES known in instruction. The connector is the strong desire for all students to use higher-order thinking—the new basic skill—evident in areas such as nonfiction writing, rich authentic tasks, and cross-curricular content. Nonnegotiable work has started in many jurisdictions to first assess students' ability to attain higher-order thinking skills and then translate the assessments into classroom instruction.

Table 4.2 illustrates progressive data from 427 students in eight grades across seven elementary schools, identified as schools in challenging circumstances, in the Catholic District School Board of Eastern Ontario. During the time period illustrated in the table, high-yield classroom strategies related to *higher-order thinking skills* (see Glossary) were implemented with the goal of increasing the number of students performing at or above the expected standard in reading (that is, at Levels 3 and 4).

Table 4.2 shows an increase in scores across all grades assessed. Whereas it demonstrates large gains from the intentional instruction in grades 1–4 and again in grade 8, results for grades 4–7 are not as strong, particularly for grades 5, 6, and 7. Teachers have agreed to continue their focus on higher-order thinking until *all* students have

Table 4.2 Percentage of Students Achieving Levels 3 and 4 in Higher-Order Thinking Skills

Grade	Pretest December 2010	Mid-test End January 2011	Posttest March 2011
1	35%	70%	80%
2	40	66	83
3	57	61	75
4	40	36	61
5	49	46	57
6	33	42	40
7	38	33	42
8	25	44	63
Average*	42	52	65

Note: *Weighted average of total $N = 427$ at seven schools.

achieved the expected gains. In summary, these results indicate that the average percentage of students achieving the expected level or higher increased from 42 percent to 65 percent. In other words, there was a 23-point gain in the percentage of students achieving at or above the expected levels of achievement. To put the FACES on the data, we would say that 99 more students from the sample achieved the expected higher-order-thinking scores in less than 16 weeks of focused instruction—another example of the limitless possibilities when we pay attention to the FACES.

Organizing for Consistency of Practice

Some of our worry about instruction is alleviated when literacy coaches come up with ways to ensure consistency in assessment and instruction across all classrooms—like the "consistency binder"—an organizer used as a collaborative, building-confidence approach with teachers.

Joy Nelson, literacy coach at Brechin Public School (see Chapter 1 case study), writes about how she has tried to ensure that all teachers have access to the same assessment and instructional practices and resources, which are discussed at least twice a month at regular meetings throughout the school year:

Our consistency binder is a compilation of all the teacher and student resources that the teachers at Brechin PS and I have compiled for the teaching of literacy. Each teacher on staff has a binder and brings it to planning meetings and to staff meetings. Using the consistency binder, we revisit the resources we used last year and then add to it as we discuss and create new items together. At the moment, our consistency binders include the following:

- School Improvement Plan
- Curriculum expectations in our areas of need (like reading and writing)
- Data about school—grade—and at-risk student performance
- Sample anchor charts—like "The First 20 Days" or "What Good Readers Do" or "Guided Reading Prompts" (M. Sharratt in *Realization,* 2009, pp. 60–63)
- Examples of learning goals and success criteria for each grade level
- Writing genres and the steps in the writing process
- Information about the gradual-release model of teaching reading and writing
- Professional resources and websites

Our consistency binder is ever-changing. New material is added, and old, out-of-date material is omitted. Culling the least effective and capturing the most effective practices and resources together provides a time for rich dialogue and debate among our teachers. That way, we all have access to the same research about new practices and resource materials. It is just one way that we can move toward our goals as a collaborative team.

Embedded instructional coaches, like Joy, make consistency of practice and alignment of support a priority when working alongside classroom teachers.

Embedded Instructional Coaches

Assessment that drives instruction through the lens of literacy and fueled by seamless technology use is easier for teachers who have the support of a coach, like Joy Nelson at Brechin PS. Joy works alongside classroom teachers, the principal, and vice principal during the school day, demonstrating proven assessment and instructional practices in classrooms and at staff meetings. Instructional coaches are co-leaders and co-learners with their administrators. These classrooms teachers, who are teaching experts across the grades, also teach in their own classrooms the rest of the day and are willing to respectfully invite other teachers into their classrooms to watch them teach.

It is critical that these coaches be selected wisely on the basis of being exemplary teachers who are respected by their peers as knowledgeable, approachable, supportive, and ongoing learners (Sharratt, 1996, p. 100). This position is the key element to making job-embedded learning viable and visible. We insist on saying that these part-time "knowledgeable others" (Sharratt, Ostinelli, & Cattaneo, 2010), often known as instructional coaches, are critical because our research tells us that professional learning, delivered by credible colleagues, must be as close as possible to the area of improvement— the classroom and the teacher. Successful instructional coaches are timetabled in, during the school day, to work with principals, focused on instructional leadership (see Chapter 5), and alongside classroom teachers to co-plan, co-teach, co-debrief, and ultimately co-reflect (Sharratt & Fullan, 2009, pp. 51–56). The singular purpose of this process is to become better at the craft of teaching—often realized when principals and teachers become co-learners in the never-ending process of improvement (M. Sharratt, 2004).

The operative word here is *embedded.* One of us, along with Jim Knight, argued recently that coaches are useless unless their role is part and parcel of an integrated strategy to achieve whole-system reform (Fullan & Knight, 2011).

Co-Teaching–Co-Planning–
Co-Debriefing–Co-Reflecting

Instructional coaches and classroom teachers or two teachers partner to read research and then embark on a process of discovering teaching and learning processes together. Lani and Colin, introduced to you in the case study at the beginning of Chapter 3, do just that. They co-plan using the data to determine a focus and create a lesson (or lessons) that are engaging for the students but very specific in terms of the purpose. They focus on the standards or curriculum expectations, use various data sources, and use co-planning as the process. They each also want to identify an area that they are working on to improve their assessment and/or instructional practices. Partners usually take at least an hour or more to co-plan a lesson and then co-teach the lesson. The data that they take from the lesson are (1) How engaged were the students? (2) Was the content understood? and (3) Was higher-order thinking visible? The co-teachers have several check-in points throughout the lesson to determine if all the students understood the content. After the co-teaching is completed, they meet to co-debrief. In the co-debrief, the partners discuss what went well, what they could tweak, and what are the next steps in thinking about all the FACES in the class. This model allows teachers to think about whether they

- Give immediate oral or written descriptive feedback and make note of it
- Develop explicit learning goals and co-constructed success criteria—in student-friendly language
- Organize groups effectively to hear if all students are engaged in accountable talk
- Engage in higher-order questioning and thus hear higher-order answers (see Appendix F)
- Achieve rich authentic tasks that make students' thinking visible
- Reach the needs of *all* the students—clearly seeing all FACES

A higher level is reached when the co-teaching partners feel comfortable enough to videotape lessons for analysis, discussion, and co-reflection. Watching the videotaped lesson together allows for honest feedback and goal setting for the next co-teaching cycle. By that point, the partners are regularly engaged in candid, open dialogue that questions their assumptions and reaches deeply into what it means to teach and learn with the needs and competencies of all students in mind.

The co-teaching cycle shown in Figure 4.4 is the most powerful way to improve teaching practice and to implement the changes in

Figure 4.4 The Co-Teaching Cycle—Deep and Deliberate Reflections on and Change in Practice with a Teaching Partner

1. Co-Planning
- Find time to plan, teach with video, debrief and reflect with trusted colleague
- Begin with curriculum expectations, Learning Goal, draft Success Criteria to co-construct with students
- Plan before during and after lesson; think about timing, flow and pace
- Use research-based, high-yield instructional strategies differentiated based on student need
- Discuss Collaborative Inquiry focus for the teaching based on assessment for learning data (determine what you want to do to improve your practice)

2. Co-Teaching
- Work side-by-side in classroom
- Co-Facilitate classroom discussion
- Focus on students' thinking
- Monitor students' engagement
- Change pace and flow if needed
- Ask "How do we know all students' are achieving?"

The Co-Teaching Cycle

4. Co-Reflecting
- Engage with co-teaching partner in candid, open, honest dialogue about their teaching and learning
- Identify and understand changes needed in practice and beliefs to become consciously skilled
- Plan next steps for student and teacher learning based on formative assessment – working from where ALL students are in their learning

3. Co-Debriefing
- Examine video clips to look/listen for student voice, questions/responses, and visibility of higher-order thinking
- Examine teaching questions and prompts used
- Consider if taught, learned and assessed curriculum were aligned
- Discuss joint teaching, thinking about what worked, didn't work, what to do differently
- Evaluate Collaborative Inquiry focus for improved practice

assessment and instruction that we've studied, observed, and discussed in this book. It pushes professionals to make their practices transparent and public in order to become increasingly more skilled, reflective, and thoughtful. Some of our co-teaching partners are now meeting with students at the end of every term to have them reflect with them on what worked or what was challenging for them, and what changes in classroom practices they, as students, would make to better meet students' needs. It has allowed teachers to be aware of the critical importance of hearing students' voices and considering their viewpoints—clearly hearing from all the FACES.

This *reflective practice* (see Glossary) occurs when teachers explore and perfect high-yield assessment and instructional strategies that improve their teaching performance. As Hattie (2012) says, "Teachers are change agents—their role is to change students from what they are to what we want them to be, what we want them to know and understand—and this, of course, highlights the moral purposes of education."

Tier 2–Case Management Approach

If Tier 1 is good classroom teaching, then most of our students will be well served by very skilled teachers who use a variety of assessment tools, continually, to keep abreast of learners' progress and to prepare for purposeful instruction. Yet there will still be students for whom teachers may find it difficult to develop just the right instructional strategies to move their learning ahead. We call the next level of intervention Tier 2—a case management approach—focusing on instruction, not dwelling on behavior.

The case management approach is used to put a spotlight on how all students are progressing. The specific intention is that not one FACE will slip through the data cracks. Timetabled case management meetings during the school day are not to be confused with multidisciplinary special education meetings, often with outside personnel attending, that focus on behavior, discipline, psychosocial assessments, and the like. Nor is it a punitive dressing down of the teacher for "failing" to achieve. The case management meeting is a forum for the discussion of student work as data, in a case-by-case approach, for those students who are plummeting, staying still, or presenting as instructional challenges for their teachers. The focus is instruction.

Case-by-Case

The case management forum provides teachers with support for working with students whom they are not able to move forward. The focus of the case management meeting is on next steps in instruction. To provide the greatest support and input, case management forum membership always includes the principal, the presenting classroom teacher, and the instructional coach. Optionally, it may include other teachers, if available (for example, the special education teacher or the teacher-librarian or Reading Recovery teacher, whose time may be freed up by teachers without classrooms, vice principals, or creative timetabling). The meeting, led by the instructional coach or principal, as chair, follows a template (see Appendix C). Because case management meetings are quick (lasting 20–30 minutes), teachers must come prepared with the student's work in the area in which instructional help is requested. The purpose is to examine the student's work, describe strengths and areas of need, and find one or two instructional strategies the teacher can try for three to six weeks, after which time the forum is reconvened so that the teacher can report back on the progress and the assembled group can offer new suggestions if the first recommendations are not working. Participants provide feedback and support to the classroom teacher and will often "walk and talk" in the classroom to see how suggested strategies are progressing and to offer encouragement to the teacher.

This approach ensures that all teachers in the school have a collective responsibility to own all students' achievement. Teachers win with every meeting—even if strategies may not work as intended for the target student, the teacher's repertoire of strategies has grown, and very often the instructional strategies tried become good for the whole class—necessary for some, good for all! In fact, this is a proven strategy that strengthens the instructional capacity of every teacher and administrator participating in the case management meeting.

Specific Steps to Success

The following provides a step-by-step process that we have used and that readers can make their own, according to their contexts:

1. Time for case management meetings is scheduled into the timetable so that all teachers have a dedicated time during which they can bring students forward.

2. The chair is either the principal (who always attends) or the instructional coach.

3. Attendance at the case management meeting is confirmed.

4. Time on task is critical. A template (see Appendix C) is followed to lend reassurance to the factual and objective nature of the ensuing conversation.

5. The classroom teacher presents student work as data and evidence of the help being sought.

6. All voices around the table are heard.

7. A clear and specific recommendation is decided on and recorded. The classroom teacher agrees to practice— deliberately practice—the chosen strategy in his or her classroom for at least three to six weeks and with continued support of colleagues present on a "reach out/go to" basis until the next meeting.

8. The next meeting of the group is scheduled.

9. The classroom teacher reports back on the success or failure of the recommendation, with the student's work as evidence at the next meeting.

10. Another cycle begins, and the school team stays the course in this explicit focus on providing a supportive forum in which classroom teachers, one at a time, can present their instructional concerns.

Love et al. (2008) write that, when a teacher brings a student forward to these group meetings, we must guard against the group's natural inclination to identify the problem as student-related: "It is easier to put the burden on students rather than examine our own practices more closely" (p. 351). In research that Love conducted, "their verification process [similar to the above case management process] proved to be a valuable learning experience, as it demonstrated the need for ensuring that a problem really did exist before throwing money and time at it in order to make it better."

Practitioners from the field who have experienced the very positive outcomes generated by case management meetings send us anecdotes, like the following, that highlight the power of the case management approach in putting FACES on the data.

Narrative from the Field

Chloe, a grade 4 student at our school, started off her school year reading at a Fountas and Pinnell level L. When looking at this in terms of grade level, Chloe was reading at a mid–grade 2 level (almost two grades below expectation). As a result of our school's strategic plan to address literacy instruction and student learning over the past two years, combined with the individual teacher's commitment to supporting his students, the teacher brought Chloe to one of our regularly scheduled case management meetings as a worry for him—and for us. It is exciting to share that Chloe is now reading independently at level Q (mid–grade 4) and is at an instructional level R (end–grade 4) as a result of our laser-like commitment to literacy and our recommended instructional strategies to improve her learning level. Chloe improved two grade levels in 9 months!

We attribute this success to the following literacy commitments we have all made as a team:

- Uninterrupted literacy blocks
- Daily small-group instruction and one-on-one conferring at the student's level
- Access to quality reading material for all students regardless of reading ability
- Teachers' commitment to using the same instructional vocabulary for students
- Use of teacher anecdotal notes to support next steps for instruction for each student
- Embedded time to meet as grade-level teams to discuss student assessment, instructional practices, and necessary interventions
- Quality professional development tied directly to supporting our literacy goals
- Our staff approach that *all* students are *our* students
- A case management approach in which individual student needs are identified, appropriate instructional strategies and supports are selected, and regular follow-up is maintained by the administrator leading the case management team

(Continued)

(Continued)

Given the intense focus on building a common commitment to our vision of literacy instruction, and rigorous analysis of teacher practice and student skill development, we have seen unprecedented growth in our students' reading abilities. Chloe's success, in leaping two grades forward to catch up to her peers, is but one of many individual stories of the data telling us that what we are doing is making a difference for all of our students.

—Joanne Pitman, principal,
Aspen Grove Public School, Grande Prairie, Alberta, Canada

Tier 3–Early Intervention

During the teaching-learning cycle (see Appendix D), teachers use ongoing assessment data to determine intervention strategies needed. All teachers thus become capable intervention teachers and teach all students in their classes in our Tier 1 and Tier 2 model. Every teacher can put FACES on the data—using the information gathered through formative assessment and using instructional interventions that meet a wide range of learning needs. This often takes the form of reteaching using varied instructional approaches and different materials, and providing more time for students to learn new concepts and to see things more clearly. Students revise and practice based on the descriptive feedback they receive (see Chapter 3), and ultimately they own their learning.

After good first teaching including classroom intervention (Tier 1), followed by case management meetings and teacher-supported interventions (Tier 2), if students are still not learning, then the next level of intervention is what we call "early intervention" (Tier 3). We don't discuss intervention at every grade level, other than early intervention here, because we believe our moral imperative is to catch children early before it's too late!

Reading Recovery

Reading Recovery is a highly successful program and an excellent example of an early intervention literacy program. Early in grade 1 (usually at age 6), the teacher identifies the lowest-achieving grade

1 students for the Reading Recovery program, which offers balanced intervention, with parental support, that moves these lowest achievers to read and write at the average level so that they are able to benefit from good, mainstream classroom instruction. Other positive consequences of early intervention are that of raising learners' mean capacity in every classroom—that is, narrowing the achievement gap between high and low achievers. In addition, the valuable instructional skills modeled in the Reading Recovery training program are transferred as best teaching practices that can benefit all classroom teachers, making this a cost-effective model. A profound example of the power of Reading Recovery is found in the story of Ethin, a six-year-old boy from Grande Prairie, Alberta, Canada.

Ethin was at Level 1 in September 2010, when he was assessed as the lowest student in grade 1, based on the Observation Survey (Clay, 2002), and was slated to be in the Reading Recovery program. His writing was an illegible scribble, as seen in Figure 4.5.

Ethin worked diligently with Reading Recovery teacher Gaye Williams for 20 minutes a day, constructing meaning through

Figure 4.5 Ethin's Writing at Week 1 of Grade 1

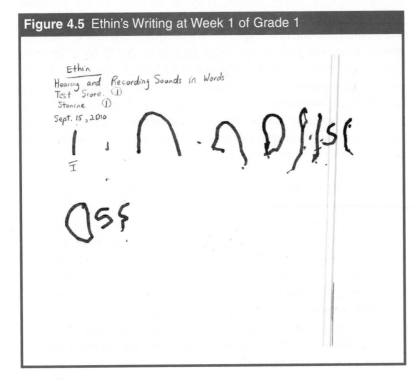

Used with permission.

interactions in daily lessons specifically crafted to meet his learning needs. Eventually, because his confidence grew with each successful lesson, he saw himself as a reader and writer. After 20 weeks of Reading Recovery lessons, with Gaye's proficient instruction, Ethin could read and write at grade and peer level. Figure 4.6 shows Ethin's dramatically improved writing after only 17 weeks of daily 20-minute lessons with Gaye.

Do all teachers know what to do when they have an Ethin in their class? Usually the answer is no. The cost-effectiveness of Reading Recovery lies in having Gaye on staff. She spends time working with primary division colleagues, sharing her expertise so that her knowledge spills over into all their early-learning class-rooms. Reading Recovery is a powerful Tier 3 intervention program that has proven to be a worthwhile financial investment for school districts. Not only are the earliest struggling learners brought quickly to reading and writing, but trained Reading Recovery teachers, like Gaye, impact the teaching and learning of the whole staff through the ongoing literacy professional learning that they lead.

Research by Emily Tanner, research director at the National Centre for Social Research in the United Kingdom, showed impres-sive results from the Reading Recovery program. Quoted in the press release (National Centre for Social Research, 2011) for a recently completed report on which she was lead author, Tanner said: "It's exciting to see how children who were struggling to read benefited from Reading Recovery after such a short time. Mastering the basic skills in literacy and finding *enjoyment* in reading during the early years at school are crucial factors underpinning later academic suc-cess." According to the press release,

> Year [grade] 1 pupils who took part in the Reading Recovery study had below average literacy levels at the start of the academic year, and 86% of these pupils attained Level 1 or above by the end of the year, showing that they had made significant improvement and had progressed towards achieving Level 2 [expected level] the following year. By comparison only 60% of similar pupils, who did not take part in the Reading Recovery program, achieved Level 1 despite receiving other types of literacy support.
>
> The National Curriculum, in the United Kingdom, states that at the end of Year 2 most children are expected to achieve Level 2 [or be able to read].

Figure 4.6 Ethin's Writing at Week 17 after Reading Recovery Lessons

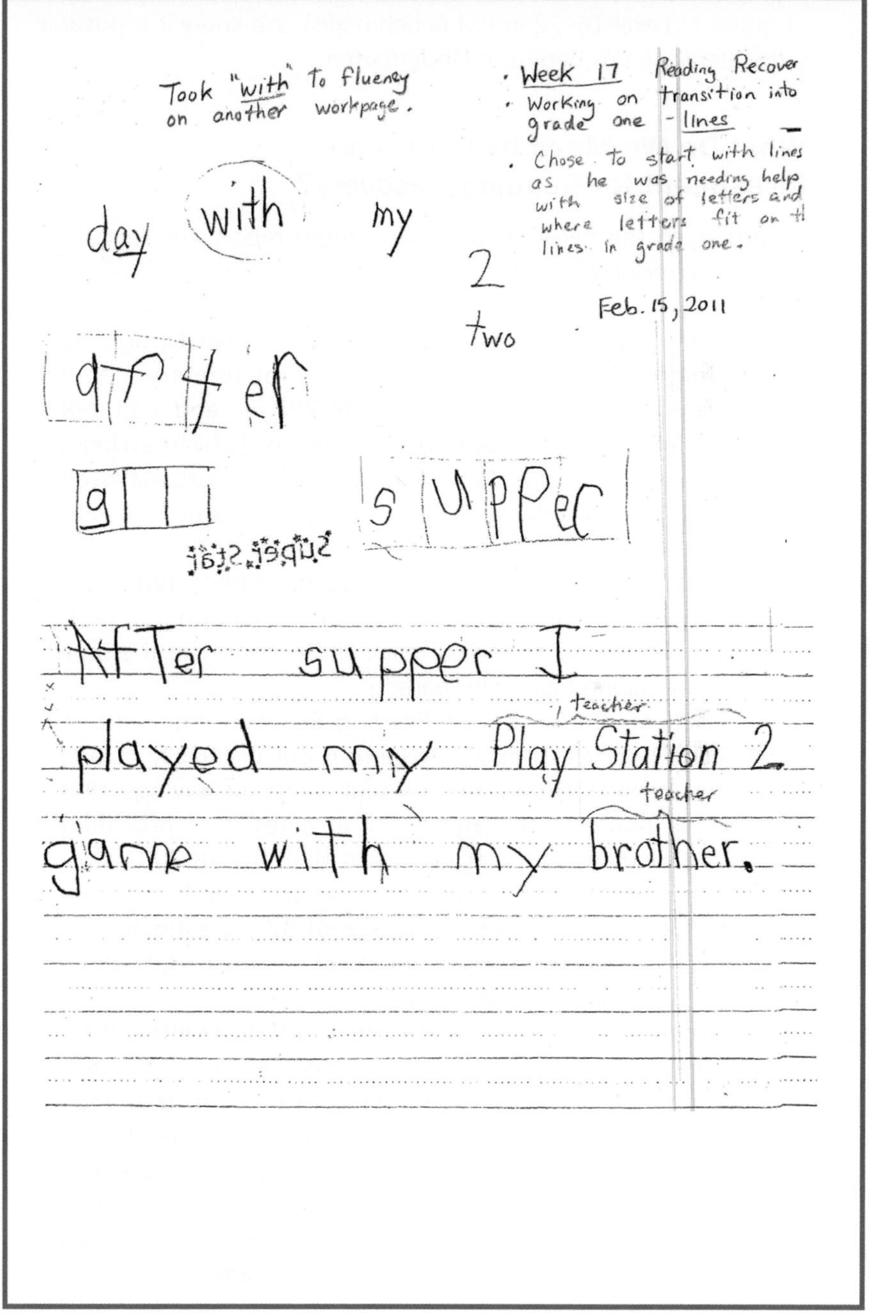

Took "with" To fluency
on another workpage.

day (with) my

af ter

g [ ][ ]

super. super

s Upper

2
two

• Week 17 Reading Recover
• Working on transition into
  grade one – lines
• Chose to start with lines
  as he was needing help
  with size of letters and
  where letters fit on th
  lines in grade one.

Feb. 15, 2011

AfTer supper I

teacher
played my Play Station 2.

teacher
game with my brother.

Used with permission.

However, in Ontario, we are saying that all six year olds are capable and can read with fluency and comprehension by the end of grade 1 (Level 16–22 in PM Benchmarks). We know it is possible if the literacy focus begins in kindergarten.

What Do We Mean by Return on Investment for Reading Recovery?

According to the KPMG Foundation (2006) report *The Long Term Costs of Literacy Difficulties,*

> The total per capita costs to the public purse to age 37 resulting from failure to learn to read in the primary school years are estimated at between £44,797 . . . and £53,098 [per student]. . . . [T]he lower-bound estimate, [which] excludes the costs of maintaining Statements of special educational need and takes a conservative approach to the costs associated with crime. . . . [T]he upper-bound estimate, [which] includes the cost of maintaining Statements and assumes higher crime costs resulting from reading failure. [*Note:* For comparison purposes, all costs are relative to the currency and economy at the time and in the nation being compared.]
>
> Based on evidence that Reading Recovery intervention will lift 79% of children who receive it out of literacy failure, . . . [the report] shows the present value of savings that would be made to the age of 37 as a result of providing Reading Recovery at the age of six to all of the 38,700 pupils per year who currently leave primary school with very low literacy skills. . . . Savings to the age of 37 are estimated at between £1,369,576,578 [in one case] and £1,623,374,471 [in the other case they reported].
>
> Based on a 79% success rate, the return on investment for every pound [sterling] spent on the Every Child A Reader programme [Reading Recovery] is estimated to be in the range £14.81 to £17.56. The long-term return on investment from the £10M spent on the Every Child A Reader initiative can therefore be estimated at between £148.1M and £175.6M over the period between 2006–8 and 2037–9, when the children currently accessing the programme reach the age of 37.

Although the U.K. researchers do not go further, it is easy to make the argument that the longer-term opportunity cost lost to a nation's economy by not using Reading Recovery in grade 1 is many times larger than the expense of implementing the program.

In Australia in April 2011, as reported in all media, the prime minister announced that 8.5 million adults were unable to be retrained for jobs requiring the ability to read because they simply could not read adequately enough to be retrained. Although these adults cannot go back to the primary grades, the new national curriculum standards and funding in Australia—which will provide intervention programs such as Reading Recovery—will ensure that, in 18 years, the children who are currently in grade 1 in Australia will not face the same economic "life sentence" that restricts them from technology or manufacturing jobs that would require them to read.

In short, we wonder what we are waiting for when we know the statistics and the costs to our nations of not doing the best for *all* children early enough. To this point, EQAO research (Calman 2010) sums up our position: "[E]ffective classroom management, effective planning, collaborative learning, formative and responsive assessment and early intervention improve the learning of all students." With so much research evidence made public, not to act reflects misguided public governance or, worse, almost criminal indecision that sentences large numbers of young students to restricted future lives. Not to act further penalizes society, in general, because of dramatically reduced earnings and other contributions that those who qualify for better educations can, and do, make to the nation.

Collaborative Inquiry

We conclude Chapter 4 by summing up the two improvement drivers that we have discussed so far—assessment and instruction—in two words: collaborative inquiry—because a focus on assessment and instruction drives inquiry. We have experienced collaborative inquiry in many guises in education: action research, reflective practice, collaborative inquiry, and, now, teacher collaborative inquiry. There must be something to it, given that it keeps coming back—if only with new titles and slightly different nuances. In fact, Kurt Lewin, the creator of the action research concept, clearly identified that action research carried out by teachers in schools should bear scientific characteristics (Ostinelli, 2008).

Then Donald Schön (1983) developed a body of knowledge, which described teachers as reflective practitioners, that made a huge impact in bringing research theory and practice together in a reflective way. At that point, educators began to write anecdotal notes and observations on what they were experiencing and thinking about in their teaching. Both the original action research theory and the later reflective practice were individualistic pursuits by teachers in classrooms without necessarily using data to inform their question of interest or connecting their learning to other colleagues or to whole school improvement. Recently, Earl and Katz (2006) highlighted the use of data for informed decision making and insisted that data must be used to serve continuous inquiry, as an aid to making wise decisions, not just to answer the question of the day.

Today, we look to whole-school approaches to inquiry and teachers, at least in pairs, questioning their practice, scrutinizing their data, and reflecting on what's working, what's not working, and what could be done differently in their classrooms.

For us, collaborative inquiry works best if it involves a whole-school approach to inquiry that focuses the work on school and student data resulting in actions from deep, collective thought and conversations over a sustained period of time. Figure 4.7 shows the

Deliberate Pause

- Are student and school achievement data driving the inquiry process?
- Are multiple data sources driving instruction in classrooms? How do you know?
- Are collaborative marking of student work, instructional coaching time, case management meetings, and collaborative inquiry the operating norm in your school? How do you know?
- Is the professional learning that you are leading making a difference to improved student learning? How do you know on a daily and monthly basis?

Figure 4.7 Collaborative Inquiry Cycle

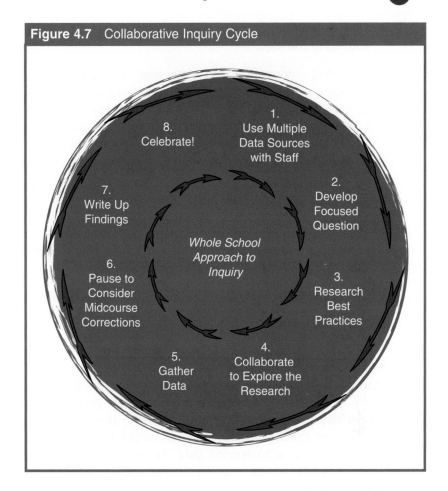

collaborative inquiry cycle graphically and includes the following components:

1. Using multiple data sources related to school and student improvement with the whole staff

2. Developing a focused question concerning school and class-room practice to increase student achievement

3. Scouring the research literature to understand current best practice pertaining to the inquiry question—teachers often conduct a book study of related research on their chosen topic

4. Finding time to collaboratively explore answers of practice aligned to the research

5. Gathering information and data from multiple sources, including district professional learning sessions, networking groups, book study, listening to experts on webcasts and at conferences, trialing new practice, observing each other's practice, and making decisions about what does and doesn't answer the initial inquiry question

6. Taking a deliberate pause to consider any midcourse corrections needed

7. Writing up findings to inform (a) professional learning sessions needed for school staff, (b) next steps in school improvement planning, and (c) annual reports of improvement

8. Celebrating the final report, which is the best part—often in a learning symposium format that mobilizes the new learning

After working together with the Catholic District School Board of Eastern Ontario, we attended their culminating event, a learning fair. There we saw the collaborative inquiry process presented by one school staff group whose members spoke to their journey to answer their collaborative inquiry question, which they created in response to student achievement data. Figure 4.8 reflects data related to students' scores in using the reading comprehension strategy of making connections. The data indicated that 52.13 percent of students were below standard (Levels 1 and 2) and only 9.40 percent were performing above the standard (Level 4), which was their target for all students.

After scrutinizing these data, the staff agreed that their whole-school collaborative inquiry question would be the following:

By using the gradual-release-of-responsibility model, how can we increase our students' ability to make connections between information and ideas in a reading selection, connections that use the reader's personal knowledge and experience?

Figure 4.8 Data Used to Make Focused Whole-School Improvement Decisions

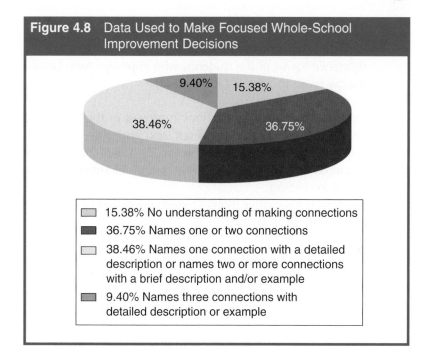

- 15.38% No understanding of making connections
- 36.75% Names one or two connections
- 38.46% Names one connection with a detailed description or names two or more connections with a brief description and/or example
- 9.40% Names three connections with detailed description or example

---

During their learning fair presentation, teachers and the principal then shared their collaborative inquiry journey of discovery. From start to finish, they

1. Focused on below-standard students

2. Established an action plan with timelines

3. Planned pre-, midcourse, and post-assessments

4. Held a book study to read recent research in evidence-proven reading strategies

5. Included modeled lessons by the literacy coach to demonstrate making connections

6. Developed classroom anchor charts, clear learning goals (tied to the curriculum expectations and standards), and co-constructed success criteria in student-friendly language

7. Practiced explicit teaching in their classrooms (a) using guided questions and (b) modeling text-to-self, text-to-text, and text-to-world connections

8. Marked common assessments collaboratively

9. Reported that in one of the classes the teacher had made a difference for 13 of the students, who improved from Level 2 (below level) to Level 3 (at standard)

In short, all students in the school improved in their ability to make connections between text and self, text and other texts, and text and the world. They are waiting for the 2011 EQAO assessment to be completed and are confident those results will show quantum improvement in reading.

In their final collaborative inquiry report, published for the learning fair, the school team wrote:

We used 3 data sources to help us determine our students' greatest need. After carefully looking at the data, we determined that students were having difficulty making meaningful connections related to personal experiences and outside materials. This also meant that students were having difficulty understanding and identifying their learning processes in reading.

Through systematic and explicit instruction, we created lessons that were centered around rich, fictional text and the use of high-yield strategies. We used our first lesson as a diagnostic to help lead us in planning the lessons that followed.

We know that we made a difference because students began to show evidence of their learning. They were able to understand the differences in the connections they had been making before to the more meaningful connections they were now able to make. Students were able to tell us how their connections helped them understand the text being read and how it helped them in their writing. Students were very receptive to the lessons and showed immediate transference of information. They began almost immediately to use the language and strategies we had modeled in class. As well, teachers were willing to share, ask questions of each other and be open to trying new instructional strategies.

For us, this example of a yearlong collaborative inquiry cycle, in which the classroom instruction planned was specific to the data, underlines the importance of using data to inform instruction. It also demonstrates our shared beliefs and understandings in parameter 1—that all teachers can clearly articulate why they do what they do to increase all students' achievement.

In Chapters 3 and 4 we have developed a "language of assessment and instruction" that will promote rich discussion and a depth of understanding among professional educators—with the sole underlying purpose of putting the FACES on the data—to make every student's progress count. When we reflect on the key topics covered in this chapter, such as instructional coaches, co-teaching, case management, and collaborative inquiry, we agree resoundingly with Chappius (2007) that these approaches are exemplary models of professional learning that work well because they are on site, job embedded, sustained over time, and centered on active learning and student outcomes.

As mentioned earlier, we worked together in a school district, outside Ottawa, Canada, in its newly created "Realization Network." The following case study illustrates how assessment (improvement driver 1) and instruction (improvement driver 2) intertwine to put FACES on the data to improve all students' learning in elementary and secondary schools in that district.

Eastern Ontario Case Study

In fall 2009, director of education William Gartland, of the Catholic District School Board of Eastern Ontario (CDSBEO), Canada, invited Fullan and Sharratt to review student achievement data, recommend an improvement plan and take action, alongside system leaders and school teams, to narrow the achievement gap and raise the overall student achievement performance bar based on using literacy as the driving reform strategy. The first thing they did was to ask for the district's improvement plan. It turns out that it was 31 pages long, with 16 goals and eight elements of action in a matrix. The ideas were fine, but our "simplexity" alarm went off. Implementation plans are for the implementers—not for the planners. They need to be clean, inspiring, actionable, memorable, or, in a word, "sticky."

(Continued)

(Continued)

We asked the district leadership team to reduce the implementation plan to three big ideas. They had little trouble doing this, settling on three stepping stones:

1. Achieving literacy for *all*

2. Living our Catholic faith

3. Making resources matter

The team was ready to roll. Senior executive council and system principals met with Sharratt and Fullan to analyze district demographic and student achievement data, review the improvement plan, and share perceived challenges with the subsequent action plan created to build collective capacity, which was becoming known as the CDSBEO Realization Network. Their work included the following:

- Collapsing the improvement plan to focus on high-yield instructional practices, assessment data, and results
- Cultivating leadership at all levels so that everyone would work together within and across the system
- Identifying key inspiring priorities that articulated the district's vision—using the three stepping stones, which everyone can recall
- Focusing on going deeper with the implementation of their rich district-developed resources

Realization Network sessions led by Sharratt and Fullan focused on implementing the 14 parameters with leadership teams from all elementary and secondary schools. Operational and strategic outcomes included the following:

- The director and his superintendents not only attended, but also actively modeled and engaged in every activity so that their leadership, thoughts, and constant belief in the potential of their school teams became the example for principals and school team members alike.
- School teams—school administrators, resource teachers, and literacy lead teachers from all elementary and secondary schools—mobilized to work through the 14 parameters of Realization (Sharratt & Fullan, 2009) and were empowered to learn and to plan for their schools. They were charged with passing along the

learning and planned input to all their teachers—building collective instructional leadership capacity in the process.

- Each session began with Sharratt putting student FACES on the district data—identifying the number of students not meeting standard so that teams could plan high-yield implementation strategies, such as
  - ○ Ensuring appropriate professional learning for all teachers
  - ○ Implementing early intervention practices in all schools
  - ○ Deploying instructional coaches and consultants to work alongside classroom teachers co-planning and co-teaching, to refine practice and focus on students' thinking
  - ○ Personalizing learning for all students
  - ○ Adopting the gradual-release model so that students would be more engaged in their own learning
  - ○ Adopting student-led conferencing (see Chapter 3)
  - ○ Involving parents more fully
  - ○ Sharing responsibility for all students through the case management approach (see earlier in this chapter)
  - ○ Building school capacity through collaborative inquiry learning (see earlier in this chapter) and Catholic professional learning communities (CPLCs), such that the Realization Network would support the collective commitment to raising the bar and closing the achievement gap

Letting the Data Tell the Story

The Realization Network professional learning sessions were an opportunity for the school system to reflect, refine, and go deeper in terms of what was needed to increase students' literacy achievement and student learning. Two school examples follow: St. Peter Elementary and Notre Dame High School. Both schools had gains that reflect their detailed implementation and monitoring plans.

St. Peter Catholic School, in Cornwall, is a community K–6 school with a diverse population of 189 students, offering both Core French and French Immersion programs.

Table 4.3 shows the EQAO results of five successive years of St. Peter's grade 3 and grade 6 classes and the overall results from the district for grades 3 and 6 during the same period. Before the Realization Network, St. Peter results were below the scores for the district in each domain in every period for grades 3 and 6. In 2009–2010, St. Peter's grades 3 and

(Continued)

(Continued)

Table 4.3 EQAO Results Showing Trends and Patterns over 5 Years for Primary and Junior Divisions—St. Peter and District

EQAO Assessment of Reading and Writing: Percentage of Students Achieving Standard, Levels 3 and 4

	Grade 3					Grade 6				
	2005–2006	2006–2007	2007–2008	2008–2009	2009–2010	2005–2006	2006–2007	2007–2008	2008–2009	2009–2010
St. Peter										
Reading	49%	56%	41%	25%	71%	53%	51%	56%	48%	75%
Writing	41	47	44	25	76	51	37	56	41	64
District										
Reading	66	64	65	62	67	67	65	67	68	74
Writing	62	60	69	69	80	60	55	67	62	71

6 scores surpassed the district scores in reading. Although St. Peter students did not surpass the district in writing in either grade 3 or 6, the St. Peter scores were significantly greater than the trend they had been following. Note that 47 percent of students at St. Peter are identified with special education needs.

Table 4.4 illustrates that, when assessed in grade 6 (2008–2009), St. Peter's cohort 1 showed almost no improvement from its scores in grade 3 (2005–2006); however, St. Peter's cohort 2 scored almost 20 points higher in both reading and writing when they were in grade 6 (2008–2009) than they did when they were in grade 3 (2005–2006). How much of that improvement was due to in-school programs and how

Table 4.4 EQAO Same-Student Results for Two St. Peter Cohorts Compared to Two District Cohorts

EQAO Assessment of Reading and Writing: Percentage of Students Achieving Standard, Levels 3 and 4

St. Peter Cohort 1	Grade 3 2005–2006	Grade 6 2008–2009
Reading	49%	48%
Writing	41	41
St. Peter Cohort 2	*Grade 3 2006–2007*	*Grade 6 2009–2010*
Reading	56	75
Writing	47	64
District Cohort 1	*Grade 3 2005–2006*	*Grade 6 2008–2009*
Reading	66	68
Writing	62	62
District Cohort 2	*Grade 3 2006–2007*	*Grade 6 2009–2010*
Reading	64	74
Writing	60	71

(Continued)

(Continued)

much to the Realization Network program can be seen by looking at the district's improvement in cohort 2 over cohort 1. The district's cohort 1 scores were approximately equal in grades 3 and 6, whereas the cohort 2 scores improved impressively by approximately 10 points on the grade 6 assessment.

Clearly the Realization Network program has had a significant impact and created a significant difference district-wide. St. Peter, perhaps motivated a little more to achieve parity, and having more room to move ahead, did in fact surpass the district. But as district 2 cohort results demonstrate, the entire district benefitted from the Realization Network.

This case study follows just two schools in their improvement processes, although many others could have been followed, as well. All school teams were galvanized for the task; however, the following notes from St. Peter may act as a proxy for the actions taken by many other schools in the district.

How Did St. Peter Catholic School Improve?

St. Peter followed five key strategies:

1. Assessment focus to drive instruction

2. Instructional focus

3. Leadership—instructional leadership

4. Professional learning for all teachers

5. Resource amplification—getting the greatest volume for the smallest investment by centralizing resources for all teachers to use

1. *Assessment*—early and ongoing intervention (parameter 5)/ case management approach (parameter 6). Evidence-based research and formal and informal assessments were necessary to clarify and deepen understanding of all students' needs. Teachers used multiple sources of data that were updated and reviewed regularly—release time was provided for each classroom teacher, special education resource teacher, differentiated instruction coach, and literacy support teacher to meet with the principal in order to regularly review initial data—these data sources were then used to develop action plans and to make decisions for strategic focus on specific issues, which in turn had a positive impact on the students. These data were also translated into priorities, goals, and strategies and linked to the school's improvement plan. Through the use of data, teachers began to intensify their ability to differentiate instruction and to collaborate on and improve in their identification of all students' learning needs. The school team was able to identify strengths and challenges at the individual and overall school levels. The school developed practices to strategically move students from one level to the next, to group students for effective instruction, and to implement an early identification and intervention plan (tutoring, guided reading groups, flexible reading groups).

2. *Instruction*—embedded literacy coaches (parameter 2)/ daily, sustained focus on literacy instruction (parameter 3)/ cross-curricular connections (parameter 13). The teachers and principal were part of both board and provincial initiatives (for example, K–1 collaborative inquiry) that helped them in implementing new approaches. Large blocks of instructional time for literacy and math were a priority. Teachers used a balanced literacy approach, clustered curriculum expectations, explored the gradual-release model, and were very conscious of spending less instructional time transitioning from subject to subject. In mathematics, teachers were able to connect math concepts to daily life and use problem-solving and comprehension strategies to enable students to develop conceptual understanding with perseverance. Teachers increasingly used anchor charts, exemplars, and open-response questions to help guide their instruction so that students were working toward the highest achievement level. Students were involved in developing success criteria, co-constructing anchor charts, and increasing their understanding of how to attain higher levels of achievement. Coaches and consultants, who supported both English and French teachers, helped to transform and build collective capacity for improved instructional practices. They helped to ensure that initiatives were carried through. Consultants and coaches provided intensive job-embedded support and release time for both English and French teachers to co-plan, co-teach, co-debrief, and co-reflect.

3. *Leadership*—principal leadership (parameter 4) and the school team (parameter 8). A key factor in the success at St. Peter is the instructional leadership of the principal. Highly knowledgeable about curriculum, special education, and instruction, she has made

(Continued)

(Continued)

an enormous contribution to the staff's professional learning. She clearly articulates, every chance she gets, that literacy, including problem solving and the gradual release model, is a focus and the top priority of the school. The principal attends and actively engages in all CPLCs, as well as professional learning sessions run by the district. She has a clearly focused and articulated vision for her school, one of academic excellence that is communicated to everyone connected to the school—the staff, the community, the parish, and the parents. She ensures the language of schooling is user-friendly for parents and community members. The principal sets high expectations for continual improvement and is a visible presence in the school—she "walks" in classrooms (see Chapter 5), observes instruction, develops capacity in her building, and is accessible to discuss matters dealing with instruction and school improvement. In addition, the principal organizes resources of time and money (through school-based budgets) to support her school's instructional agenda. She ensures that teachers have the materials needed to give their students rich instructional experiences. The provision of appropriate teaching materials, specifically books, has been a priority of hers.

While the principal is indeed the leader, she builds trust to ensure that the members of the school team are in fact part of the leadership team. They do not just "practice followership." They engage in data analysis, debate the merits of planned items, and learn as they go along to become powerful partners with the principal—as do the teams in the other CDSBEO schools.

4. Professional learning for all teachers—shared beliefs and understandings (parameter 1). Teachers began to work together to share the common goal for increased student achievement at school staff meetings and CPLCs. They held regular meetings and gathered in CPLCs to co-plan and co-teach, they shared an action research project (parameter 11), and they opened their classroom doors. They began to share a collective responsibility for *all* students in the school through celebrating and sharing small successes.

Through the teacher moderation process (collaborative marking of student work), teachers reviewed the data to examine trends and identify areas of strength and areas for improvement; they examined classroom data results (PM Benchmark, CASI, the Ontario Writing Assessment, and

EQAO) to determine goals and put FACES on the data, monitored and adjusted their instructional strategies, and moved students forward. Through this process, teachers came to understand the expectations for each level and how they could help their students to achieve the provincial standards. They asked questions, discussed results, and provided their students with descriptive feedback (see Chapter 3) in a timely fashion to help them improve their performance. Now, teachers are well equipped to proficiently share successful and effective strategies in planning next steps for instruction.

5. Resource amplification—centralized resources (parameter 9). St. Peter's book room houses literacy and cross-curricular resources in English and French for teachers to use in their classrooms. The book room centralizes the school's collection of books and multimedia resources that promote balanced literacy, literature study, and cross-curricular literacy. The resources are organized in a variety of ways (leveled books for guided reading, mentor texts that support the Catholic faith and cultural traditions, and books to use in *think-alouds* (see Glossary) to model particular reading comprehension skills or writing traits. The centralized resources make it easy for teachers to find the materials they need for the strategy or task they are planning. Teachers use a simple library card system for signing out books. The books and resources are selected strategically to support instruction; they are engaging, are of high quality, support the Ontario curriculum, and promote student learning. Teachers have also experienced success using assistive technology, with the use of Kurzweil, Dragon Naturally Speaking, document cameras, and an interactive white board to support students with special needs. These resources not only support student needs as indicated on the students' individualized education plans (IEPs) but also help all students to engage actively in classroom learning.

These five elements are not all that mysterious. They are "simplexity" at its best—a small number of core elements well implemented in concert. Synergy is multiplicative.

How Did Notre Dame High School Improve?

An analysis of Notre Dame's achievement data indicated that students in grades 7–12, particularly students in locally developed courses, typically had difficulty in the thinking and communication

(Continued)

(Continued)

areas of achievement. Successful scores in these areas were thought to correlate with successful scores on the province's grade 10 language assessment, the Ontario Secondary School Language Test (OSSLT), which students must pass in order to graduate. Knowing this, the school was determined to be better—the target was to have all teachers working together toward precise common literacy goals so that all students would be completely prepared to pass the OSSLT as first-time takers. The data-savvy teachers knew that passing OSSLT was heavily correlated to students having achieved Level 3 or 4 on the EQAO reading and writing assessments in grade 6. Because Notre Dame is a grade 7–12 school, teachers felt that intervening early, beginning in grade 7, with those students who were below Level 3 or 4 in grade 6, would provide their future grade 10 students with the best opportunity to pass the OSSLT and, equally valuable, to do better in all other subjects.

The first step was for the elementary and the secondary leadership teams to review their data together—taking responsibility for *all* students (parameter 14). They discovered that the data from the Ontario Writing Assessment, CASI, STOMP (Success Through Optimizing My Potential—a district framework that supports critical and creative thinking for intermediate students), and the OSSLT indicated that students had difficulty with thinking and communication skills. The team recognized that some teachers had been using high-yield literacy strategies, especially in English Language Arts (parameter 3); however, consistency of practice across all grades was lacking.

The team felt that greater collaboration would be fostered if all staff members were involved in setting the focus. The elementary teachers were developing common assessments, practicing teacher moderation, and exploring ways of incorporating high-yield literacy strategies in all content areas (parameter 13). The differentiated instruction support teacher (parameter 2) worked closely with the elementary team to ensure that instructional methodology was consistent.

The secondary leadership team gathered evidence from staff as to what their professional learning needs were through discussions at meetings, surveys, and a reflective "classroom practices inventory." All teachers were asked to visit another teacher's classroom to observe literacy practices. After much discussion, it was determined that a common assessment task, called a "higher-order thinking (HOT) paragraph" would be used to monitor student learning in each and every secondary classroom.

All secondary teachers were expected to explicitly teach students how to respond to HOT questions related to their course material. Supports such as graphic organizers and posters were developed to guide instruction. The math department developed an organizer consistent with the HOT paragraph framework for problem solving. Near the end of the semester, teachers came together in mixed subject groupings to moderate their paragraphs using a common assessment tool that they had developed (parameter 13).

Lively professional dialogue emerged from the *teacher moderation* sessions (see Glossary), which facilitated more reflection on instruction, assessment, and student learning. The principal and district curriculum consultant were able to have "courageous conversations" with staff as they raised their challenges and concerns during the teacher moderation process. The assessment data collected by the principal were shared with staff.

Figure 4.9 shows the early positive impact of the HOT paragraph writing program for a period of time in which all staff members at Notre Dame were involved in helping *all* students to attain needed literacy skills. The level of collaboration and professional dialogue that was focused on instruction and on student learning at Notre Dame increased dramatically. Teachers were urged to review their results honestly together, to make their strategies even more precise.

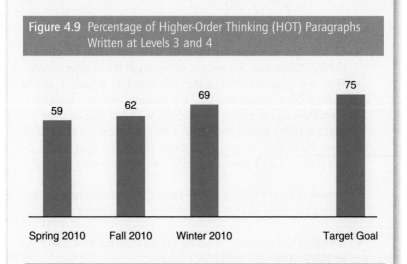

Figure 4.9 Percentage of Higher-Order Thinking (HOT) Paragraphs Written at Levels 3 and 4

Spring 2010	Fall 2010	Winter 2010	Target Goal
59	62	69	75

(Continued)

(Continued)

After the moderation of the winter 2010 HOT paragraphs (see Figure 4.9), teachers realized that the development of future HOT questions required more attention and they felt they needed more support in delivering explicit instruction on the communication elements of the paragraphs. Teachers also realized the success criteria needed to be refined. These steps—assessing their own teaching and learning tools—have allowed staff to be even more precise in next-cycle instruction, and staff teams have created a new baseline for evaluation.

The Realization Network process has enabled a culture of continuous improvement to grow at Notre Dame. Further, the new moderation methodology will link the scoring of the HOT paragraph to Student's Achieve, the district's online program for tracking data, which was piloted and is currently being rolled out to all district high schools. Now teachers will be able to pull data by subject, grade, student, and level of difficulty and then target instruction to individual students—putting FACES on the data.

Figures 4.10 and 4.11 show the result of the HOT paragraph writing program in improving Notre Dame students' OSSLT results. Figure 4.10 illustrates the underlying notion that achieving a Level 3 or 4 on the EQAO grade 6 reading assessment correlates with first-time-taker success on the OSSLT in grade 10. Below are some important details related to the data reflected in the figure:

- A total of 125 students, including 15 new students, took the OSSLT in 2009–2010.
- Of the 125 participating students, 110 had data for grade 6 (2005–2006); thus, 88 percent were part of the original cohort.
- From the original cohort, 3 students who had a Level 1 on the grade 6 EQAO passed the OSSLT; 3 students were not successful.
- From the original cohort, 16 students who had a Level 2 on the grade 6 EQAO passed the OSSLT; 5 students were not successful.
- From the original cohort, 83 students who had a Level 3 or 4 on the grade 6 EQAO passed the OSSLT; all students were successful.

In summary, from the original grade 6 cohort, 102 students were successful in passing the grade 10 OSSLT the first time, and 8 students were not.

- A total of 125 students, including 15 new students, took the OSSLT in 2009–2010.
- Of the 125 participating students, 88 percent were part of the original cohort.

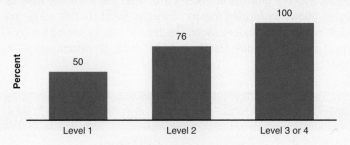

Figure 4.10 Percentage of Students Passing the OSSLT in 2009–2010, by Grade 6 EQAO Reading Score in 2005–2006

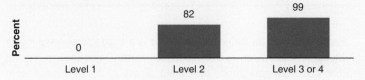

Figure 4.11 Percentage of Students Passing the OSSLT in 2009–2010, by Grade 6 EQAO Writing Score in 2005–2006

- From the original cohort, no students who had a Level 1 on the grade 6 EQAO passed the OSSLT; 1 student was not successful.
- From the original cohort, 28 students who had a Level 2 on the grade 6 EQAO passed the OSSLT; 5 students were not successful.
- From the original cohort, 75 students who had a Level 3 or 4 on the grade 6 EQAO passed the OSSLT; 1 student was not successful.

In summary, from the original grade 6 cohort, 103 students were successful in passing the grade 10 OSSLT the first time, and 7 students were not.

(Continued)

(Continued)

Table 4.5 compares OSSLT results for Notre Dame High School, the district, and the province in 2009–2010, after the incredible work discussed above, on focused literacy strategies in all content areas, individualized for each student. (*Note:* The deferral rate for writing the OSSLT was 0 percent at Notre Dame, compared with 11 percent across the province.)

Table 4.5 Percentage of Students Passing the OSSLT at Three Levels, 2009–2010

	OSSLT Results		
	Notre Dame High School	*District*	*Province*
First-Time Eligible	93%	90%	84%
Previously Eligible	83	59	51
Special Needs—First Time	69	65	54

Remember that the subject of this case is a high school—perennially problematic when it comes to change. But Notre Dame took to it quite readily. The HOT paragraphs developed across all content areas were tied to student FACES; they were implementable; and the ideas were manageable, albeit requiring commitment, focus, and follow through by every teacher across all traditional vertical subject disciplines.

High school reform is possible on a large scale using these strategies as endorsed by the remarkable gains made across the 900 schools in Ontario that have increased their graduation rates from 68 percent to 81 percent in six years. Our colleague Ben Levin (2012) explains our core strategy in terms of four pillars:

1. Know the status and progress of every student, know the reasons for any problems, and intervene as soon as there are signs of difficulties.

2. Provide a program mix and approach that enables a good outcome for every student.

3. Improve daily teaching and learning—it is essential to achieving better high school outcomes; to do this requires a thoughtful and specific strategy.

4. Connect schools deeply to their local and broader community.

It is amazing what can be accomplished by putting FACES on the data and doing something precise about it (or precisely defining the instruction required to make the difference in student achievement).

The Culminating Event—The Learning Fair!

The Realization Network mobilized CDSBEO to pursue the goal of literacy for all students in a personalized and precise way. Between each network session, school teams shared information with their staff and put into practice the elements of the 14 parameters that were most urgent at their schools.

A learning fair was held for school teams to celebrate their success. In groups of four schools, each team explained in detail how they had achieved an increase in student achievement, built collective capacity, and established Catholic professional learning communities. Teams presented evidence of their success, gave each other suggestions, and brainstormed together on how to deal with the challenges that remained.

A portion of the day was reserved for educators to visit other school presentations to learn about the high-yield strategies that were making a difference to student achievement elsewhere. A highlight sheet for each presentation was compiled into a book that was shared system-wide. The rich dialogue that emerged during the learning fair created the excitement and energy needed to deepen the implementation of the 14 parameters. The data sources indicate that the district has begun to truly realize its commitment to achieving literacy for all FACES. This process has engaged the whole school system in an energetic and sustainable way.

Source: William Gartland, director of education, Catholic District School Board of Eastern Ontario, Canada.

Narrative from the Field

Several years ago, in June, Alistair arrived in my secondary year 5 class to do higher maths. He started by telling me that he was no good at maths and his secondary year 4 and 5 teachers had confirmed this by telling him that he would probably not stay in my class once he received his results in August. In August, he got a pass at the lowest grade for the credit, but it meant he could stay in my class. We got on well, and I noticed that he was good at seeking clarification on many points. He said he had always been told that if he didn't understand something straight off, then he probably would never "get it." The different approach in my class (of ask and discuss) made him feel more confident. Regular chats with me about his work settled him into a pattern of working hard and achieving. He passed (with a B), went on to do advanced higher math (got a C), then went on to university to do maths teaching. He keeps in touch with me and has now changed his path to a straightforward maths program to widen his options. I know my instructional approaches made a difference to Alistair. He might be a teacher yet!

—Pauline Ward, maths teacher,
St. John's Academy, Perth and Kinross Council, Scotland

So far we have shown that powerful impact is achieved by putting FACES on the data and by zeroing in on assessment and instruction made precise by putting FACES on the data. We saw this most vividly in CDSBEO. After being flatlined on most student achievement scores for four years, they leapt ahead by some 8% in one year. It happened because of widespread focused action in elementary and high schools alike. But this applied energy was *unleashed* by leadership—the subject of Chapter 5.

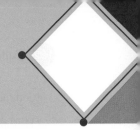

CHAPTER FIVE

Leadership— Individualizing for Improvement

In previous chapters we detailed the skills and practices that underlie our improvement drivers 1 and 2—assessment and instruction. Here we look at improvement driver 3—leadership—as identified by our research respondents, beginning with a case study from the Diocese of Broken Bay in Australia.

Leading-by-Example Case Study

St. Joseph's Catholic Primary School, in Narrabeen, is a small school on Sydney's northern beaches, one of two Catholic primary schools in the parish. By 2006, some staff and parents felt the school was in peril. The student population had fallen, from 242 in 1992 to 103 in 2006; student achievement scores were very low; most teachers were not interested in improvement; and parents seemingly had lost any interest in catholicity being taught in the school. Data compiled at the national level also showed that the school was underperforming. The school's "index of community socio-educational advantage" (ICSEA), retrieved from Australia's "My School" national database (www.myschool.edu.au), is 1125.18. The average national index is 1000, which means that St. Joseph's has a higher socioeconomic advantage than the results portrayed. The school had a relatively low number of students from non-English-speaking backgrounds

(Continued)

(Continued)

(11.8 percent) and no children identifying themselves as having Aboriginal or Torres Strait Islander background. Finally, the ICSEA methodology claimed to account for around 68 percent of primary school performance, meaning that the remaining 32 percent of variance is attributable to in-school factors. Therefore, as the school's principal, Don O'Brien said, "[T]he staff team and I surmised that low performance could be—must be—reversed."

Declining enrollment was interpreted by teachers and families alike as foreshadowing school closure, which led to a siege mentality, notably paranoia, and a status-quo performance style that led to continued downward spiraling. The school population was simply and clearly underachieving, and the results reflected very low expectations and general malaise. On all counts, St. Joseph's was underperforming and in jeopardy.

Could Student Achievement Scores Improve?

After a lengthy period of stakeholder consultation—through staff meetings, surveys, reviewing of external standard testing data, and parishioner input—Don and the staff found that the results and enrollment issues were associated directly with a lack of attention to the 14 parameters (Sharratt & Fullan, 2009). As such, the results of triangulating the data sources showed the following:

- Lack of a shared vision for the school—evidenced by a "disidentification" and disengagement with the Catholic community and a deep-seated suspicion of the educational administrative arm of the diocese, the Catholic Schools Office (parameter 1)
- Low levels of professional cohesion and professional learning (parameters 2, 7, 8, and 11)
- Low academic achievement and inconsistent academic standards (parameter 3)
- Leadership instability—six principals between 1992 and 2005 (parameter 4)
- Poor identification of and attention to children with learning needs (parameters 5 and 6)
- Disengagement of parents and the community, manifested in steadily declining enrollments (parameter 12)

At the conclusion of the review process, it was determined that the school required work in three broad domains—commitment, curriculum, and culture. Don and the staff set out their work plan as follows:

1. Clarifying of and recommitting to the basic mission and identity as a Catholic school

2. Reconceptualizing the school's curriculum to be evidence based to meet the needs of all learners and emphasizing high student achievement expectations

3. Establishing the philosophical and pragmatic nexus between positive pastoral outcomes and improved student learning

Focused Actions for Improvement

The strategic plan developed was succinct with a powerful collaborative mantra—"all of us, all the time—no exceptions!" The process, while urgent, was not rushed. Don and the staff recognized that, according to the literature, the change process takes two or more years before any real change is evident. But they also saw that, with focus, the timeline for initial success could become more compressed. They did not have the luxury of waiting—student improvement could not wait! Insistence on change and progress toward change were not without challenges. According to O'Brien, "We lost several longstanding staff members and several families, but as painful as this was, those who remained were clear, committed, and articulate about the change process."

It began with shared beliefs and understandings (parameter 1) and strategies that staff and the community could all support. Don and his staff team expected participation in the school improvement process from all stakeholders, honoring the Catholic belief that people or groups affected ought to have key decision-making roles.

More specifically, as a school team they agreed to do the following:

- Focus on literacy, given its central and ubiquitous place in the primary school curriculum in Australia (parameters 3 and 13). In addition to reading current literature, O'Brien and his staff visited several colleague schools that had strong literacy results or had been identified at the system level as having effective instruction in place. Ultimately this experience proved to be an effective introduction to differentiation of learning for all learners and a practical example of embedded professional learning premised on authentic teacher inquiry (parameter 11).

(Continued)

(Continued)

- Collect, interpret, and use data to guide instruction and to see how the whole school performed. Regularly scheduled and budgeted "learning team meetings" involving classroom teachers, school leadership, and the learning support teacher were established to review student learning and set targets for all children (parameters 4 and 8).
- Engage with research that addresses the needs of children with learning difficulties (parameter 5). (*Note:* Approximately 18 percent of the school population required special learning support.)
- Adopt a case management approach (see Chapter 4) to adjust the instruction for children at risk (parameter 6). (*Note:* These case management meetings proved to be effective not only in reviewing the data but also in talking with colleagues about pedagogical issues and solutions [parameter 7].)
- Give teachers time to co-plan with their grade-level partner, school leadership team, and the school's teacher-librarian (or instructional coach) regarding the newly developed integrated curriculum (parameters 2, 8, and 13).
- Re-imagine professional learning to focus on sustained teacher inquiry; the collaborative inquiry question that staff wanted answered was, What practices make a difference in classrooms in order to increase student learning outcomes? (parameter 11).
- Develop clear statements of how the literacy and numeracy blocks were to be structured (parameter 3).
- Procure the resources necessary to deliver on the focus (parameter 9).
- Implement a system of student behavior management called positive behavior for learning (PBL). (*Note:* Over three years of PBL, the school showed a sharp decline in behavior referrals, paralleling a sharp improvement in student learning.)

What Were the Results?

The plan made a difference to student population size and student achievement. After falling from 242 students in 1992 to 103 students in 2006, the student population has now risen to 161 children. In the new federal scheme, assessment and literacy are assessed and tracked through the National Assessment Plan for Literacy and Numeracy (NAPLAN; Australian Curriculum, Assessment and Reporting Authority, 2008, 2009, 2010). Figure 5.1 shows that in every assessed domain, St. Joseph's improved in 2010 over 2008.

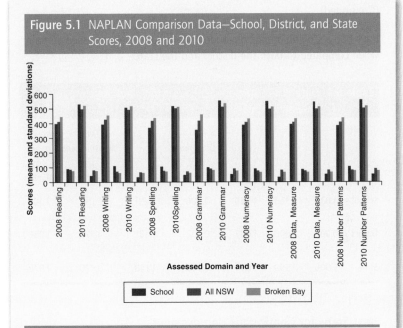

Figure 5.1 NAPLAN Comparison Data—School, District, and State Scores, 2008 and 2010

In 2010, St. Joseph's exceeded the district (Broken Bay) score in every domain except writing, and the school exceeded the state (New South Wales—NSW) score in every domain. Figure 5.1 also shows that the district's purposeful plan was effective in raising overall district scores in NAPLAN such that the district outperformed the state on every domain assessed in 2010. This district improvement makes the St. Joseph's leap over the district scores even more astonishing. Figure 5.1 also demonstrates raising the bar of performance and narrowing the achievement gap between high performers and lower performers, given that the standard deviation at St. Joseph's has been reduced from 2008 to 2010 scores. (*Note:* In the figure, the standard deviations for the domains are represented by the smaller sets of bars.)

The most impressive part of this story is the analysis of effect size. Essentially, many of the increased scores at the school can be explained by measures made within the community, but at least 32 percent of the improvement can be attributed directly to the school's intentional plan and focused efforts. Table 5.1 uses the data in Figure 5.1 to show that, in terms of effect size, the St. Joseph's school improvement initiatives

(Continued)

(Continued)

have had a striking impact on student learning in every assessed domain, when compared to both the district and the state.

	Reading	Writing	Spelling	Grammar and Punctuation	Numeracy	Data, Measurement, and Geometry	Number Patterns and Algebra
School	1.839	1.353	1.788	2.406	2.291	2.091	2.107
District	0.960	1.006	1.087	0.992	1.181	1.178	1.056
State	1.006	0.959	1.095	1.045	1.148	1.120	1.078

Table 5.1 Data Effect Sizes for School, District, and State on Assessed Domains

Next Steps for Continuous Improvement

Sustaining the gains is the next challenge for O'Brien. The driving strategies are subject to continuous evaluation and reflection. Are students and staff doing as well as they can be doing? In that regard, the habit of teacher collaborative inquiry (parameter 11) is well established. In 2011, O'Brien revised the mode of learning team meetings to give greater attention to the students in the middle of the cohort range (parameter 8).

Consistency of teacher assessment practices remains an ongoing challenge. Teachers are now planning to mark student work collaboratively (see Chapter 4) and assess it against agreed-upon criteria to develop consistent standards across classes. School assessment tools and success criteria will remain central to this work. Continuing ongoing engagement and involvement with parents and the community are necessary to ensure that the hard-won shared understandings of the school's mission remain current and well understood with each generation of newly enrolled families (parameter 12).

More Than Numbers Tell the Success Story at St. Joseph's

The numbers speak for themselves and are, of course, critical, but it is the human FACE of the improvement agenda that offers the most compelling evidence—the emotional connections made. Don and his staff write that a strong endorsement of their school improvement agenda on all three fronts (commitment, curriculum, and culture) has come recently from two parents on behalf of one of the school's students:

> At a recent parent and faculty meeting, a parent of one of our children living with disability spoke eloquently as to the great sense of gratitude she felt towards the school community for the care her daughter had received. She said her daughter had previously never believed she would learn to read, have friends or be able do anything independently. After being at our school for the past five years, her daughter was reading, had friends, was self-confident and had the opportunity to represent our diocese at a state-wide sporting carnival.
>
> Clearly moved, and unprompted, another parent responded by saying that she felt both her children had been enriched by being at a school that so actively sought to meet the needs of all children, including children living with disability. She said, "My children are better, stronger human beings for having known your daughter. Isn't this what we're on about as a Catholic school?"

Sources: Tony Bracken, superintendent of school effectiveness improvement, and Don O'Brien, principal, St. Joseph's Catholic Primary School, Narrabeen, Diocese of Broken Bay, Sydney, Australia.

Know-ability, Mobilize-ability, Sustain-ability

The St. Joseph's story of school improvement almost parallels our research findings. Recall that in our survey we asked educators, "What are the top three leadership skills needed to put FACES on the data?" In response, 45 percent said that, to lead with credibility, leaders must first model knowledge of classroom practice—assessment and instruction—what we call *know-ability*. Further, 33 percent said that the ability to inspire and mobilize others through clear communication of commitment was essential—what we call *mobilize-ability*. Finally, 21 percent said that knowing how to establish a lasting culture of shared responsibility and accountability was crucial—what we call *sustain-ability*. These are three factors that represent a specific focus by leaders to get results—exactly what Don O'Brien modeled for us in the case study that opened this chapter. We expand on each of these three areas to clarify what great leaders do—to put FACES on the data.

1. Know-ability

Principals need to have a strong and compelling message, but they also must know their stuff. Don O'Brien's first step was to analyze student achievement data to gain knowledge of students, not only to make well-informed decisions but also to have a compelling message that made teachers and parents want to buy in to the hard work ahead. A nearly universal finding in school improvement efforts has been "the need for strong, academically-focused principal leadership" (Calman, 2009, p. 17). Principals must be knowledgeable about high-yield classroom practices if they are to "champion the importance of assessment for [and as] learning [and instruction, discussed in Chapters 3 and 4] by ensuring a consistent and continuous school-wide focus on student learning; and by using classroom, school, and system data to monitor progress" (Ontario Ministry of Education, 2010a). However, recent research literature has not articulated clearly what academically focused instructional leaders must do, nor are there any strong examples in the literature of just how principals use data to monitor progress so that they can lead in a school where putting FACES on the data is a daily occurrence. Know-ability begins with prowess in teaching, learning, and leading. Andreas Schleicher (2011) further defines its impact by saying that the quality of an education system cannot exceed the quality of its teachers and principals.

Our intent is to uncover the "how" of being a knowledgeable leader and describe it clearly, using examples, as we delve into the complexities of the leadership skills needed to put the FACES on the data.

Know-ability: Knowledgeable Other

According to the respondents in our research, the key is principals' deep structured understanding of evidence-based assessment and instructional practices in classrooms. The principal must be the lead learner, modeling continuous learning, committing to being a co-leader and co-learner with teachers, and participating in tangible assessment and instructional practices as "knowledgeable other" (Sharratt, Ostinelli, & Cattaneo, 2010). As knowledgeable others, school leaders know what it looks like to use data to improve instruction in each class across the school. They are mindful to stay the course by maintaining, reviewing, and monitoring lesson plans and school improvement plans to ensure alignment between the vision in the plan on paper and classroom practices recorded in lesson plans.

Data-driven instruction and the ubiquitous presence and use of data are core themes for promoting and maintaining effort to improve. Principals lead the case management approach, in which (1) individual students are tracked and corrective action takes place on an ongoing basis (see Chapter 3) and (2) teachers have a forum to discuss students who present them with instructional conundrums (see Chapter 4).

Principals know how to improve the performance of teachers who are struggling and how to reward their best teachers. They provide environments in which teachers work together to frame good practice. That is where teachers and principals conduct field-based research (collaborative inquiry/action research; see Chapter 4) to confirm or disprove the approaches they develop and implement on behalf of students. This demands that high-quality school systems, in general, and school leaders, specifically, pay attention to how they select and train their staff (Schleicher, 2011).

Know-ability: High Expectations

"Challenging satisfactory teachers (and leaders) to be good and the good to be outstanding is a significant factor in creating high-performing schools" (Davies & Davies, 2011, p. 178). Leaders who are outstanding continually ask themselves these questions: Are our expectations high enough? Are all students excelling—not just getting by—or going unnoticed? Am I leading by example? Then they clearly articulate the expected use of data to drive instruction (see Chapters 3 and 4), provide differentiated professional learning opportunities for teachers to see and experience it in action, and monitor the implementation of data use and differentiated instruction by being in classrooms conducting learning walks and talks (L. Sharratt, 2011) and following up with teacher conferences.

Teddlie, Reynolds, and Sammons (2000) identified the following five high expectations of staff that principals need to address:

- Expecting new teachers to have a good understanding of the school before they arrive
- Expecting a high level of teacher participation in professional development activities
- Expecting detailed monitoring by staff of student activities, including homework
- Expecting staff to make the academic achievement of their students their first priority
- Expecting staff to manage their time effectively to ensure maximum student time on task

To this list we add, expecting staff to use data to inform instruction for every student every day.

Know-ability: Data Use

In a study conducted by Louis et al. (2010), principals and teachers reported increasing efforts to develop the capacity of teachers to engage collectively in data analysis for instructional decision making, often associated with professional learning communities initiated and assisted by district training. They found that principals played a key leadership role in establishing the purposes and expectations for data use, in providing structured opportunities (collegial groups and time) for data-use training and assistance, and in providing access to expertise and follow-up actions. However, they said that they saw no evidence that teachers do this on their own . . . and if the district wasn't using the data to make educational decisions for educational improvement actions, it was unlikely to be happening at the school level.

Therefore, alignment of know-ability, is an issue. If districts expect that teachers are using data for instruction, then they had better be modeling how and monitoring the implementation of data use. As well, if principals expect teachers to be using data for instruction, then they must provide the primary leadership. What does this mean in real time in a big or small but always busy school? In response to this notion, the Ontario Ministry of Education (2010a) documents that principals must champion the importance of assessment for and as learning (see Chapter 3) by ensuring a consistent and continuous school-wide focus on student learning and by using classroom, school, and system data to monitor progress.

We describe here an exemplary model of how to use data for school and student improvement, implemented by Jill Maar, principal of Armadale Public School (see Sharratt & Fullan, 2009, pp. 85–88), and many of her principal colleagues. Working with her vice principal, Cal Darby, Jill works diligently to improve all students' performance—one teacher and one student at a time. In short, Jill and her team know how to put the FACES on the data and make every student matter! Let's take a walk and talk with her.

Know-ability: Data Drives Instruction

At Armadale, learners' progress is monitored with rigor at four- to six-week intervals, when teachers bring their data, using a Venn diagram format (Figure 5.2), for frank discussions of where and how students are progressing in each class—rating them "below," "at," or "above" standard, using *running records* (see Glossary) in grades K–3 classrooms, and *higher-order thinking (HOT) skills* (see Glossary), for example, in junior and intermediate classrooms. Figure 5.2 shows where each student is in a mixed grade 1 and 2 class. The focus of each teacher conference with Jill is to determine strengths, needs, and next steps for each and every individual learner. These courageous conversations put the spotlight on what teachers are doing (or not doing) for individual students in every class—kindergarten to grade 8. Teachers articulate why they are doing what they do and how it is going (parameter 1). Red flags indicate where different intervention strategies are needed for struggling students, and discussions follow about what teachers will be teaching in the next four to six weeks and where the flagged students will be when the next check-in with Jill is planned. In that way, she has a pulse on the achievement of every FACE in her school. Figure 5.2 shows a powerful, simple visual that has made a difference to putting FACES on data so that students who need to be noticed and require interventions are indeed noticed and interventions are indeed applied.

Figure 5.3 illustrates a developmental learner profile that Jill and her leadership team developed to put FACES on every student. It shows a kindergarten profile—note the specificity of the data collected. Teachers develop a learner profile for every student in every class at Armadale and these profiles are examined regularly with Jill and Cal. These two powerful examples of data use by administrators and teachers reflect Shulman's belief (2010, p. 2) that data represent "[t]he most common, profound and pervasive catalyst for improvement" that schools have identified. In Shulman's study, "[S]chool

Figure 5.2 Venn Diagram Showing Movement of Students in a Class against Expectations

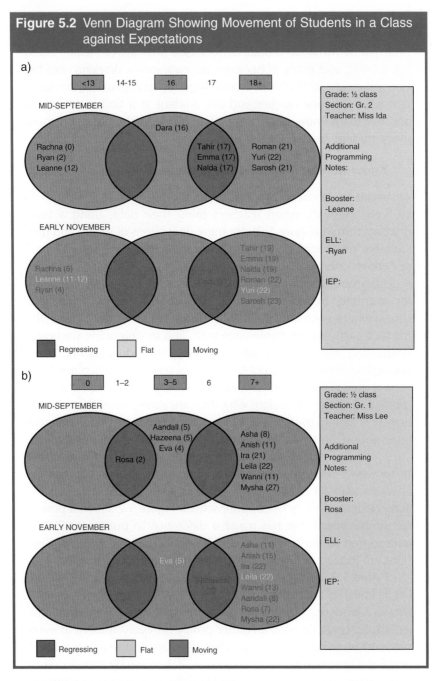

Developed by Armadale PS Literacy Leadership Team.

Figure 5.3a Developmental Learner Profile for a Pre-Primary/Kindergarten Class

Two-Year Developmental Learner Profile—Kindergarten

Junior Kindergarten (JK): 4-year-olds / Senior Kindergarten (SK): 5-year-olds   M F

Phonological Awareness

	Oct	Mar	Oct	Mar	Oct	Mar
1. Sentences to words						
2. Words to syllables						
3a. Hearing rhymes						
3b. Producing rhymes						
4. Sounds to words						
5. Words to sounds						

I = Independent   S = With support   N = Not yet

Letter ID and Sounds

○ Can identify letter name   ▦ Can identify letter name and sound

	A	K	I	T	D	O	W	C	L	M	V	F	S	Y	E	G	P	X	J	Q	H	B	R	Z	N	U
JK																										
SK																										

	c	k	l	t	d	o	w	c	l	m	v	f	s	y	e	g	p	x	j	q	h	b	r	z	n	u
JK																										
SK																										

(Continued)

(Continued)

Concepts of Written Materials When Reading (R) and Writing (W) (Check when concept is demonstrated)

Front cover	Title	Text starting point for reading	Text is written from left to right	Return sweep (text is written from top to bottom)	Voice/print match (1 to 1)	Leaves spaces between words	Identifies beginning and end of a sentence	Reads left page before right	Punctuation ? " " . , !	Identifies a letter	Identifies a word	Capital letter	Lower-case letter
JK R													
JK W													
SK R													
SK W													

Reading Text Level (Record date: M/D/Y)

0	1	2	3	4	5	6	7	8	9	10	11	12	13	14	15	16	17	18	19	20	21

Developed by Armadale PS Literacy Leadership Team

Figure 5.3b Developmental Learner Profile for a Pre-Primary/Kindergarten Class

Two-Year Developmental Learner Profile—Kindergarten

Junior Kindergarten (JK): 4-year-olds / Senior Kindergarten (SK): 5-year-olds   M F

Student Name: _____   Date of Birth: _____   Home Language: _____

Oral Language

Understanding	Oct	Feb	Oct	Feb	Using	Oct	Feb	Oct	Feb
Words					Words				
Sentences					Sentences				
Story/ Paragraph					Story/ Paragraph				

I = Independent   S = With support   N = Not yet

Date: JK Talk Sample 1 (Assessment SET 1) Context:	Date: JK Talk Sample 2 Context:	Date: JK Talk Sample 3 (Assessment SET 2) Context:	Date: JK Talk Sample 4 Context:
Date: SK Talk Sample 1 (Assessment SET 1) Context:	Date: SK Talk Sample 2 Context:	Date: SK Talk Sample 3 (Assessment SET 2) Context:	Date: SK Talk Sample 4 Context:

Developed by Armadale PS Literacy Leadership Team

teams systematically identified strengths and challenges at the individual-student, grade and overall school levels. The information obtained was used to set goals and identify target areas for improvement; it often laid the foundation for the school [improvement] plan," as is the case at Armadale.

All decisions about the focus of instructional programs and practices, training needs, resource requirements, identity of support for student needs, and the placement of support staff are grounded in the outcomes of the data analyses. Our research suggests that principals must be committed to looking for living data by "walking" in classrooms both to observe and note successful practice, and to confer with teachers regularly.

Know-ability: "Walking and Talking"

In between data conferences with teachers, Jill and Cal walk with intentionality, daily, in the school to see how the students are doing. They always check in on the six kindergarten classes with an intentional focus for the walks. In Figure 4.2, the focus of the walk was looking for evidence of shared/interactive writing; they also make a point of walking with a purpose to one wing of this very large school each day.

Reeves (2010, p. 59) says that it is "essential that school leaders distinguish evaluation—a process bounded by the constraints of legal precedent and collective bargaining—from assessment"—a process to promote growth through learning. For us, this relates to the monitoring job that principals can do either by clipboard evaluations or by learning walks and data talks, wherein they walk in classrooms to observe and learn daily and have focused follow-up conversations with teachers about assessment and instruction.

Jill and Cal have chosen to monitor their school's improvement plan by walking with purpose and talking with teachers daily. Administrators, like Jill and Cal, champion the importance of ongoing assessment of practice by ensuring a consistent and continuous school-wide focus on student learning and by using classroom, school, and system data to monitor progress.

Does monitoring student progress using the Venn diagram process make a difference?

In September 2010, assessments showed that 31 of 75 kindergarten students were at risk of not reading at the expected level. With focused literacy intervention, Jill and Cal and their kindergarten teachers reduced the at-risk population to only 8 of 75 students by June 2011, with all of the 8 reading above a Level 0. This is an outstanding example of the principal and vice principal as knowledgeable others, and the leadership team's sharing that knowledgeable other role throughout the school, in both data-informed and hands-on practitioner modes.

According to our research respondents, principals' deep structural understanding of successful literacy practices in classrooms is a key. Therefore, principals must be committed to walking in classrooms daily—not to visiting or wandering around, but to walking in classrooms to observe and note successful practice and to confer with teachers. We often make assumptions about what is going on in classrooms unless, as principals and district staff, we make a conscientious effort to walk in classrooms. Learning walks and talks (L. Sharratt, 2011) is a way of monitoring expected practices in all classrooms.

The classroom walks and talks not only give principals the opportunity to see what is being taught but also provide them with the opportunity to address the issues that come up by offering ongoing professional learning at staff meetings and by pairing up teachers with other teachers who are delivering the expected practices. Focused daily walks in all classrooms make monitoring enjoyable and are a habit worth acquiring.

Senge (1990) reminds us so eloquently:

> **Deliberate Pause**
>
> - How is the impact on student learning monitored?
> - Who monitors student learning?
> - Are learning goals aligned to standards or curriculum expectations?
> - How are success criteria aligned to learning goals, and how are they differentiated for students?
> - Is feedback to students and teachers factual, objective, immediate, and helpfully aligned with learning goals?
> - What examples do you have of putting FACES on the data at the district, school, and classroom levels? What professional learning is in place to learn from it?

"[L]eader as teacher" is not about "teaching" people how to achieve their visions. It is about fostering learning for everyone.

Such leaders help people throughout the organization to develop systemic understandings. Accepting this responsibility is the antidote to one of the most common downfalls of otherwise gifted leaders—losing their commitment to tell the truth. (p. 356)

Principals model leadership and learnership by being committed to the truth and by taking responsibility, accountability, and ownership for student learning. In that way, they "mobilize" teachers to action.

2. Mobilize-ability

Don O'Brien mobilized and galvanized his staff and community to focus on all students. He did this skillfully by getting teachers to collectively scrutinize the data, develop a plan of action, and seek input from the parents in the community before moving forward together. As the U.K. Office for Standards in Education, Children's Services and Skills (Ofsted) report aptly concludes, "[A]ll staff members need to be 'aboard the bus' when the school embarks on its journey of improvement" (cited in Calman, 2010, p. 25).

Mobilize-ability: Magic Happens!

As one of our principal interviewees expressed, "Support and encouragement are crucial. Pushing too hard never works. Magic happens when teachers take initiative within a framework which has been developed by the district, like the 14 parameters. Incorporating professional learning into staff and division meetings needs to be led by staff not just the principal. When teachers share their best practices, things happen."

Providing both time and resources for mentoring, coaching, and co-teaching (see Chapter 4) ensures that literacy becomes and remains a focus. Walking the fine line between push and pull is always an exciting challenge and worth the time it takes to build strong leaders in a school (Fullan & Sharratt, 2007). Such leaders put FACES not only on student data but also on teacher performance data. They mobilize teachers in a positive, unthreatening manner by knowing their personal and professional goals, aspirations, and motivations.

As with students, leaders build teachers' capacity to accurately self-assess their teaching abilities and to seek collaborative learning opportunities when needed to ultimately benefit both teachers and students. When teachers become leaders, in *distributed leadership* roles (see Glossary), everyone benefits from the capacities of more of its members. Distributed leadership develops a fuller appreciation of interdependence and how one's behavior affects the organization as a whole (Leithwood, Mascall, & Strauss, 2009; Louis et al., 2010).

Mobilize-ability: De-privatizing Practice

Leaders de-privatize practice, making teaching and learning transparent to all and debatable by all. How does that happen? EQAO research (Rogers, 2009) reported that "a school culture that focuses on learning for *all* students was repeatedly described as an important factor in enabling each student to experience some measure of success. . . . [Principals mobilize stakeholders by openly]

- holding and sustaining high academic, social and behavioral expectations;
- using a variety of teaching methods to meet, in real ways, the needs of different students;
- creating a consistently positive and caring school community;
- encouraging positive role models to whom students can relate;
- ensuring strong and effective educational leadership from the principal and
- maintaining ongoing active engagement of parents in the school." (p. 4)

The mobilization of these factors and de-privatizing practice happens naturally when school district and school leaders organize an annual learning fair—a culminating celebration and "live" report of evidence related to student achievement. This is not an exercise in bureaucratic accountability reporting. Put one way, we did not *start* with accountability but rather *ended* with it. Put still another way, after all schools were steeped in capacity-building, we sought a natural reinforcer that integrated "accountability and responsibility" and fed more positive energy into the cycle at the school level (Sharratt & Fullan, 2009, pp. 90–92).

Interdependent leadership practice and the 14th parameter are evident in the annual learning fairs held now in many of the jurisdictions with which we work (see the case studies in Chapters 2–4). For these events, all elementary and secondary schools prepare a half-hour multimedia presentation based on the following:

1. What the school set out to do that year

2. Evidence to support their students' increased literacy achievement

3. What assessment and instructional strategies they used

4. Lessons learned

5. Challenges they are currently facing

What is most impressive about these learning fairs is how articulate, consistent, and specific educators have become when they discuss the what, the why, the how, and the assessed impact of their work. Every school in the district participates in teams. There are, in other words, many change agents spread across all schools, all engaged in the same phenomenon—all using precise language, all pushing practice to the next level.

Every school administrator and teacher team prepares an evidenced-based report (focused on student data) and then submits it to their district leaders. The reports show their improved school results and their intentional next steps for the following year that are to be incorporated in their updated school improvement plans. Low-performing leaders are supported, "pulled along," and energized in this process by strong leaders who reach out—as the 14th parameter is about shared accountability and responsibility for all our students. The annual reporting serves as a collaborative dialogue across schools and deepens participants' understanding of their own individual and the collective learning that leads to the generation of additional next steps to be taken in their schools. As well as generating new teaching strategies, it also broadens the interdependency from intraschool to interschool with one critical result being a reduction in the overall performance gap between schools—definitely an energizing way to de-privatize practice across schools in a district.

Mobilize-ability: Having an Urgent Craving

As Bill Gates (1995) says, "to be highly productive, we should introduce a sense of urgency into our lives." To us, it is urgent to get serious about putting FACES on the data and executing what we call the three tiers of instruction (see Chapter 4) in support of all students. In our view, strategic leaders throughout the system—from elected officials to superintendents, principals, and teacher-leaders—energize and mobilize by doing the following:

- "Walking the talk" that models our shared beliefs and understandings, even when things are chaotic and budgets are pressed
- Remaining focused and staying the course on supporting evidence-proven classroom practices
- Having a laser-like focus on targeted high achievement levels

In our work these are recurring themes; however, here they are even more precise. Shared beliefs and understandings are more of an outcome of a quality process than a precondition. Put differently, one condition for mobilize-ability involves working on defining, shaping, and refining the school's sense of shared moral purpose, using relevant data sources in relation to student improvement.

The more that beliefs are shared, the greater the ongoing effort, and the efficiency of the effort. As one principal reported, "[W]hen we reflect on the impact of our instructional decisions and what the data tell us about students' increased learning, it creates 'intellectual energy'" (Fullan & Sharratt, 2007). It becomes a craving to impact the learning of every student.

3. Sustain-ability

Achieving and sustaining substantial improvement for all students all the time is complex. Sustainability at Don O'Brien's school will be experienced when students continue to achieve; decisions continue to reflect caring about students and teachers; and parents continue to feel part of the fabric of school life—no matter who is the principal. O'Brien has a good start toward what Louis et al. (2010) say that instructional leadership is: both climate and actions. The former relates to the steps that principals take to establish a culture that supports ongoing professional learning of research-based instructional strategies; the latter refers to the explicit steps that principals take to engage with individual teachers about their own growth. According to this measure, Don has done well in a relatively short time.

Some time ago we worried about the conditions in which school leaders can sustain reform efforts individually and collectively (Fullan & Sharratt, 2007), as state- and district-wide reform relies heavily on mobilizing leadership at all levels of the system. Hargreaves and Fink (2006) define sustainability in this way:

> Sustainability does not simply mean whether something will last. It addresses how particular initiatives can be developed without compromising the development of others in the environment now or in the future. (p. 30)

Sustain-ability: We-we

We believe that intentional leadership models must unfold in a way that all schools benefit. The spirit underlying such approaches attempts to create a "we-we" mindset at every level. As a result of purposeful interaction within and across schools, school leaders become more aware of, and indeed more committed to, the success of other schools in addition to their own.

Although individual leaders, like Don O'Brien, can and must work on sustaining their own energies, the conditions for sustaining large numbers of people can be fostered only if the organization as a whole is working in this direction (Fullan & Sharratt, 2007). Moreover, we maintain that focusing on sustainability must become more deliberate and precise. Synergy is created when sustainability is worked on in a self-conscious and organizationally conscious manner.

Sustain-ability: Energy Creates Synergy

Sustainability conditions are those that motivate people to continue to invest their energies in working with others to accomplish greater student improvement. In 2007, we asked almost 100 elementary and secondary principals, "How do you as leader sustain your schools' literacy initiative?" We found that most responses reflected the themes in our 14 parameters research at the time and could be categorized into five major areas:

1. Shared beliefs, goals, and vision

2. Distributed leadership and professional learning cultures

3. Data-based decisions/impact measures/celebrating success

4. Resources

5. School-community/home relations

These findings parallel O'Brien's story at St. Joseph's and our current research here in identifying the top three leadership skills necessary to put FACES on the data—know-ability, mobilize-ability, and sustain-ability.

Successful sustainability is often related in the literature to what we have come to call the presence of dedicated "second change agents" or what is sometimes referred to as distributive leadership— a critical mass of leaders led by the principal working on establishing a culture of ongoing learning. The principal is the first change agent—the lead learner. Having one or more "second change agents" is crucial—for example, a teacher-leader or embedded instructional coach (parameter 2) with direct responsibility and time during the school day to work alongside other teachers in their classrooms, to link teachers with each other internally and across schools, to help set up data management systems, and to work with the principal on school improvement agenda. One principal summed this up by saying, "Sustaining the momentum within the school is possible because of the many levels of support available to our school. The staffing made available for literacy coaches has been critical. This has given our school a teacher-leader who is working to increase the knowledge of all those around her" (Fullan & Sharratt, 2007).

Sustain-ability: Waste Not

Human and materials resources management is part and parcel of continued success, provided that the resources selected are part of a focused cycle of success. Kick-start your improvement processes with new resources, and then have your success "chase the money"—this year's success is next year's additional resources. For example, Armadale Public School has just received a grant from Indigo Books for $176,000 to purchase resources for their library— the largest grant ever to be awarded to a school in Canada! This grant followed on tremendous initial success and honors the amazing work the entire staff has done. Bravo to Jill and her incredible team!

Publicly elected officials and district and school administrators must agree to allocate funding for "just-right" resources aligned to the priority and continue to fund them through tough economic times. Consideration for human and materials resources must focus on equity of outcomes for all students and learning for all teachers. However, wastes of time and material resources are also equity issues that cause leadership frustration at every level.

James Bond, the principal of Park Manor Senior Public School in Waterloo, Canada, had his first career at Toyota. He learned about quality assurance from this beginning. One of the things he thinks about now as a principal is "lean learning"—that is, determining "what is value-added" and "what is waste"—in improving all students' performance. James writes, "Before determining what is value-added and what is waste, a school administrator or classroom teacher needs to have a vision of what their success criteria look like"—in other words, at departure, know where you're going and what it will look like on arrival.

Once leadership teams have a vision for each graduating student, anything that helps the student achieve that vision is value-added. On the other hand, any action that does not help the student move closer to that expectation is considered waste. For example, time can be a waste when it's lost due to inefficient transitions from class to class; undifferentiated instruction can be a waste if it causes many students to be retaught what they already know. Another type of waste is lack of knowledge- or skills-sharing, when students or staff don't work collaboratively and share ideas.

When these wastes plus the many other forms of waste are reduced, students are able to add more value to their learning as they work toward the desired success criteria. James encourages his staff to look at any school or system initiative in the same manner, which helps his school to be more precise and aligned toward the expected outcomes. What is the principal's role in determining "waste" in reaching the goal of every student excelling?

Sustain-ability: Developing Other Leaders

It is well-known that one dimension of the leader's job is to focus on developing other leaders. However, as Reeves (2010) points out, "[S]ustained capacity-building for high-impact learning depends upon the development of teacher-leadership as well—those teachers who provide feedback to help their colleagues [see Chapter 4] and who receive feedback on the impact of their coaching" (p. 71). Teacher leadership must be a co-leadership endeavor with principals—establishing trusting relationships and equal partnerships as the work progresses (M. Sharratt, 2004). According to Davies and Davies (2011), "[I]t should be a mindset of 'doing with' and not 'doing to' that enables us to build engagement with others" (p. 174) to co-lead in the work of explicitly putting FACES on the data—what great leaders do!

Careful attention must be given to ensuring that aspiring principals have the opportunity to learn the necessary skills. System leadership is challenged in today's context to find, train, and keep young leaders who are motivated to continue the work of reform, given its very public pressures and its considerable personal and professional demands. We note that leaders selected for the role of school principal should be able to create the conditions under which other leaders will flourish. There is no more neglected topic in research policy or practice. Supports and opportunities must be available for leaders that show the way to greater understanding of how they can bring these conditions about in their schools. We know that if these processes are not effective, schools pay a considerable price. Ineffective leadership can sabotage school reform processes in many different ways.

In short, it is not so much that leaders need to believe that know-ability, mobilize-ability, and sustain-ability are possible, but rather that the only way to move forward is to be "in the game"—to be skilled (knowledgeable), engaged and engaging (mobilizing), and committed to (sustaining) the FACES of improvement.

The benefits of principals' understanding the impact of know-ability, mobilize-ability, and sustain-ability on their all-inclusive approach to leadership is critical to their success in putting FACES on the data and making every student count. In Chapter 6, we look to how these three dimensions extend to taking ownership (driver 4), for putting FACES on the data at the district, state, and national levels.

We began with Don O'Brien, principal of a school in Australia, and we close with a case study of Cal Baker, chief superintendent of the Vail Unified School District in Arizona. Both leaders remarkably and capably reflect our top leadership characteristics in putting FACES on the data—although each has a very different leadership position.

Case Study from Vail Unified School District, Vail, Arizona

When teacher Jeremy Gypton was reviewing the Civil War material for his American History class at Empire High School in Vail, Arizona, he found something on the internet that he'd never read before, even though he has a degree in history—the complete Constitution of the Confederate States of America—what a find for teaching his next history class! There's nothing unusual about a teacher finding resources for a class, right? Wrong. Jeremy Gypton teaches at a school with no textbooks—every teacher and every student has a laptop. For Jeremy, the search—while normal—and the finding—while exciting—was another important instance of "teacher as leader" or "guide-on-the-side" finding new, stimulating material for his classes. It definitely won't be "same old, same old" in Gypton's class.

The powerful use of technology supports a strong, focused approach to teaching and learning in Arizona's Vail Unified School District (VUSD). Calvin Baker, superintendent for the past 24 years, leads VUSD, a district with a mixed population of 11,000 students from lower- and middle-income families where Jeremy teaches in one of the high schools. Baker embodies the three key leadership dimensions—know-ability, mobilize-ability, and sustain-ability—as the research respondents defined them. His program, too, is a textbook response to many of the 14 parameters, as you can see and judge for yourself in the commentary below from VUSD. When we talked to Calvin Baker, Baker attributed the school district's unprecedented successes to a whole series of factors, not just one indicator. Our discussion covered key improvement topics such as

1. A consistent direction—articulated often, clearly understood, and embraced by all—has (a) a strong academic focus and

(b) enhanced community engagement, as evidenced by the lived motto: "where education is a community effort."

2. Staff members are exceptionally strong. Cal interviews each new teacher that principals recommend to be hired (he says principals are especially careful in interviewing as they don't want any of their recommendations to be turned down after the interview). Baker has personally interviewed all 600 teachers now employed in the district. Dr. Kris Bosworth also added that each year when the "new-to-the-district" teachers have their five-day orientation in August, Baker himself rides with them in a school bus on a tour of the district highlights so that they better understand their new school community.

3. Baker believes that his leaders at every level need to start in the VUSD classrooms, and he can now say that all have—in that way they know firsthand the priorities of the system and the uniqueness of the communities that make up the district.

4. Cal says that staff members do the "hard work" of getting along. He feels that, because VUSD is a smaller district, the staff must work through the power struggles together—and that makes them stronger and more cohesive.

5. There is ample use of data to drive instruction, and it shows, given that VUSD is the top-performing district in Arizona. As well, VUSD has just won the International Society for Technology in Education (ISTE) award for "outstanding innovation in education" with its Beyond Textbooks program in grades 9–12.

6. Professional learning is ongoing and accompanied by aggressive learning walks and talks with principals and teachers walking in others' classrooms to witness effective practices. Professional learning is evident at every staff meeting led by principals and staff with a focus on instruction. As Cal says, "There are no drive-by in-service sessions." His vision is to set targets that are reachable and relevant, and then deliver ongoing support to all classrooms.

He is proud of the award from ITSE, but Cal is really proud of the teachers in the district for their focus on instruction. They follow a framework for reading instruction called balanced literacy (see Chapter 4). The framework is implemented across grade levels and across schools and

(Continued)

(Continued)

results in consistency for students. Further, teachers are able to collaborate around common expectations and a common language. The framework provides small-group instruction at ability level with the goal of moving all students to proficiency and on to exceeding expectations. Within the small groups, instruction is focused on identified state standards and on comprehension strategies. Students also experience whole-group instruction, shared reading, and *read alouds* (see Glossary). Student progress toward mastering state standards is assessed quarterly, and additional instruction is provided to students who have not demonstrated mastery.

New teachers are trained in using the balanced literacy approach at the beginning of the school year. Although they do not have literacy coaches at each site, new teachers are assigned for one year a literacy coach, who is a practicing classroom teacher (parameter 2). This approach is instrumental in developing the teachers' skill with balanced literacy and for ensuring that the framework is implemented with fidelity.

Achievement Teacher Position

When the district began its concentrated effort to improve academic achievement approximately 10 years ago, it struggled with the reality that the principals were stretched too thin. Almost everyone insists that the principal must be the instructional leader. Indeed, principals better have a pretty solid grasp of instruction . . . given that they are the school leaders and do set expectations. However, the simple, inescapable reality is that when a parent comes in angry because of an incident in the parking lot or a disagreement with a teacher, they want to speak to the principal, period. Similarly, a single disciplinary issue or building emergency can easily demand a principal's complete attention for an entire day. Meanwhile, analysis of instruction, coaching, data team meetings, and other "instructional leadership" activities are ignored. Not only are things left undone, but every time a meeting is missed due to a conflict of duties, the message is sent that instruction really isn't the priority. Giving the principal an assistant or office manager (as many other districts have done) simply does not resolve the problem satisfactorily because the principal is still called away due to his or her title and responsibilities.

VUSD's response was to create the position of achievement teacher at every school (parameter 2). That person has no other charge than to improve instruction at that school. They analyze data, lead instructional planning meetings, organize accountability measures, coach teachers, and the like. They are not assigned any administrative duties (for example, supervising aides, disciplining students, or completing evaluations). Achievement teachers always show up for those important group and individual meetings with teachers—because that is their clear priority. In Cal's judgment, the impact of this position has been key to academic achievement gains in VUSD. The position has given schools a clear focus and sent a strong message to staff regarding the importance of instruction that is carefully planned—and of instruction that is responsive to data. In addition to literacy coaches for new teachers, there is an "achievement teacher" in every school. The position has survived major budget cuts—an indicator of the value placed upon it by trustees and leadership alike. Everyone owns the pursuit of achievement.

Cal's newest secondary school is textbook-less and rich in giving each student a laptop; however, he believes that the teachers who have the support of an achievement teacher at that school, like Jeremy Gypton, would excel with or without laptops. He believes it is the teachers' instruction that makes the difference and that technology is simply a powerful enhancement.

The education superintendent for the state of Arizona, John Huppenthal, recognized Cal Baker and the VUSD staff team in May 2011, when they received the ISTE award, by saying, "Your continuing leadership role in digital content and establishing an excellent culture of learning are extraordinary and from personal experience, your recognition is well-deserved and your willingness to take risks is to be commended."

VUSD is very pleased with its scores in the AIMS Arizona State Assessments, shown in Figure 5.4. Is there room for growth? Yes, but they are moving quickly in the right direction! We can see that VUSD outperforms both the county and the state of Arizona—and this case study tells why—Cal's and the staff's explicit attention to detail in ensuring that all teachers are selected carefully, that they understand the district's context, and that they are then supported with resources to humanize their data. Is it any wonder that the data are reflective of a strong vision that is well supported by knowing and hiring every staff member personally—Cal Baker puts teacher and student FACES on the data!

To get a deeper sense of VUSD achievement, see Tables 5.2 and 5.3, which drill into the excellent disaggregated reading results by grade and by number of students assessed, revealing the precise number of students who were "below standard." Using this type of drill-down technique has become a VUSD standard operating practice, which keeps all

(Continued)

(Continued)

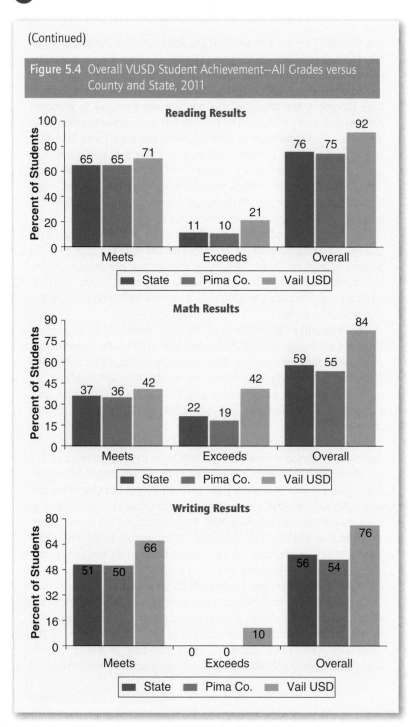

Figure 5.4 Overall VUSD Student Achievement—All Grades versus County and State, 2011

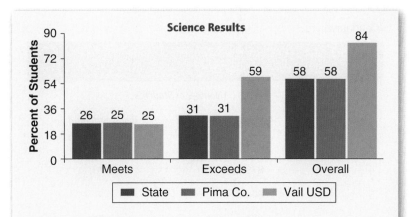

eyes on the FACES of those students who need intervention in each class and in each school so that they can "meet standard" or move from "at standard" to "exceeds standard."

Table 5.2 Student Achievement—Reading: Vail and State of Arizona				
Percentage Meeting or Exceeding Standard—Reading				
Grade	Vail 2009	Vail 2010	Vail 2011	State 2011
3	88%	89%	90%	76%
4	89	91	92	75
5	91	91	94	78
6	92	92	94	81
7	93	95	94	81
8	88	92	91	71
10	88	91	92	77

In summary, Cal Baker has led his district with that combination of emotional connection and cognitive insights that we spoke about earlier. He leads and has developed leadership team members in VUSD who

(Continued)

(Continued)

Table 5.3 Student Achievement: Number of Students below Standard—Reading, 2011

	Number of Students	
Grade	Assessed	Below Standard
3	783	78
4	879	70
5	844	51
6	850	51
7	827	50
8	773	70
10	752	60

understand and execute the elements of know-ability, mobilize-ability, and sustain-ability that our research respondents so adamantly and consistently told us were the keys to good school principal and system leadership.

Source: Calvin Baker, superintendent, Vail Unified School District, Vail, Arizona, United States of America.

Deliberate Pause

- Who is in my class? (*Note:* Everyone has "a class" to teach and learn from—state and district leaders, administrators, teachers, elected officials, and community members.)
- Whose learning is my responsibility?
- How do we ensure that the use of data considers emotional connectedness and cognitive insights?

Narrative from the Field

Pupils are setting up e-portfolios through "Glow," a personal blog which allows pupils to record success either through text or by uploading media: photographic, scanned, audio, or video. Pupils can tag their posts against the curriculum content areas for CfE (National Curriculum for Excellence). All school staff, pupils, and parents have access and can contribute or comment on the pupils' work and/or the content they have added. I think this is important as it enables pupils to make decisions over their own successes and share them with a wider community. It allows them to receive constructive feedback in a relatively private environment. It also builds as a record throughout their education from primary to secondary as pupils are able to track their ongoing learning journey.

—Wendy McNaught, head teacher,
Auchenlodment Primary, Renfrewshire Council, Scotland

As we have said in our "Motion Leadership" work, leadership is about causing positive movement in individuals, schools, and systems (Fullan, 2010a). Put more dramatically, leadership stimulates large numbers of people to put in the energy to get better results when at the outset they are not motivated to do so. This is the magic of FACES.

We close this chapter with a reflection from Sir John Jones (personal communication, November 2011) on the power of leaders to know and understand the relevant data so that all FACES may be put sensitively and skillfully on the data:

Data is a clever seductress and those who are fixated by it often hide behind phrases like "What gets measured gets done." That may or may not be true. What is certain is that a leader who merely cognitively connects with numbers on a page or dots on a graph can never fully grasp the truth behind that detail. At best, the data tell half a story and, at worst, become a dangerous weapon in the leader's hands. It is only through emotional connectedness with the dots and the digits that the whole tale can be told and the data understood. Behind every dot and digit is a story of triumph over adversity, heroic failure or missed opportunity.

CHAPTER SIX

Ownership—Of
All the FACES

Our culminating task is to represent all of our research and the many hundreds of participants in our work across the globe in a single, reflective question: who "owns" the FACES? We begin with a case study that scrutinizes that question from a whole state's point of view.

An Entire State as a Case Study

The Australian Capital Territory (ACT) is one of eight states in the Commonwealth of Australia. Although each state has constitutional responsibility for primary and secondary education delivered through public and private schools, the Australian government is increasingly driving national educational policy by providing significant resources to public and private schools and systems in an effort to improve and make the overall base of national education achievement consistent across Australia.

The Education and Training Directorate has primary responsibility for the ACT public school system, educating over 39,000 students in 84 schools. The directorate operates primary schools (preschool to year 6), high schools (years 7–10), colleges (years 11 and 12); early childhood schools (birth to year 2); and specialist schools for students with severe intellectual disability.

The general population of ACT is relatively highly educated, and the student population is somewhat diverse, with 11 percent of students identified as requiring additional support in English as a Second

Language (ESL), and 3.3 percent of students of Aboriginal and Torres Strait Islander descent. On the national "index of socio-educational advantage" (ICSEA), the majority of ACT public schools draw from relatively advantaged communities; however, every public school has a proportion of students from disadvantaged backgrounds. An increasing number of schools, particularly those in outer suburbs, serve communities with comparatively high levels of social disadvantage.

Recognizing the Gaps—Nationally, Internationally, and Locally

In the annual National Assessment of Performance in Literacy and Numeracy (NAPLAN; Australian Curriculum, Assessment and Reporting Authority, 2008, 2009, 2010), ACT is consistently ranked as one of the top two performing educational jurisdictions in Australia. In the 2009 Program for International Student Assessment (PISA), 15 year olds from ACT schools outperformed other Australian states in measures of reading literacy, mathematical literacy, and scientific literacy. Closer analysis of the national, international, and system data, however, revealed the following:

- ACT performance was not improving relative to other states.
- International-level performance was slipping, especially for ACT's top-tier students.
- Student outcomes varied significantly across and within schools (inconsistency across ACT).
- Many schools were underperforming compared to similar schools, and within schools some students were failing to progress at expected rates.
- Aboriginal and Torres Strait Islander students were overrepresented in the lower-achieving cohorts, as were students from non-English-speaking backgrounds.
- For many schools, the January 2010 comparative data from the "My School" website were surprising, suggesting that their performance was not as strong as they had believed.

Data Analysis Drives School and System Improvement

A joint focus in late 2009 on the analysis of school- and system-level data established a consensus for action around (1) improving the literacy and numeracy outcomes for every student (including high levels of critical reasoning and problem solving), (2) reducing the

(Continued)

(Continued)

achievement gap between the highest and lowest performers, and (3) ensuring student well-being. Ensuring that every student experiences success at school and is equipped with the skills to lead a fulfilling, productive, and responsible life has become a shared moral imperative across the system.

Fullan agreed to work with ACT, to guide and critique directions and strategies. He helped the system to focus relentlessly on the essential components for whole-system reform: activating its moral purpose and setting high expectations, building individual and collective capacity, engaging in intelligent accountability, and providing resolute leadership (Fullan, 2010b, pp. 61–80). Sharratt began working with the system to sharpen its focus on high-yield assessment and instructional practices.

Core Principles for School Improvement

The new strategic plan *Everyone Matters,* and school improvement strategy, *School Improvement in ACT Public Schools: Directions 2010–2013,* formally established the system's priorities and core principles—which they share and believe, to which they intend to adhere, and to which they are to be held accountable at all levels—in individual schools, networks of schools, and the system as a whole:

1. Every principal is the instructional leader in his or her school.

2. Every student will be taught by highly effective teachers.

3. Improving teacher capacity is the most effective way to improve student performance. Their strategy of choice is in-class support through coaching.

4. Every teacher and school leader deserves purposeful and regular feedback through high-quality performance and development processes.

5. There is strength in collaboration. As a team they will take responsibility for each other's work.

6. *Everyone matters.* They will do whatever it takes to ensure every young person can learn and thrive in their schools.

These six core principles refer to assessment driving informed instruction, and to instructional leadership and effective teaching practices in every school, with every teacher and school leader. Therefore, key elements of the improvement strategy include the following:

- Establishing four school networks, with experienced network leaders, working together to build collective capacity and sharing responsibility for improving the learning outcomes of each and every student in each network
- Building collective capacity: school leaders as instructional leaders and teachers explicitly teaching literacy and numeracy instructional strategies
- Increasing the use of valid and reliable data to inform classroom instruction and broader school improvement practices, and to monitor progress
- Increasing the autonomy and accountability of principals to enable school-led innovation and improvement, leading to growing school-based accountability for student outcomes

Progress to Date

In less than 18 months, significant investments were made at the school, network, and system levels to establish the conditions and supports that they believe will lead to improved learning across all schools, for every student.

A target for system improvement was building a performance and development culture in every school, where teachers and school leaders regularly work together to identify, assess, and share the most effective instructional practices and learn from each other in order to increase the collective capacity of their school and network. Through networks, principals are engaged in observation and coaching within and across schools, developing their understandings and capacities to analyze classroom practice, identify and lead whole-school strategies, and provide fair and constructive feedback. Every primary and high school has a literacy and numeracy coordinator, and 21 full-time literacy and numeracy coaches (called field officers) are working in the neediest schools. Both the field officers and literacy and numeracy coordinators work directly with teachers, providing in-class coaching and support for planning and assessment. A small central team supports the field officers and coordinators by assisting with the development of consistent understandings and approaches to literacy and numeracy assessment and instruction, and ensuring those effective practices are shared across schools and networks.

(Continued)

(Continued)

Schools such as Charles Conder Primary School are developing more systematic processes to use their student performance data for diagnostic purposes, investigating patterns in their data, and identifying students who require specific and ongoing intervention. As shown in Figure 6.1, teachers are using data to confidently identify students whose needs are not being met and then are participating in collaborative processes to develop personalized learning plans for those students. Has this worked at Charles Conder Primary? Yes, and it's another interesting and powerful example of how one school has improved by putting FACES on the data. In fact, Charles Conder Primary has moved from being the very lowest achieving school in ACT to a much higher position within ACT primary schools' ranks. The new principal, Jennifer Dawes, with great support from ACT central staff, with renewed vigor from her staff, and with the support of her network colleagues under network leader Tanya Nelipa, has made great strides in improving student achievement scores. As Jennifer has described it, but using our terms, the data wall has helped Conder teachers make an emotional connection with all students that has enabled the new cognitive insights to take hold.

Figure 6.1 Putting FACES on the Data Wall at Charles Conder Primary School, ACT

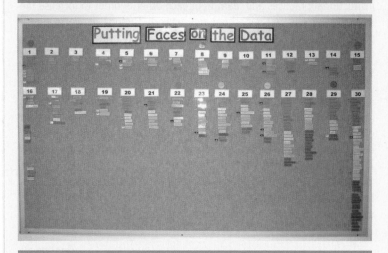

As described above, through regular network meetings, in which they share evidence-proven practices, schools are beginning to work together to do the following:

- Identify how best to meet the needs of all their students
- Develop a common language of instruction
- Engage in collaborative marking of student work to make cross-school and cross-classroom assessments consistent
- Establish consistent approaches to student assessment, behavior management, and pastoral care
- Create new, specific strategies to meet the needs of students of Aboriginal and Torres Strait Islander descent

At the system's annual school leadership conference, held in April 2011, Sharratt worked with each network leadership group to review their student achievement data, to discuss network priorities, and to introduce powerful instructional practices that have been successful in other jurisdictions. At the conference, Fullan emphasized the power of collaboration in driving whole-system change, reminding them of the need to ensure that ACT strategies engaged every teacher and student across the system. These timely interventions have led to refinement of school and network plans.

In November 2011, we filmed in three schools—a primary school, a middle school, and a college—and found impressive consistency of practice including widespread use of classroom observation and feedback.

Results So Far

NAPLAN testing takes place in May each year. Data from 2009 will be the ACT baseline against which progress is tracked. The impact of the school improvement strategy will be more evident when the 2011 data are released.

The currently available 2010 data (see Table 6.1) suggest some improvement from 2009 in mean scores in reading and writing in all years (except years 5 and 9). ACT students are performing well above the national mean, and the gain from 2009 to 2010 is modestly greater for ACT students compared to the gain nationally. In the three domains where ACT scores were lower in 2010 than in 2009, the national scores were lower, too; however, the ACT directorate and school teams do not believe that it is acceptable for assessment scores to drop. Further, the improvement in NAPLAN scores shown here, while not dramatic, has been recognized internally as a positive beginning, a very solid platform upon which to build future gains.

(Continued)

(Continued)

Table 6.1 NAPLAN Mean Scores in Reading and Writing for ACT, 2009 and 2010

Year		ACT 2009	2010	National 2009	2010
3	Reading	433.6	439.1	410.8	414.3
	Writing	421.6	434.0	414.5	418.6
5	Reading	512.7	508.6	493.9	487.4
	Writing	489.5	494.7	484.7	485.2
7	Reading	558.3	567.3	541.1	546.0
	Writing	538.7	541.4	532.4	533.5
9	Reading	598.0	594.8	580.5	573.7
	Writing	578.0	575.9	568.9	567.7

Sources: Jim Watterston, director general; and Jayne Johnston, executive director, school improvement, Education and Training Directorate, ACT, Australia.

Public Policy Implications

The ACT case study demonstrates what it takes as a state or province to put FACES on the data. The process is the essence of public education—the very core. Education systems were not and are not passive entities developed to warehouse children. Governments spend big tax dollars on education—the education portfolio is often the largest component of a public budget. The underlying rationale is to educate all children. Specific mission statements between systems may differ, but the expense is not divided by child—it is universal for *all* children in the jurisdiction. That is, governments support education financially because they believe it a right for every child to be educated.

What are our roles in advocating for every student to receive the help they require to achieve the highest possible grades they can? Leaders in schools must not only believe but act, like ACT did, to demonstrate that they believe all children can learn and thus commit to having every teacher equipped with intervention skills so that each child does indeed learn to his or her potential. So what should that look like in all schools, in all nations?

In a presentation in Japan, Andreas Schleicher (2011), head of the Indicators and Analysis Division of the OECD Directorate for Education (PISA), stated:

> [T]here is no question that most nations declare that education is important. But the test comes when these commitments are weighed against others. How do countries pay teachers, compared to other highly-skilled workers? How are education credentials weighed against other qualifications when people are being considered for jobs? Would you want your child to be a teacher? How much attention do the media pay to schools and schooling? What we have learned from PISA is that in high performing systems political and social leaders have persuaded citizens to make choices that show they value education more than other things.
>
> But placing a high value on education is only part of the equation. Another part is belief in the possibilities for all children to achieve success. In some countries, students are separated into different tracks at an early age, reflecting a notion shared by teachers, parents, and citizens that only a subset of the nation's children [FACES] can or need to achieve world class standards. Our analysis shows that systems that track students in this way, based [on] differing expectations for different destinations, tend to be fraught with large social disparities.
>
> By contrast, the best performing systems deliver strong and equitable learning outcomes [for all FACES] across very different cultural and economic contexts. In Finland, Japan, Singapore, Shanghai-China and Hong Kong-China, parents, teachers and the public at large share the belief that all students are capable of achieving high standards and need to do so, and they provide great examples for how public policy can support the achievement of universal high standards.

We have written here that it is imperative that there is a commitment to education and the belief that competencies can be learned and therefore all children can achieve. High-performing education systems share clear and ambitious standards across the board. Everyone knows what is required to get a given qualification, both in terms of the content studied and the level of performance needed to earn it. Students cannot go on to the next stage—be it in work or in further education—unless they show that they are qualified to do so. They know what they have to do to realize their dreams, and they put in the work that is needed to do it.

As Schleicher emphasizes,

> The most impressive outcome of world class education systems is perhaps that they deliver high quality learning consistently across the entire education system [and own all students' achievement] so that every student benefits from excellent learning opportunity. To achieve this, they invest educational resources where they can make the greatest difference, they attract the most talented teachers into the most challenging classroom, and they establish effective spending choices that prioritize the quality of teachers. Some of the most successful systems are also actively looking outward, realizing that the benchmark for success is no longer simply improvement by national standards, but the best performing systems internationally.

"Last but not least, in high performing systems these policies and practices are aligned across all aspects of the system, they are coherent over sustained periods of time, and they are consistently implemented. . . . And PISA shows," insists Schleicher, "that success is within the reach for nations that have the capacity to create and execute policies with maximum coherence in the system. . . ." So, for us, this is all about focus on commitment to the whole data story that leads to increasing and owning *all* students' achievement.

Increasing students' achievement is the core business of education. Ownership of student improvement at all levels ensures that high expectations are set and students, parents, and staff are clear about the expectations and standards. Lead by example, demonstrating high standards for teaching and learning. Then monitor high expectations for all students and teachers by walking and talking daily, to look for and to celebrate examples of success against the high expectations (see Chapter 5).

Parents and Communities Are "Owners," Too!

Remember the example of Luis, in Chapter 1? Luis graduated—note that we didn't say "he was graduated"—no, Luis graduated! The vice principal, his literacy coach, and his teachers "owned" Luis as a problem that needed to be solved. They engaged his parents honestly and brought them into the solution; Luis took the opportunity and ran excitedly with it to the finish line.

Just as the school staff worked with Luis's parents, it is imperative that parents, students' first teachers, become our valuable resources as partners at all grade levels and not just in primary schools.

We know from our research respondents that making a connection with parents was a strong reason for putting FACES on the data, and we know from our research for parameter 12 (parental and community involvement) that families who are involved in their students' schooling significantly increase their performance (Epstein, 1995; cited in M. Sharratt, 2004). By taking a collaborative approach to the development of family involvement programs, schools can form successful partnerships with families and community groups to improve the educational achievement of all students. "With frequent interactions among school, families, and communities," notes Epstein, "more students are more likely to receive common messages from various people about the importance of school, of working hard, of thinking creatively, of helping one another, and of staying in school" (p. 701). As a result, school-family-community partnerships enable students and families to produce and own their own successes.

Some commentators on public education make a point that student performance in any school is the direct effect of socioeconomic measures in the school area—the higher the status, the higher the scores. This myth has been shattered many times, especially by results from schools in challenging circumstances, where administrators' and teachers' knowledge of each learner, precise assessment and instruction, and concerted efforts to involve parents and community have made remarkable differences for all students (see Sharratt & Fullan, 2009, pp. 68–90).

As we noted in Chapter 3, student-led conferences engage and inspire parents and the community to become active participants in schools' safe and supportive learning environments. Inviting local media to share in school celebrations such as these is a powerful way to share students' achievement with the broader community. On an ongoing basis, students, principals, and teachers need to be able to confidently articulate to parents and the community the why, what, and how of what they do in the classrooms.

Finding relevant ways to invite parents and community members in schools to be an integral part of the focus on students is critical. Learning environments must be redesigned by the use of new technologies to ensure continuous communication so that student learning at home and at school is seamless. Successful district leaders and principals find ways to involve social agencies to support families and hire community liaison workers to focus on bringing parents and community members into schools to contribute to the learning environment. In that way, parents and students see schools as a collection of resources for their own learning. Teachers and leaders who work diligently on open communication with parents bring about a change in attitude toward parents who are seen as important contributors to children's education. Then we experience a strategic and necessary paradigm shift from blaming parents for their children to celebrating all the children that parents send us.

Vidya Shah's work demonstrates that it takes a whole community to raise a child and put FACES on the data. Vidya, lead teacher in the Model Schools for Inner Cities Program in the Toronto District School Board (TDSB) in Canada, writes that they are taking community walks with district leaders, administrators, teachers and community members, together, to "look in on" and "listen to" communities to better understand how to serve *all* students everywhere within this very large urban school district (personal communication, November 2011). The TDSB program is committed to making their schools the heart of the community, where students, parents, and community partners feel welcome, and where the home, school, and community collectively support student success. They are also committed to closing the achievement and opportunity gaps by using culturally relevant and responsive practices and high-yield instructional strategies.

Case Studies Reveal "Ownership by *All*"

The case studies we have presented in this book have "ownership"— shared responsibility and accountability (parameter 14)—as a central component. In Simcoe County's Brechin Public School, Jeff and his colleague Shelley, from Rama Public School, took on the school's performance, and in developing their plan, they engaged teachers and staff to own the new standards, the new expectations, and the new style of working together for every student across the school—not for the singularity of one classroom. This know-ability—shown by the two principals and their willingness to get involved and to learn how to remedy the situation with their teachers—led to working collaboratively, to increase student achievement and to reach a sense of collective responsibility or ownership (Sharratt & Fullan, 2009, pp. 84–102).

Bear Paw's results have risen steadily during the past 18 months because the leaders "own" the actions they have undertaken—they have reattached the human-emotional connection and attacked the leadership side of the equation with equal strength.

Saskatoon continues to drive ahead with the professional learning of everyone across all schools and is developing a secondary school approach to improving student graduation rates. Leadership "owns" the need and the development of the new programs.

At Clarendon College, Jan, Colin, and Lani took on the process of differentiating math instruction so that every student would be able to improve. They did so in such a thoughtful and well-evaluated manner that the new processes and their continuous improvement steps have become institutionalized.

Park Manor principal James Bond has worked with teachers to improve the "stickies" used on the data wall, demonstrating that the concept is no longer singularly his. Teachers have quickly offered suggestions due to the positive human-emotional connection they felt, as well as to their reaction to the positive interaction across the staff in helping to resolve specific student performance problems. By the way, Park Manor achieved a greater than 8-percent improvement in reading and writing scores in the latest EQAO assessments! Focus and ownership are paying off.

Armadale continues to achieve at very high levels. A school with assessment scores exceeding 90 percent has to drive hard every year with new students in grades 3 and 6 in order to maintain its very high standard. Because the leadership team "owns" and stays the course in putting FACES on the data with every class, because the teachers "own" the need to help every child to achieve, and because they start with high learning expectations in kindergarten, the overall assessment results remain at very high levels.

Grande Prairie's success at having over 90 percent of teachers collaboratively marking student work in order to create the cross-classroom and cross-school language of success is a good example of leadership bringing "ownership" of student achievement to the classroom. Teachers want to grow the human-emotional connection, as well, to bring a higher level of performance to every Grande Prairie school because now they feel a collective responsibility to act as a whole system.

St. Peter in CDSBEO improved its assessment scores because of the work of the Realization Improvement Network. They worked to ensure that their learning permeated the entire staff at the school. The teachers there and in the other schools across the district appear to have bought in to and, therefore, "own" the FACES program created by William Gartland's district team and all school team participants. The five key strategies bear repeating: (1) assessment that improves instruction, (2) a focus on instruction, (3) instructional leadership—know-ability, (4) planned professional learning for all teachers, and (5) resource amplification—getting the greatest return for the smallest investment by centralizing resources for all teachers to use.

At Notre Dame in CDSBEO, the teachers created and "owned" the process for cross-curricular higher-order thinking (HOT) paragraph writing that improved success rates for first-time writers of the OSSLT (especially for students who had been assessed on the grade 6 EQAO writing tasks at below the expected Level 3). As interesting and positive as this process was, even more interesting in leadership and engagement terms was the follow-up action of the teachers involved. When, after several months of working together and realizing their program was not producing the desired positive effect, cross-curricular secondary teacher teams analyzed and rebuilt it. That is, they spontaneously and collaboratively made their program a better program so that it would deliver the improved results. That is the "ownership effect" by committed teachers in action. Committed leadership enabled that effect to occur.

At St Joseph's Primary School, Don O'Brien's team worked together—not without initial difficulties, but together, nevertheless—and together they "owned" and continue to own the need for changing the future of the school and the success of all students.

The ownership has already paid off for the students and the school as the academic results and increased student enrollment numbers demonstrate. The ownership will continue to do so into the future because the parents and community are also owners of the process that they helped to create.

Calvin Baker, superintendent of the Vail, Arizona, schools, continues to tour the district with his new teachers every August prior to the new school year so that they truly understand the community and the overall Vail strategy of high expectations for all students. He and his leadership team, who share common values and beliefs, all "own" the Vail program and continue to work on focused instruction to maintain exemplary reading assessment scores while at the same time constantly looking to improve in all domains assessed.

Leaders at all levels within the state of ACT have adopted the student improvement program and are rightfully proud of their early gains in improving student achievement. Not because of the gains but by putting FACES on the data, ACT leadership team and their network school staff teams have begun to create a strong tradition of "owning" success for all their students, as the Charles Conder Primary School example shows so clearly.

Deliberate Pause

- Who owns the responsibility for all your students' achievement?
- How do you support parents and the community to take ownership for student achievement?
- What supports are in place to encourage all employees to own student achievement with emotional connections and cognitive insights?

Narrative from the Field

It's about all students' learning—each and every student. And it's about recognizing and celebrating the small wins!

During a Fountas and Pinnell Level 1 reading assessment, a grade 1 student is reading a book about a little boy who is going out to a farm to choose a pet cat for the family. In reading the passage, he comes

(Continued)

(Continued)

across the word *tongue* and tries to sound out the word. He cannot figure it out so he tries to sound out the word again, flipping the vowel sound to the long /o/ sound. He is still stumped so he shares with the teacher that he is now going to look at the picture and find something that is pink in the picture. Since there is no pink tongue in the picture, he turns to his teacher and tells her that he is now going to "skip the word and keep reading." Wow! At last he got it—then the teacher knew that he had mastered what to do when he came to a word that he didn't know—what good readers do unconsciously. The teacher's patient waiting and believing in him had paid off—hooray!

—Sheena Ness and Raechelle Goretzky,
teachers, Alexander Forbes School,
Grande Prairie Public School District, Alberta, Canada

Ownership is not an end product; rather, it is a new foundation for going further. In fact, we have found that while moral purpose can drive implementation, the reverse causal sequence is a more powerful driver. To be crystal clear, realizing success may form or deepen a teacher's sense of moral imperative (Fullan, 2011a). As one of us proved in practice (Sharratt) and we discussed together in *Realization* (2009), "putting FACES on the data" is very powerful indeed.

EPILOGUE

In this book we have used a range of case examples. Each case has its own context, but the message of success is remarkably consistent. Every situation of success has focused leadership. Such leadership sees the assessment-instruction nexus as the core work. They mobilize all others toward this task. They want to impact the whole system whether that is a school, a district, a province or state, or a country. But they do it in a way that pinpoints each and every individual. The only way to make this memorable is to conjure human FACES out of what are otherwise impersonal, and therefore meaningless, statistics. FACES make the whole enterprise meaningful. A leader's most significant measure of success is evidence-based impact, including individual success stories that are part and parcel of a larger story line.

This ability to focus and mobilize is crucial these days when there is so much contentious noise in the larger context. In a recent paper, one of us examined system-wide reform from the vantage point of "wrong" and "right" drivers (Fullan, 2011b). A driver is a policy and set of related strategies that is intended to affect the whole system positively. Wrong drivers have that intention but fail to have an impact; right drivers have positive intentions but *do* have an impact. The four wrong (and right in parentheses) drivers are external accountability (vs. collective capacity-building), individual development (vs. team or group development), technology (vs. strong pedagogy—assessment and instruction), and fragmented (vs. systemic) actions.

The leaders that we have featured in this book are all on the side of the right drivers. To be a proactive leader these days is essential when you consider what is happening. In the United States, for example, the introduction of common core state standards is a welcome addition to the reform scene. But when you couple the standards with two cross-state consortia responsible for developing specific assessment items and systems for each standard, you get a fairly unwieldy proposition. We are not against these developments per se. But we do know that for the next four or five years, this new system will lurch forward. What will be underdeveloped unless we do something forceful about it, will be assessment linked to instruction linked to leadership linked to ownership. What will be missing will be millions of individual FACES.

Our case-featured leaders do not wait for clarity or assume that the system will eventually solve problems for them. Rather, they lead by carving out a clear reality with those with whom they work. FACES is their mantra, because it gets at three key things:

1. Who are the humans behind the numbers? How can they understand the individuals as bundles of human desire and inadequacies? Their modus operandi is to make emotional connections in their everyday work.

2. But they also know that caring and passion is not enough. They have to know how to make a difference—have cognitive insights, in every classroom, with every student.

3. They have commitment and techniques for identifying FACES in the crowd because they want to make a big difference—for the whole organization or system—not just for a handful of individual students.

In a very basic way, our case study leaders use their "know-ability" and "mobilize-ability," that is, they are able to model, motivate, and inspire; and their "sustain-ability" as advocates for learners. Don't these skills reflect why most teachers come into teaching so that they can make a difference? What we have done in the case studies is to show how to make this commitment a lived reality. That "lived reality" requires leadership if it is going to happen on any scale.

In today's schools and tomorrow's schools we will need still more—leadership skills and new, powerful resources.

We will need both new ideas (innovation) and powerful systems of implementation. As we mentioned earlier, we are working on one such big example. We call it ML/Madcap (Fullan, Devine, Sharratt, Cuttress, Butler, & Mozer, 2011). It combines, into a single package, digital media dimensions that are to be purposefully made (like all good lesson plans) to highlight desired learning outcomes; specific teacher supports to generate great pedagogy; and an integrated tracking and assessment support system for implementation. The idea is to develop digital innovations in relation to core standards to engage, entertain, and immerse students and their teachers in irresistible learning experiences. We would do this across the curriculum—arts as well as science. You can be sure that FACES will be a cornerstone of this work.

Information overload will only expand in the future as the public demands more accountability, and the awesome power of technology has a life of its own. You will be lost without the focusing power of FACES. Whatever is going on in your environment, you have a responsibility to focus and to "own" the work to make teaching come alive for all those you encounter. Do this by making the FACES stand out from the statistics. Make those FACES brighter and more knowing. Go back to the human roots of education—the human-emotional connections and the professional cognitive insights—and make learning flourish on a grand scale.

GLOSSARY OF TERMS

Action Research/Collaborative Inquiry A process in which a question, arising from data, is the focus for all staff for at least a year. It is often a problem-based question arising from an area of whole-school need in order to get focused on improvement. Most successfully completed by whole staffs collaboratively inquiring after a problem of practice in their school.

Accountable Talk Teachers and students engaging in dialogue to understand their own perspectives and the perspectives of others in seeking clarity.

Anchor Charts Classroom charts that prompt students to remember their learning, their work, and the processes they've explored. Most useful are those that are visible in the classroom and that are co-constructed by teachers and students to provide clarity.

Assessment A process that takes place between teachers and students so that students can understand where they are, how they are doing, and where they are going.

> **Assessment *for* and *as* Learning (Formative)** Seamless integration of information about a student's learning that turns into the instruction needed in a timely way with multiple opportunities for students to demonstrate the new learning. During lessons, teachers instantly use the information given by students to clarify meaning and go deeper into the demonstration and sharing of their learning. Assessment that drives instruction is a never-ending cycle in which one informs the other daily: assessment becomes instruction that becomes assessment. Thus data today is instruction tomorrow.

> **Assessment *of* Learning (Summative)** Assessment at the end of a unit of study or a term—through observation; conversations with students; or an examination of products, comparing them against the established success criteria.

Diagnostic Assessment   Varied forms of assessment to determine the instructional starting points for each student at every grade level.

Self-Assessment   Students' assessment of their own work against the success criteria to determine their next steps in their learning.

Authentic Learning   Learning related to students' real-life experiences that are relevant to them, their context, and their culture.

Big Ideas   "Educational leaders are coming to understand that the notion of teaching through 'big ideas' is about teaching the higher-order thinking skills of analysis, interpretation, evaluation and synthesis of a text or curriculum unit. The term 'big idea' does not mean naming a theme unit such as 'Friendship' and selecting a bunch of books and activities that go along with the Friendship Theme, but rather providing students with the modeling of higher-order thinking skills and opportunities to think through text or essential questions critically, bringing them to levels of deep understanding, creativity and new learning. 'Big Ideas' can be addressed through the reading of individual texts or through a unit of study but they need to cause and stretch student thinking by highlighting what is essential in the text or learning experience and connecting these ideas meaningfully to students' lives and the world."—Melanie Greenan, doctoral candidate, OISE/University of Toronto, personal communication, August 2011.

Bloom's Taxonomy   A system, developed by Benjamin Bloom at the University of Chicago in 1984, to describe thinking skills as a hierarchy with knowledge and memory as foundational skills, followed progressively by comprehension, application, analysis, and evaluation skills.

Comprehension   The ability to draw meaning from written text, visual media and the spoken word.

Developmental Learner Profile   Student information is kept in files that show all aspects of the student as a learner: his or her social, emotional, and academic achievement. Samples of current student work are kept and results of assessments housed for reference by students and teachers in setting new learning goals. They can be accessed readily by teachers for colleague discussions and

transitioning to the next teacher—so that instructional time is not lost in conducting diagnostic assessments with each new teacher.

Differentiated Instruction   An approach to maximize each student's learning by assessing student need and designing instruction to match the need, thus moving the student forward.

Distributed Leadership   Leadership is the art of influence. Distributed leadership is when leadership is shared influence with the attached accountability and responsibility.

EQAO   The Education Quality and Accountability Office (EQAO) assessment is the standards-based test given to Ontario, Canada, students in grades 3 and 6 in reading, writing, and mathematics and in grade 9 in mathematics. The office also develops and administers the Ontario Secondary School Literacy Test (OSSLT) for all grade 10 students, which is a diploma-bearing assessment, as students cannot graduate from an Ontario high school without passing this test.

Graphic Organizer   A visual framework that helps students organize and chunk their ideas to make processes and content more easily understood.

Higher-Order Thinking (HOT) Skills   The skills to be able to develop a critical stance through inference; by making connections and predictions; and by analyzing, synthesizing, and developing a supportable argument or opinion.

Inquiry-Based Classroom Learning   Learning in which students ask questions and solve problems to develop knowledge and skills in their areas of interest, allowing them to find new areas of interest.

Instructional Intelligence   Being consciously skilled in integrating the use of clusters of skills, strategies, tactics and organizers. Often highly effective teachers work intuitively. Their work is exemplary, but they are not able to describe what they do. Instructional intelligence provides a language to describe instructional methodology. Teachers can then share their expertise as well as assess and refine their own practice. Instructional intelligence includes reflective use of such skills and strategies as effective (cooperative) group work, concept attainment, inductive thinking, thinking strategies, and framing questions. Instructional intelligence means weaving these tactics, skills, and strategies together into effective instruction for each student (Sharratt et al., 2002).

Independent Reading and Writing The ultimate goal in the gradual-release-of-responsibility model: readers and writers who can enjoy both reading and writing on their own. The primary responsibility for reading and writing is with the student when he or she is independent, which becomes the gradual-acceptance-of-responsibility model.

Learning Goal We have chosen to use Learning Goal in this book; however, other terms that are similar are Learning Intention or Learning Target. The Learning Goal is directly developed from the Curriculum Expectations. It can be several of the Curriculum Expectations clustered together for teaching purposes. Success Criteria for students are directly developed from the Learning Goal and most effective when co-constructed with the teacher. The Learning Goal must be in student-friendly language and be visible in classrooms for students to reference.

Leveled Books Teacher assesses a student's appropriate developmental level of reading unseen text and the readiness of a student to progress to the next reading level. This process allows for flexible groupings of students for guided reading groups.

Literacy Begins with the basic skills of being able to read, write, speak, listen, view, represent, and do mathematics. It becomes the ability to comprehend, think critically, resolve problems, and use higher-order thinking skills independently. We have added higher-order, critical thinking skills to the list of basic literacy skills for 21st-century learners.

Balanced Literacy Composed of oral language and modeled, shared, guided, and independent reading and writing; includes media literacy.

Critical Literacy A process of going beyond the literal text to realize an author's deeper meaning. Often focuses on issues of equity, fairness, and social justice. Critically literate students can determine if a point of view is justified from their point of view.

Cross-Curricular Literacy When literacy curriculum expectations or concepts or skills are specifically taught in the subject areas.

Multi-Literacies Include the traditional literacy definition (above) and may extend to include information, cultural, financial, critical, media, digital and environmental.

Mentor Texts Rich pieces of literature that teachers can use to demonstrate or model the teaching points they are making, such as reading comprehension strategies. These teacher-selected texts create common conversations with students that result in students' becoming critical consumers of varied forms of texts.

Modeled–Shared–Guided–Interdependent Practice Progression of learning about practice that is scaffolded (see below), beginning with *modeled* (demonstrated by leader) practice, then moving to *shared* (leader and learner) practice, scaffolded to *guided* (demonstrated by the learner) practice, and then self-actualized in *interdependent* practice (learners and leaders flying together).

Oral Language The foundational skill that underscores all learning to read, write and comprehend.

PISA (Program for International Student Assessment) International assessment of the learning performance of 15 years olds from over 65 countries, focused on literacy, math, and science and conducted every two years. PISA is operated by the Organisation for Economic Co-operation and Development (OECD).

PM Benchmark Assessment Tool Kit An assessment tool produced by Nelson Publishers to provide comprehensive reading assessment resources using 30 unseen leveled texts.

Prior Knowledge What students already know at the outset of a lesson. Should be assessed before teaching new information, to allow for differentiation of instruction.

Read Aloud When teachers share rich literature with students by reading out loud to them.

Reflective Practice Ongoing habit of mind that teachers and leaders use to think critically about their work. Reflective practitioners ask, often, What worked? What didn't work? and What can I do differently? Students learn this habit as well from teachers who make this practice visible.

Running Record Determining the level at which students are reading can be accomplished by taking a running record using a book that is close to the child's developmental level. Assessing children's reading progress is key to moving them along at the proper developmental rate. The running record allows you to record a child's reading behavior as he or she reads from the book. Careful analysis of the running record assessment help teachers gain insights into a child's reading, assign children to the appropriate developmental level for guided reading groups, and determine what next steps in reading instruction are needed.

Scaffolding   Supported progressive learning during which knowledge is built-up. New knowledge is brought into play and is connected with prior knowledge. Each layer is built on a solid foundation created by previous learning.

Success Criteria   Criteria tied directly to learning goals, which are developed from (clustered) curriculum expectations. Should be visible and available in classrooms so that students can use them as a reference while they are doing their work and against which they can measure progress toward their own goals for improvement. They are most effective when co-constructed by teachers and students.

Teacher Moderation   A process of teachers working together to collaboratively score commonly developed assessments to ensure consistency of practice across a grade or subject area. Through moderation, teachers work together to share beliefs and practices, enhance their understanding, compare their interpretations of student results, and confirm their judgments about each student's level of work.

Think Alouds (Modeled Reading)   The teacher makes her thinking "visible" as she reads a text out loud to students modeling her thinking so that the students can gather information, develop insights, solve problems, or correct any confusion about how a good reader reads and thinks about the text during the process.

Word Study   Systematic exploration of the patterns and irregularities in working with words. Teachers often use Word Walls to work with word patterns or families of words or to introduce words that will be used in a new learning unit.

APPENDIX A

*Matrix of Scaffolded Learning Using the
Gradual-Release-of-Responsibility Model:
From Modeled to Shared to Guided to
Interdependent Practice for Practitioners*

Appendix A 14 Parameter Matrix of Scaffolded Learning Using the Gradual-Release Model

Parameter	Modeled Practice	Shared Practice	Guided Practice	Interdependent Practice
1. Shared Beliefs and Understandings				
All students can achieve high standards given sufficient time and the right support.	District and school leaders and teachers articulate vision everywhere, at any time (professional learning sessions, staff meetings, board meetings).	Leaders and teachers work in smaller clusters or networks with "accountable talk," i.e., teachers can articulate why and how they teach what they do.	All teachers receive intensive and ongoing training focused on classroom practice (e.g., literacy walks, Reading Recovery, action research, and lesson study).	Special education and regular education assessment and instruction are seamless; all students are engaged and achieving, and all parents are involved.
High expectations and early and ongoing intervention are essential.	They use data in the district and schools to set targets; intervention practices are in place in all schools.	They discuss how to use data to differentiate instruction; intervention techniques are discussed and in place at every level.	Teachers moderate student work; performance targets are visible in every classroom.	The case management approach is used for each struggling student; all students can articulate performance targets and their work to be done.
All teachers can teach to high standards given the right assistance.	Administrators and literacy leads model and work alongside classroom teachers.	They use video clips to discuss best practices and build on clips.	Literacy coaches now embedded; demonstrate assessment and instructional strategies and model descriptive feedback.	Teachers (and administrators) co-teach, question as critical friends, and examine students' thinking.

(Continued)

(Continued)

Parameter	Modeled Practice	Shared Practice	Guided Practice	Interdependent Practice
Teachers can articulate what they do and why they teach the way they do.	■ Teachers can articulate to colleagues and parents why they are instructing as they are.	■ Teachers share practice through demonstration class visits, opening their doors.	■ Teachers plan and watch each other teach (lesson study) and demonstrate student improvement using samples of student work.	■ Students can articulate why and how they learn, using the same language and evidence from their work.
2. **Embedded Literacy/ Instructional Coaches**	■ Partial staffing is allocated during school day to model successful literacy instruction in every school. ■ Selection is critical: they must be "knowledgeable others," credible, supportive, approachable.	■ Ongoing dialogue with principal and leadership team focuses on school and student data.	■ Districts find the funding to hire/ carefully select literacy coaches in every school ■ Literacy coaches work alongside classroom teachers in planning. ■ They demonstrate literacy assessment and instructional practices during the literacy block. ■ They demonstrate how technology is an integral instructional tool.	■ Step back—lead from behind. ■ Students consistently use strategies and skills; teachers and literacy coaches support when necessary. ■ Literacy coaches co-teach with teachers across all divisions to refine practice and focus on students' thinking.

Parameter	Modeled Practice	Shared Practice	Guided Practice	Interdependent Practice
3. Daily, Sustained Focus on Literacy Instruction	■ Minimum 100-minute block is time-tabled for literacy instruction. ■ Minimum 60-minute block is time-tabled for mathematics instruction. ■ Interruptions are eliminated during literacy block and time is protected for instruction.	■ Literacy instruction progresses from modeled to shared to guided to interdependent. ■ Teachers move from whole- to small-group to individual differentiated literacy instruction.	■ Data determine which students need more daily guided practice. Assessment informs all instruction. ■ Literacy skills are observed and demonstrated through lesson study sessions. ■ Higher-order questions promote critical thinking.	■ Students' voice is heard frequently. ■ Students work independently using explicit, timely formative feedback from teachers' assessments (e.g., one praise point and one instructional point). ■ Students use multiple forms of technology to demonstrate their literacy learning.
4. Principal Leadership	■ Principals can articulate deep, structured understanding of assessment that drives literacy instruction for all staff. ■ They use technology for effectiveness and efficiency. ■ They have an instructional coach if needed.	■ Principals are part of literacy leadership team and attend professional learning (PL) with staff; no other priority is more important to spend time on. ■ Superintendents, curriculum staff, and principals lead PL sessions.	■ Principals and staff use data to drive school plans and guide selection of resources and instructional strategies. ■ They provide focused PL and resources that reflect district sessions.	■ Principals and teachers support all students' learning through frequent, nonevaluative classroom literacy walks and follow-up reflective conversations about practice. ■ They ensure that all teachers and students have opportunities to learn with and through appropriate technology.

(Continued)

(Continued)

Parameter	Modeled Practice	Shared Practice	Guided Practice	Interdependent Practice
5. **Early and Ongoing Intervention**	■ Data are used to identify struggling students' strengths and areas of need early in each school year at every grade level in order to put interventions in place immediately.	■ Assessment data are shared with all teachers in order to make collaborative decisions about how to move all struggling learners forward.	■ Guided instructional training, in literacy interventions such as Reading Recovery, is provided for some teachers who form first cohort, and a systematic plan is developed to provide training for all teachers in district over a five-year period.	■ Wait lists are a thing of the past—no students wait! All students are actively engaged in relevant and appropriate learning. ■ Students use technology to support their individual differentiated learning.
6. **Case Management Approach**	■ Administrators and literacy leadership teams gather, triangulate, and report data for schools and students. ■ Display performance data (data walls, data folders, smart boards, etc.) for staff to discuss and take collective responsibility for all students' improvement.	■ Teachers identify the students with whom they need instructional help. ■ Time tables reflect that specialist teachers in school provide instruction in classrooms to free up classroom teachers to attend case management meetings.	■ Principals, literacy coaches, and classroom teachers come together in scheduled case management meetings during the school day. ■ Classroom teachers present struggling students' work for collective problem solving. ■ The team recommends instructional strategies to try, taking ownership.	■ Teachers implement instructional strategies recommended in case management meetings. ■ They return to follow-up meetings until student improvement is achieved. ■ Many or all students benefit from the strategies tried for one student.

Parameter	Modeled Practice	Shared Practice	Guided Practice	Interdependent Practice
7. **Professional Learning at School Staff Meetings**	■ Principals and literacy leadership teams as lead-learners model district key messages and embed PL from district sessions at all staff meetings.	■ Principals, literacy leads, and teachers, using diagnostic data, determine staff learning needs and lead differentiated PL. ■ Teachers use technology to get just-in-time personal literacy PL beyond the PL at staff meetings.	■ Principals and literacy coaches use school data to identify the parameter(s) that need focused PL. (Parameter 1 is most challenging and is always a given.) ■ They develop a key action research (AR) question that reflects the parameters chosen (see parameter 11) and work on finding answers all year.	■ Beliefs match practice and become a habit of mind. ■ School and classroom learning environments are characterized by high energy, staff room conversations focus on students' improvement, and students use common language modeled by K–12 teachers.
8. **In-School Grade/Subject Meetings**	■ Literacy leads/department heads model what literacy looks like in all curriculum areas at every large- and small-group teacher and administrative meeting; operational issues are reduced to memo format.	■ Weekly discussions of student work at grade or division meetings lead to common language and understanding of curriculum expectation and explicit assessment that informs instructional strategies.	■ Administrators and literacy coaches build and share a varied repertoire of high-yield assessment and instructional strategies to support teachers.	■ Students benefit from immediate, explicit feedback from teachers about their work and are given on-the-spot instruction to move them forward.

(Continued)

(Continued)

Parameter	Modeled Practice	Shared Practice	Guided Practice	Interdependent Practice
		■ Teachers have common planning time to collaboratively assess student work and reach consensus through rich dialogue on the level of each piece of work.	■ Teachers learn from each other by modeling what is working for them; they visit other classrooms together to see others' practice and discuss refining their own.	
9. Centralized Resources	■ Administrators, literacy leads, and teacher-librarians collect school resources and locate them in a central location for all teachers to use. ■ Analyze gaps to determine what further resources are needed.	■ Teachers share the use of leveled texts and multidimensional resources, all labeled appropriately according to learners' stages. ■ Resources are also categorized by authors, genres, and publishers, and include graphic novels, bibliographies, software, etc. ■ Administrators and teachers select professional resource books to read and discuss at book studies.	■ Literacy coaches and teachers collaboratively plan and teach lessons using a variety of resources and instructional approaches. ■ Teachers use software to discuss, share, and guide use of exemplary resources with others.	■ Students see themselves reflected in the classroom resources used. ■ Students know how to use web technology to find resources and information and know how to apply it. ■ Students share their resources in collaboratively designed group work with built-in individual student accountability.

Parameter	Modeled Practice	Shared Practice	Guided Practice	Interdependent Practice
10. Commitment of District and School Budgets for Literacy Learning and Resources	■ Senior management and elected officials (trustees) continue to fund literacy resources (human and material) in tough economic times by finding operational areas in which to cut costs; they are united in staying the course.	■ District curriculum consultants share how to use resources and instructional approaches, using blended learning model (face-to-face time and interactive technology time) to reach all teachers. ■ Teachers in small groups are expected to try out resources and apply their new skills to refine their practice.	■ Literacy coaches support the selection and use of resources for classrooms and book rooms. ■ Carefully selected resources mirror the diversity in classrooms and enable students to relate to the resources.	■ Equity of outcomes for all students is experienced and acknowledged through data—all students are meeting the high performance targets set for them. ■ Students, parents, and the community see schools as resources for their own learning; schools find many contextually unique ways to accomplish this.

(Continued)

(Continued)

Parameter	Modeled Practice	Shared Practice	Guided Practice	Interdependent Practice
11. Action Research/ Collaborative Inquiry (AR/CI)	▪ Principals and literacy leadership teams model the exploration of school literacy data to determine areas of students' strength and need.	▪ Principals and literacy leadership teams share data with staff and discuss teaching outcomes necessary to increase achievement for all students.	▪ District PL is provided to guide staff to focus on developing one AR/CI question that they need to know more about, based on multiple data sets. ▪ Time is set aside throughout the year for discussion focused on finding answers to the AR/CI question—an example of accountable staff talk.	▪ The district gives money for in-school PL days to consolidate findings in order to answer and write a report on the AR/CI question. ▪ All teachers are committed to applying discussed assessment and instruction approaches needed to answer the AR/CI question to ensure that all students are learning.
12. Parental and Community Involvement	▪ Everyone models the belief that parents are students' first and most important teachers: sending us their best for us to ensure that they reach their potential.	▪ Principals and teachers reach out to the community to bring parents in to schools. Schools host adult learning session day/ night. ▪ Use of technology and software to learn at home is supported through take-home programs.	▪ Principals and teachers are able to confidently articulate to parents and the community why, what, and how they do what they do in the classrooms.	▪ Parents and students know what, why, and how students are doing and have a clear understanding of learning expectations and what students need to do to reach the next learning level.

Parameter	Modeled Practice	Shared Practice	Guided Practice	Interdependent Practice
13. Cross-Curricular Connections	■ The language of the discipline is modeled in every subject area. ■ Modeled, shared, guided, and independent approaches are used to differentiate instruction and scaffold literacy learning in all subjects.	■ Discussion groups, demonstration classrooms, video streaming, and web technologies are used to share examples of cross-curricular instruction for all teachers.	■ Curriculum consultants, literacy coaches, and knowledgeable others work alongside classroom teachers to integrate literacy into all subject areas.	■ Students experience that the taught, learned, and assessed curriculum align. ■ Students make connections to text as media and media as text. ■ Students work collaboratively online, building projects together.
14. Shared Responsibility and Accountability	■ The focused literacy priority of the province, district, school, and classroom is aligned, clear, precise, and intentional. ■ Everyone knows and can articulate the priority.	■ All elementary and secondary school teams participate in evidence-based literacy improvement presentations at district learning fairs.	■ All schools host their own Literacy Learning Fairs for parents and community members. ■ Teams of teachers present their AR findings at Literacy Learning Fairs that evidence increased students' literacy achievement.	■ The case management approach (parameter 6), with time during the day, is available to any teacher who is struggling to reach a student; teachers and administrators, assisted by colleagues, find assessment and

(Continued)

(Continued)

Parameter	Modeled Practice	Shared Practice	Guided Practice	Interdependent Practice
	■ The priority is clearly reflected in the AR/CI question developed (parameter 11) in every school using triangulation of data.	■ Principals and teachers conduct nonevaluative literacy walks together to ask reflective questions about practice that goes deeper. ■ Classroom teachers open doors to each other, making practice public.	■ Streaming technology is used to make the Literacy Learning Fairs accessible to the broader community. ■ All teachers use data to drive differentiated instruction. ■ Assessment data are delivered to administrators' and teachers' desktops, making everyone accountable and responsible for putting individual student FACES on the data and taking action for all students. ■ Principals and teachers conduct nonevaluative literacy walks together, which result in coaching	instructional strategies that work with each student brought forward (and continue until they do), thus becoming accountable and responsible for all students. ■ Students, facilitated by teachers, present at Literacy Learning Fairs in their schools and can articulate to parents and the broader community why they have improved in literacy and what the next steps will be; they show how their work is connected to the district work at the district Literacy Learning Fairs.

Parameter	Modeled Practice	Shared Practice	Guided Practice	Interdependent Practice
			conversations to go deeply into practice that supports all students' achievement.	■ Students and teachers develop Sharepoint or other technology to communicate their achievements continuously to those beyond their schools (superintendents, community members, trustees, etc.). ■ Coaching conversations focused on increasing student achievement occur throughout the school day by all staff and students who make classrooms public places of learning.

Data Collection Placemat for Research

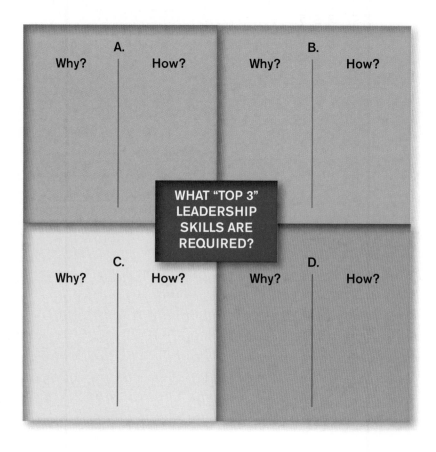

A.
Why? | How?

B.
Why? | How?

WHAT "TOP 3" LEADERSHIP SKILLS ARE REQUIRED?

C.
Why? | How?

D.
Why? | How?

Instructions for using the placemat:

1. Divide your chart paper into four equal sections and letter them A, B, C, and D.

2. Individually write in your section the answers to these questions:
   a. Why do we put FACES on the data?
   b. How do we put FACES on the data?

3. As a team, reach consensus on what leadership skills are required to put the FACES on the data.

4. Record your top three leadership skills in the center of the paper.

5. Give us some concrete examples or stories of where this is happening.

Case Management Template

Student's Name: _____

Grade: _____ Date: _____

Reading Comprehension Strategy Focus (if appropriate): _____

Background Information:
Interests:
Strengths:
Identifications/Accommodations:
Other Important Learning Info:

Observation:

Background Info (lesson objective, instructional strategy used, teacher observations):

Analysis of work sample:

What are the strengths of this student?	*What are the areas of need for this student?*

Which area is critical to student achievement?

Plan:
What is a reasonable next short-term goal for this student? Why?

What instructional strategies will you try and WHY do you think they will work?

Strategy	Rationale	Modeled	Shared	Guided	Independent

What resources would you need to implement this plan?

Evidence and Follow Up:

What kind of work samples from this student will you bring to the next meeting?

Next Meeting Date:

THINK ABOUT: What other instructional practices from our **Balanced Literacy Program** might this student respond to?

READING

MODELED	SHARED	GUIDED	INDEPENDENT
☐ Read-Aloud	☐ Book Talks	☐ Instructional Level Reading	☐ Self-Selected
☐ Think-Aloud	☐ Story Theatre	☐ Focus: Comprehension	☐ Literature Circle
☐ Different Genre/ Reading	☐ Reader's Theater	☐ Before Reading	☐ Reading Workshop
☐ Whole Class	☐ Paired Reading	☐ During Reading	☐ Conferencing
☐ Broaden Interests	☐ Choral Reading/ Speaking	☐ After Reading	☐ Buddy/Partner Reading
☐ Thinking and Problem Solving	☐ Whole Class (same reading material)	☐ Small Flexible Groups	☐ Book Club
☐ Student Engagement/ Motivate	☐ Build Skills and Strategies	☐ Groups Based on Needs	☐ Pursue Areas of Interest
☐ Students Develop Appreciations	☐ Framing Questions	☐ Reinforce Strategies Taught	☐ Books Easily Accessible
	☐ Student Engagement/ Motivation		☐ Diversity

WRITING

MODELED	**SHARED**	**GUIDED**	**INDEPENDENT**
☐ Teacher Write-Aloud ☐ Show Process in mini lesson ☐ Thinking/ Problem Solving ☐ Whole Class ☐ FOCUS (week, month, term) ☐ Use of Resources	☐ Teacher and students write story together with the teacher as scribe ☐ Students share the pen to complete a story after talking about a shared event	☐ Focused Mini-Lessons ☐ Small Flexible Groups (needs) ☐ Reinforce Strategies Taught ☐ Groups Based on Needs	☐ Journal ☐ Constructed Response ☐ Writing Workshop ☐ Conferencing ☐ Process Writing ☐ Flexibility of Topic ☐ Pursuit of Interests

THINK ABOUT:

LEARNING GOAL

SUCCESS CRITERIA

FORMATIVE and/or SUMMATIVE ASSESSMENT

DESCRIPTIVE FEEDBACK

CO-CONSTRUCTED ANCHOR CHARTS

EXEMPLARS

RICH TASKS

OTHER:

Source: Adapted from York Region District School Board (2011).

The Teaching-Learning Cycle

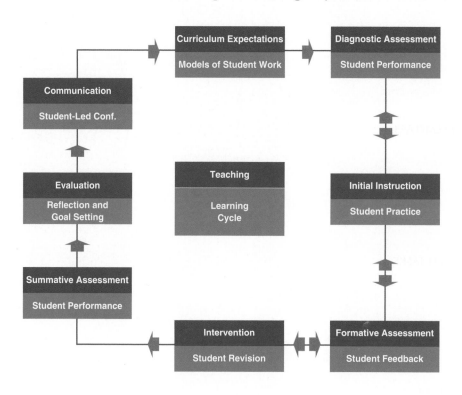

Source: Printed with permission from York Regional District School Board (2007).

APPENDIX E

Weekly Literacy Block Planner

Week of: _____   Literacy Focus: _____

Suggested Weekly Literacy Block Planner

Time	Component	Monday	Tuesday	Wednesday	Thursday	Friday
Suggested Guidelines	Entry: Welcome students into classroom and promote polite and respectful interactions. Support students as they get organized for the literacy block.	Literacy Learning Goal: □ Clustered curriculum expectations and big idea	Literacy Learning Goal: □ Clustered curriculum expectations and big idea	Literacy Learning Goal: □ Clustered curriculum expectations and big idea	Literacy Learning Goal: □ Clustered curriculum expectations and big idea	Literacy Learning Goal: □ Clustered curriculum expectations and big idea
10–20 min.	Modeled or Shared Reading □ Comprehension strategies □ Author study / genre study □ Think aloud with focus □ Critical literacy analysis □ Poem/cross-curricular □ Article/poster/graphic text	Text: Focus:	Text: Focus:	Text: Focus:	Text: Focus:	Text: Focus:
10–20 min.	Language & Word Study/Book Talks □ Word sorting/making words □ Fix-up strategies □ Grammar □ Fluency and phrasing □ Word wall □ Centers	Text or Comprehension or Critical Literacy Focus:	Text or Comprehension or Critical Literacy Focus:	Text or Comprehension or Critical Literacy Focus:	Text or Comprehension or Critical Literacy Focus:	Text or Comprehension or Critical Literacy Focus:

			Students to one-on-one conference with:	Students to one-on-one conference with:	Students to one-on-one conference with:	Students to one-on-one conference with:	Students to one-on-one conference with:

20–30 min.	**Independent Reading** ▫ Book talks ▫ Reading response ▫ "Just right" books ▫ Reading logs ▫ Poetry reading ▫ Current events	Students to one-on-one conference with: ▫ ▫ ▫ ▫ ▫	Students to one-on-one conference with: ▫ ▫ ▫ ▫ ▫	Students to one-on-one conference with: ▫ ▫ ▫ ▫ ▫	Students to one-on-one conference with: ▫ ▫ ▫ ▫ ▫	Students to one-on-one conference with: ▫ ▫ ▫ ▫ ▫
20–30 min.	<u>Guided Reading</u> ▫ See resources (i.e., guided reading folders) for student groupings, focus, prompting questions, and assessment	GR Group # ___ Text: Focus: GR Group # ___ Text: Focus:	GR Group # ___ Text: Focus: GR Group # ___ Text: Focus:	GR Group # ___ Text: Focus: GR Group # ___ Text: Focus:	GR Group # ___ Text: Focus: GR Group # ___ Text: Focus:	GR Group # ___ Text: Focus: GR Group # ___ Text: Focus:
10–20 min.	<u>Writer's Workshop</u> Mini-Lessons: ▫ Modeled writing ▫ Shared writing ▫ Interactive writing (primary) Practice: ▫ Independent writing	Form and Focus of Writing:	Form and Focus of Writing:	Form and Focus of Writing:	Form and Focus of Writing:	Form and Focus of Writing:

(Continued)

(Continued)

	Guided Writing	Guided Writing	Guided Writing	Guided Writing	Guided Writing	Guided Writing
20–30 min.	<u>Guided Writing</u> ▫ Writing form, feature, and genre ▫ Writing traits (ideas, organization) ▫ Structure ▫ Grammar and punctuation ▫ Details and descriptive vocabulary ▫ Writing process	Focus: Names of Students in Small Group: ▫ ▫ ▫ ▫	Focus: Names of Students in Small Group: ▫ ▫ ▫ ▫	Focus: Names of Students in Small Group: ▫ ▫ ▫ ▫	Focus: Names of Students in Small Group: ▫ ▫ ▫ ▫	Focus: Names of Students in Small Group: ▫ ▫ ▫ ▫
Next Steps	Reflection from today's literacy block and whole-group, small-group, and individual instruction in order to plan for tomorrow	Reflection:	Reflection:	Reflection:	Reflection:	Reflection:

- Important to note that oral language, media literacy, critical literacy, and higher order thinking skills are all interwoven throughout the literacy block and all other subject areas
- The focus and order of the literacy block will change depending on student need – more time may need to be given for modelled practice and learning styles, social/emotional skills, multiple intelligence, and student voice and interest will be taken into account when planning.

Task-Oriented Question Construction Wheel Based on Bloom's Taxonomy

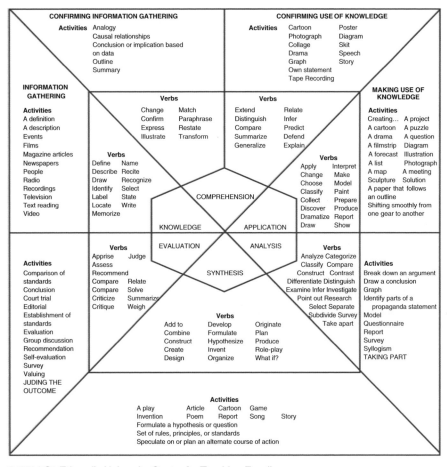

CONFIRMING INFORMATION GATHERING

Activities
Analogy
Causal relationships
Conclusion or implication based
on data
Outline
Summary

CONFIRMING USE OF KNOWLEDGE

Activities
Cartoon   Poster
Photograph   Diagram
Collage   Skit
Drama   Speech
Graph   Story
Own statement
Tape Recording

INFORMATION GATHERING

Activities
A definition
A description
Events
Films
Magazine articles
Newspapers
People
Radio
Recordings
Television
Text reading
Video

Verbs
Change   Match
Confirm   Paraphrase
Express   Restate
Illustrate Transform

Verbs
Extend   Relate
Distinguish Infer
Compare   Predict
Summarize   Defend
Generalize   Explain

MAKING USE OF KNOWLEDGE

Activities
Creating...   A project
A cartoon   A puzzle
A drama   A question
A filmstrip   Diagram
A forecast   Illustration
A list   Photograph
A map   A meeting
Sculpture   Solution
A paper that follows
an outline
Shifting smoothly from
one gear to another

Verbs
Define   Name
Describe   Recite
Draw   Recognize
Identify   Select
Label   State
Locate   Write
Memorize

COMPREHENSION

Verbs
Apply   Interpret
Change   Make
Choose   Model
Classify   Paint
Collect   Prepare
Discover   Produce
Dramatize   Report
Draw   Show

KNOWLEDGE   **APPLICATION**

EVALUATION   **ANALYSIS**

Verbs
Apprise   Judge
Assess
Recommend
Compare   Relate
Compare   Solve
Criticize   Summarize
Critique   Weigh

SYNTHESIS

Verbs
Analyze Categorize
Classify Compare
Construct Contrast
Differentiate Distinguish
Examine Infer Investigate
Point out Research
Select Separate
Subdivide Survey
Take apart

Activities
Comparison of
standards
Conclusion
Court trial
Editorial
Establishment of
standards
Evaluation
Group discussion
Recommendation
Self-evaluation
Survey
Valuing
JUDING THE
OUTCOME

Activities
Break down an argument
Draw a conclusion
Graph
Identify parts of a
propaganda statement
Model
Questionnaire
Report
Survey
Syllogism
TAKING PART

Verbs
Add to   Develop   Originate
Combine   Formulate   Plan
Construct   Hypothesize Produce
Create   Invent   Role-play
Design   Organize   What if?

Activities
A play   Article   Cartoon   Game
Invention   Poem   Report   Song   Story
Formulate a hypothesis or question
Set of rules, principles, or standards
Speculate on or plan an alternate course of action

APPENDIX G

*Cross-Curricular Literacy
Indicators of Success*

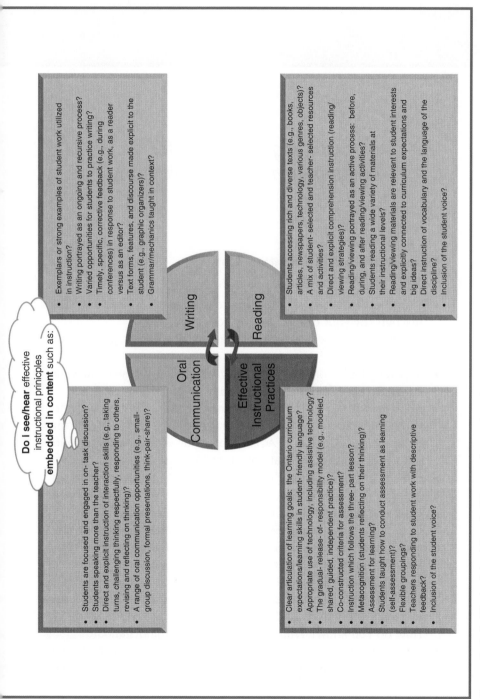

Source: Catholic District School Board of Eastern Ontario (2011).

APPENDIX H

Guiding Questions for
Collaborative Team Book Study

Chapter 1: From Information Glut to Well-Known FACES

- Create an inventory of the data-generating tools used by your teachers, by your district, and by your state.
- Of all the data available, which are most critical? Justify your thinking.
- In putting FACES on your data, analyze and discuss how useful your data have been to district leaders, administrators, and teachers.
- Examine what is available and what your staff members want to know more about. List the data that might be useful to you for determining students' FACES that your state, districts, and schools are missing or that appear to be missing.
- Give examples from your data that demonstrate that every child is learning to his or her maximum potential—and that every teacher is teaching to his or her maximum potential.
- Determine how many FACES—not the percentages, but the actual number of students—are exempted from assessments. Why were these exemptions granted? Is the reasoning for these exemptions legitimate? How do you know?
- What percentage of students (in your state, school, or classroom) can read with fluency and comprehension by the end of grade 1? How do you know? What determines the reading standard?
- Define literacy in your context. What does cross-curricular literacy look like, K–12? What criteria do you use to measure an effective literacy program?

- What is the collective plan for improvement—how do you build consensus so that all staff commit to improvement?
- What resources are available to you to implement this focused improvement?
- Critique your implementation of value-added support for *all* students' learning. How are your instructional coaches offering added value to the professional learning of administrators and teachers?
- Review the 14-parameter framework in Appendix A. Identify your strengths and areas of need. Develop a plan to implement parameter 1 and two others. Build this into your improvement plan, thinking about how you will scaffold the learning from modeled to shared to guided and ultimately to achieve interdependent practice by all staff.
- Compare the implementation lessons learned at Brechin Public School and discuss how they might apply to your context.

Chapter 2: The Power of Putting FACES on the Data

- Think about the three research questions presented in FACES. How do your answers compare to the research data? How do they fit into the chart and summary responses in this chapter?
  - Why do we put FACES on the data?
  - How do we put FACES on the data?
  - What are the top three leadership skills needed to put FACES on the data?
- Relate how state and district reviewing of and knowledge about the performance data affect your leadership and what teachers teach and what students learn?
- Do teachers know what data sets look like for the whole school and system—beyond their class? In other words, consider how all teachers get to see and understand the big picture in your school (and district), too.

Chapter 3: Making It Work in Practice—Assessment

- Construct a mind map of the processes involved in knowing each and every learner.
- How do you determine what is to be taught and who needs to be coached and about what?

- How do you make a learning goal easily understood to all students? To all teachers? Explain why it is critically important to identify big ideas with students.
- Point out and visit all classrooms where teachers display Success Criteria that have been co-constructed with students.
- Explain all the components of assessment—check for understanding by consulting the glossary.
- Are all students and teachers improving? How do you know? Examine the data wall process that Principal James Bond uses. How can you adapt that process to your situation? Where can the confidential data wall be located in your context? Define the implementation process for using a data wall. List the steps involved. What will you consider strategically in implementing the data wall process in your state? District? School? Classroom?
- Take a moment to think about yourself as leader and what you can do to improve as leader by looking at and comparing your work to the mythical cohort described in the chapter. Select a group of students for which a snapshot of each grade score across all grades in your school could represent a cohort of students going through all grades in your school. Calculate the students' scores across disciplines (for example, reading, writing, math or numeracy, and other literacy measures). Do they increase as the grades increase, do they decrease, or are they sustained at a high level from the beginning grades? Is there fluctuation at certain grade levels? Predict and discuss how that fluctuation will represent leadership opportunities for you with teachers who may require additional support.
- Confirm with evidence that your teachers and leaders give descriptive feedback that is factual and objective and that outlines how to improve as a student or as a teacher.
- Recommend to others where you could go for help as an instructional leader or a teacher. Reflect and give evidence of whether students in your system, school, and classroom
  - Set their own individual goals and monitor progress toward achieving them
  - Seek clarification or assistance when needed
  - Assess and reflect critically on their own strengths, needs, and interests
  - Identify learning opportunities, choices, and strategies to meet personal needs and achieve goals
  - Persevere and make an effort when responding to challenges

- Compare the Ballarat Clarendon College case study and lessons learned to your situation. What will you add or delete from your improvement plan after discussing this case study? How will you become more focused on assessment that improves instruction?

Chapter 4: Making It Work in Practice—Instruction

- In your school, does everyone believe that every student can and will learn?
- How do you know that your collective expectations for all FACES are high enough? Is there planned and purposeful literacy learning in kindergarten?
- Defend oral language as the foundation of all instruction, K–12?
- Do all teachers model, share, and guide reading and writing beginning in kindergarten? What strategies do we recommend to ensure that these happen?
- Research to discover if your teachers can answer these four fundamental questions:
  - What am I teaching?
  - Why am I teaching it?
  - How will I teach it?
  - How will I know when all students have learned it? What then?
- Define and list the characteristics of your literate graduate.
- Identify the components of an effective literacy program by referring to Appendix A. How does your program compare?
- Explore if students in your school are required to use new ways to think about and solve problems. Make a list of what this looks like and sounds like in classrooms.
- Are tasks relevant to and authentic for students? How do you know?
- Do disciplines come together, and can they be explored in the performance tasks that teachers select?
- Examine if the subject disciplines use a common language and common assessments of written work and thinking skills so that students can transition readily from year to year and across all disciplines.
- Collect evidence that all learning tasks prompt thinking and creativity and stimulate curiosity.

- Give examples that support students' ability to confer, consult, and communicate with others.
- List all the ways that your teachers make their students' thinking visible.
- Assess if your students are required to write down and reflect on their thoughts and learning each day. Explain how and when that happens.
- Reflect on how Principal Joanne Pitman and her staff use case management meetings to support all students and all teachers. How would you make this work in your context? What operational issues need to be considered in making this approach successful?
- Role-play a case management meeting with your staff using the template in Appendix C.
- If we were to watch you teach over a two-month period, elaborate on what we would see that would increase the learning and life chances of *all* your students.
- If we were to watch you lead as principal over a two-month period, reflect on what we would see that would increase the professional learning of your teachers.
- When a teacher is having difficulty making progress with a specific student, how does the teacher come to you with a statement of need, or how would you notice the apparent difficulty? Assess the attributes of the case management approach to instructing each student.
- Defend or negate the following statement (provide reasons for your point of view): Inquiry is driving the learning and thinking of all students at this school.
- Are multiple data sources driving instruction in classrooms? How do you know?
- Are collaborative marking of student work, instructional coaching time, case management meetings, and collaborative inquiry the operating norm in your system? School? How do you know? What successful learning interventions do you deploy in your school? What is the success rate in bringing underachieving students to acceptable or above acceptable levels of performance? Do the interventions enable your teachers to close the gap between lower performers and higher performers on assessments? What criteria are used to evaluate successful interventions (use Reading Recovery as the model)?

- Make a list of conclusions that we came to in determining the powerful advantages of the co-teaching model. Explain the cycle. Discuss how this can be set in motion in your context.

Chapter 5: Leadership—Individualizing for Improvement

- Is the professional learning that you are leading making a difference to improved student learning? How do you know on a daily, weekly and monthly basis?
- As leader, how do you monitor your impact on student learning? Explain how your thinking about the monitoring of student achievement is transformed into action.
- Who monitors student achievement across the entire school? System? Who reports that improvement or no improvement in a timely fashion to the teacher, looking for answers, not to the question "why aren't they learning?" but rather to the question "how can we help you to improve all students' achievement?" How early in the semester or learning cycle do you have this progress information so that you can offer interventions when required? Compare your actions to those used by Principal Jill Maar at her school.
- What examples do you have of putting FACES on the data at the district, school, and classroom levels? What professional learning is in place for leaders to learn from data? How do you define instructional leadership? What professional learning is in place for administrators to become instructional leaders?
- Who is in my class? (*Note:* Everyone has "a class" to teach and from which to learn—district leaders, administrators, teachers, elected officials, and community members.)
- Whose learning is my responsibility?
- Summarize the strategies that you use to ensure that the use of data considers emotional connectedness and cognitive insights?
- How does your leadership compare to the strategies used by Don O'Brien and Calvin Baker?

Chapter 6: Ownership—Of All the FACES

- Discuss who owns the responsibility for all your students' achievement.
- Deconstruct the support you give to parents and the community so that they can assist in taking ownership for student

achievement. Compare and contrast your work to the strategies we discuss for enhancing parental and community involvement.

- Formulate a to-do list after discussion about the ACT case study and how they achieved improvement in their entire state.
- Reflect and collate what supports are in place to encourage all your employees—not only teachers—to own all students' achievement with emotional connections and cognitive insights? In your opinion, what is missing? Who needs to know what is needed?
- What are your narratives from the field?
- Write your own case study of improvement in putting FACES on the data.

REFERENCES

Alberta Teachers' Association. (2010). *Professional learning for informed transformation: The 2010 professional development survey.* Calgary, Canada: Author.

Allen, R. (2003). *Expanding writing's role in learning.* Curriculum update. Alexandria, VA: Association for Supervision and Curriculum Development.

Australian Curriculum, Assessment and Reporting Authority. (2008). *NAPLAN achievement in reading, writing, language conventions and numeracy: National report for 2008.* Sydney, Australia: Author.

Australian Curriculum, Assessment and Reporting Authority. (2009). *NAPLAN achievement in reading, writing, language conventions and numeracy: National report for 2009.* Sydney, Australia: Author.

Australian Curriculum, Assessment and Reporting Authority. (2010). *NAPLAN achievement in reading, writing, language conventions and numeracy: National report for 2010.* Sydney, Australia: Author.

Barber, M., Moffit, A., & Kihn, P. (2011). *Deliverology 101.* Thousand Oaks, CA: Corwin.

Bennett, B., & Rolheiser, C. (2001). *Beyond Monet: The artful science of instructional integration.* Toronto, Canada: Bookation.

Bennett, B., Sharratt, L., & Sangster, S. (2001). *Systemic change: A focus on instructional intelligence . . . two and one-half years into a five year journey.* Toronto, Canada: OISE.

Calman, R. C., for the EQAO. (2010). *Exploring the underlying traits of high-performing schools.* Toronto, Canada: Queen's Printer.

Carr, N. (2010). *The shallows.* New York: Norton Publishing.

Chambers, A. (1985). *Book talk.* London: Bodley Head Limited.

Chappius, J. (2007). *Learning team facilitator handbook.* Portland, OR: Educational Testing Service.

City, E., Elmore, R., Flarman, S., & Teitel, L. (2009). *Instructional rounds in education.* Cambridge, MA: Harvard Education Press.

Clay, M. (2002). *The observation survey.* Auckland, NZ: Heineman Education.

Cornelius-White, J. (2007). Learner-centred teacher-student relationships are effective: A meta-analysis. *Review of Educational Research, 77*(1), 113–143.

Davies, B., & Davies, B. (2011). *Talent management in education.* London: Sage.

Dufour, R., & Marzano, R. J. (2011). *Leaders of learning: How district, school, and classroom leaders improve student achievement.* Bloomington, IN: Solution Tree Press.

Duke, C., & Duke, P. (2006). Special education: An integral part of small schools in high schools. *High School Journal, 89*(3), 1–9.

Earl, L., & Katz, S. (2006). *Leading schools in a data rich world: Harnessing data for school improvement.* Thousand Oaks, CA: Corwin.

Epstein, J. (1995). School/family/community partnerships: Caring for the children we share. *Phi Delta Kappan, 76,* 701–712.

Friedrich, R., Peterson, M., & Koster, A. (2011). The rise of generation c. *Journal of Strategy + Business, 62*(spring), 55–61.

Fullan, M. (2010a). *Motion leadership: The skinny on becoming change savvy.* Thousand Oaks, CA: Corwin.

Fullan, M. (2010b). *All systems go.* Thousand Oaks, CA: Corwin.

Fullan, M. (2011a). *Moral imperative realized.* Thousand Oaks, CA: Corwin.

Fullan, M. (2011b). *Choosing the wrong drivers for whole system reform.* Victoria, Australia: CSE.

Fullan, M. (in press). *Stratosphere: Integrating technology, pedagogy and change knowledge.* New York, Toronto: Pearson.

Fullan, M., Devine, D., Sharratt, L., Butler, G., Cuttress, C., & Mozer, R. (2011). *The "how" of the common core state standards: Implementation and innovation in grades 3 through 9.* Unpublished project planning document for Gates Foundation, Toronto, Canada.

Fullan, M., & Knight, J. (2011). Coaches as system leaders. *Educational Leadership, 69*(2), 50–53.

Fullan, M., & Sharratt, L. (2007). Sustaining leadership in complex times: an individual and system solution. In B. Davies (Ed.), *Developing sustainable leadership.* London: Sage.

Fullan, M., & Watson, N. (2011). *The slow road to higher order skills.* Report to Stupski Foundation.

Galileo Educational Network. (2008). *Evidence of learning in the 21st century classroom: Classroom observation rubric and leadership for learning by instructional leaders.* Calgary, Canada: Author.

Gates, W., Myhrvold, N., & Rinearson, P. (1995). *The road ahead.* New York: Viking Press.

Greenan, M. (2011a). The secret of success criteria. *Principal Connections, 14*(3), 10–13.

Greenan, M. (2011b). *Teaching "big ideas" to little kids.* Mississauga, Canada: Dufferin-Peel Catholic District School Board.

Hanson, R., & Farrell, D. (1995). The long-term effects on high school seniors of learning to read in kindergarten. *Reading Research Quarterly, 30*(4), 908–933.

Hargreaves, A., & Fink, D. (2006). *Sustainable leadership.* San Francisco: Jossey-Bass.

Hargreaves, A., & Shirley, D. (2006). *The fourth way.* Thousand Oaks, CA: Corwin.

Harlen, W. (2006). *Teaching, learning and assessing science 5–12,* 4th revised ed. London: Chapman.

Harste, J. C. (2003). What do we mean by literacy now? *Voices from the Middle, 10*(3), 8–12.

Hattie, J. (2009). *Visible learning: Synthesis of over 800 meta-analyses relating to achievement.* New York: Routledge.

Hattie, J. (2012). *Visible learning for teachers: Maximizing impact on learning.* New York: Routledge.

Hattie, J., & Timperley, H. (2007). The power of feedback. *Review of Educational Research, 77*(1), 81–112.

Hill, P. W., & Crévola, C. A. (1999). The role of standards in educational reform for the 21st century. In D. D. Marsh (Ed.), *ASCD Yearbook 1999: Preparing our schools for the 21st century* (pp. 117–142). Alexandria, VA: Association for Supervision and Curriculum Development.

Hopper, K., & Hopper, W. (2009). *The puritan gift: Reclaiming the American dream amidst global financial chaos.* London: Tauris.

Jackson, M. (2009). *Distracted.* New York: Prometheus.

KPMG Foundation. (2006). *The long term costs of literacy difficulties.* London: What Works Clearinghouse.

Leithwood, K., Mascall, B., & Strauss, T. (2009). *Distributed leadership according to the evidence.* New York: Taylor & Francis.

Levin, B. (2009). *How to change 5000 schools.* Boston: Harvard University Press.

Levin, B. (2012). *More high school graduates: Helping more students succeed in secondary schools.* Thousand Oaks, CA: Corwin.

Louis, K. S., Leithwood, K., Wahlstrom, K., Anderson, S., Michlin, M., Mascall, B., et al. (2010). *Learning from districts' efforts to improve student achievement: Final report of research to the Wallace Foundation.* New York: Wallace Foundation.

Love, N., Stiles, K. E., Mundry, S., & DiRanna, K. (2008). *The data coach's guide to improving learning for all students.* Thousand Oaks, CA: Corwin.

McCormick Calkins, L. (2001). *The art of teaching reading.* Portsmouth, NH: Heinemann.

Meek, M. (1991). *On being literate.* Portsmouth, NH: Heinemann.

Millar-Grant, J., Heffler, B., & Mereweather, K. (1995). *Student-led conferences.* Markham, Canada: Pembroke.

Moss, C., & Brookhart, S. (2009). *Advancing formative assessment in every classroom—A guide for instructional leaders.* Alexandria, VA: Association for Supervision and Curriculum Development.

National Centre for Social Research. (2011). *Reading Recovery programme significantly improves literacy for primary pupils* [press release]. Retrieved from www.natcen.ac.uk/media-centre/press-releases/2011-press-releases/reading-programme-significantly-improves-literacy-for-primary-pupils.

Ontario Ministry of Education. (2003). *A guide to effective instruction in reading: Kindergarten to grade 3.* Toronto, Canada: Queen's Printer.

Ontario Ministry of Education. (2004). *Literacy for learning: Report of the expert panel on literacy in grades 4 to 6 in Ontario.* Toronto, Canada: Queen's Printer.

Ontario Ministry of Education. (2010a). *Growing success.* Toronto, Canada: Queen's Printer.

Ontario Ministry of Education. (2010b). *Ontario language arts curriculum.* Toronto, Canada: Queen's Printer.

Ostinelli, G. (2008). *The school improvement advisor/researcher SIA: Helping the individual school in the self-management of improvement.* Research paper presented to the Admee Meeting, Geneva, Switzerland.

Paris, E. (2011). *Filter bubble.* New York: Penguin Press.

Reeves, D. B. (2010). *Transforming professional development into student results.* Alexandria, VA: Association for Supervision and Curriculum Development.

Reeves, D. B. (2011). *Elements of grading: A guide to effective practice.* Alexandria, VA: Association for Supervision and Curriculum Development.

Robinson, K. (2009). *The element.* New York: Viking.

Rogers, W. T. (2009). *Towards an understanding of gender differences in literacy achievement.* EQAO Research Bulletin #5. Toronto, Canada: EQAO.

Schleicher, A. (2011). OECD *presentation to world education ministers in Japan.* Tokyo, Japan.

Schön, D. (1983). *The reflective practitioner.* New York: Basic Books.

Senge P. M. (1990). *The fifth discipline: The art and practice of the learning organization.* New York: Doubleday.

Sharratt, L. (1996). *The influence of electronically available information on the stimulation of knowledge use and organizational learning in schools.* Doctoral dissertation. University of Toronto, Canada.

Sharratt, L. (2011). *Learning walks and talks* [training materials]. Alberta, Saskatchewan, and Ontario, Canada.

Sharratt, L., & Fullan, M. (2005). The school district that did the right things right. Annenberg Institute for School Reform, Brown University, *Voices in Urban Education,* Fall, 5–13.

Sharratt, L., & Fullan, M. (2006). Accomplishing district wide reform. *Journal of School Leadership, 16,* 583–595.

Sharratt, L., & Fullan M. (2009). *Realization: The change imperative for deepening district-wide reform.* Thousand Oaks, CA: Corwin

Sharratt, L., Ostinelli, G., & Cattaneo, A. (2010). *The role of the "knowledgeable other" in improving student achievement, school culture and teacher efficacy: Two case studies from Canadian and Swiss perspectives and experiences.* Paper presented at the International Congress for School Effectiveness and Improvement, Kuala Lumpur, Malaysia.

Sharratt, M. (2004). *The impact of teacher leadership on students' literacy learning* [master's thesis], University of Toronto, Canada.

Shulman, R., for the EQAO. (2010). *Strategies that work for schools: Thinking globally in a postmodern world.* Toronto, Canada: Queen's Printer of Ontario.

Teddlie, C., Reynolds, D., & Sammons, P. (2000). The methodology and scientific properties of school effectiveness research. In C. Teddlie & D. Reynolds (Eds.), *The international handbook of school effectiveness research* (pp. 55–133). London: Flamer.

Temple, J. A., Reynolds, A. J., & Miedel, W. T. (1998). *Research on Chicago Child-Parent Centers.* Chicago: Sector and Charles Stewart Mott Foundation.

UNESCO. (2006). *Education for all global monitoring report.* Retrieved from www.unesco.org/education/GMR2006/full/chapt1_eng.pdf.

Wiliam, D. (2011). *Embedded formative assessment.* Bloomington, IN: Solution Tree.

Willms, J. D., Friesen, S., & Milton, P. (2009). *What did you do in school today? Transforming classrooms through social, academic, and intellectual engagement: First national report.* Toronto, Canada: Canadian Education Association.

York Region District School Board. (2004). *The literate graduate.* Aurora, Canada: Author.

York Region District School Board. (2007). *Guidelines for curriculum implementation: A curriculum expectations document.* Aurora, Canada: Author.

INDEX

CORWIN
A SAGE Company

The Corwin logo—a raven striding across an open book—represents the union of courage and learning. Corwin is committed to improving education for all learners by publishing books and other professional development resources for those serving the field of PreK–12 education. By providing practical, hands-on materials, Corwin continues to carry out the promise of its motto: **"Helping Educators Do Their Work Better."**

The Ontario Principals' Council (OPC) is a voluntary association for principals and vice-principals in Ontario's public school system. We believe that exemplary leadership results in outstanding schools and improved student achievement. To this end, we foster quality leadership through world-class professional services and supports. As an ISO 9001 registered organization, we are committed to **"quality leadership—our principal product."**

Learning Forward (formerly National Staff Development Council) is an international association of learning educators committed to one purpose in K–12 education: Every educator engages in effective professional learning every day so every student achieves.